An Inside Account of Life in the Army by One of West Point's First Female Graduates

★

CPT. CAROL BARKALOW

with Andrea Raab

Poseidon Press

New York   London   Toronto

IN THE MEN'S HOUSE

Sydney   Tokyo   Singapore

Poseidon Press

Simon & Schuster Building
Rockefeller Center
1230 Avenue of the Americas
New York, New York 10020

POSEIDON PRESS *is a registered trademark*
of Simon & Schuster Inc.

POSEIDON PRESS *colophon is a trademark*
of Simon & Schuster Inc.

Designed by Liney Li
Manufactured in the United States of America

1 3 5 7 9 10 8 6 4 2

Library of Congress Cataloging in Publication Data
Barkalow, Carol.
In the men's house: an inside account of life in the Army by one of West Point's
first female graduates/Carol Barkalow, with Andrea Raab.
p. cm.
1. Barkalow, Carol. 2. United States Military Academy—Biography. 3. United
States. Army—Biography. 4. United States. Army—Women. 5. Women
soldiers—United States—Biography. I. Raab, Andrea. II. Title.
U410.M1B372 1990
355'.0092—dc20 90-37076
CIP

ISBN 0-671-67312-2

Photo credits:
pages 3, 21: U.S. Army
page 141: Author's Collection
page 199: Anthony Edgeworth

Acknowledgments

Thanks to David Black, our literary agent, who initiated this project and whose caring hand guided us along the way; to Ann Patty, our publisher at Poseidon Press, for her patience, enthusiasm, and continued support; and to our editor, Kathleen Anderson, whose extraordinary talent, energy, faith, and commitment were rare and wonderful gifts for which we will always be profoundly grateful.

An added word of thanks to our copyeditor; and to Lydia Buechler, copy supervisor; Liney Li, designer; and Karolina Harris, associate art director, for contributing their skills and expertise.

Thanks to everyone at West Point who helped us: Andrea Hamburger, Col. Jack Yeagley, Col. James N. Hawthorne, Col. Howard T. Prince II, Ph.D., Col. Hawley Oakes (Ret), Lt. Col. Jerome Adams, Dr. James A. Peterson, Mrs. Caroline Gaspard, Mr. Alan C. Aimone, and others who preferred to remain anonymous. To Capt. Mary Clark, Capt. Lissa Young, 2d. Lt. Kristin Baker, and the cadets we spoke to from the classes of '86, '87, and '88—your thoughts and reflections were invaluable. To Joan Jordan, whose documentary film about the women of West Point's Class of '80 gave us the opportunity to relive the history those women were making. And to those men and women of the classes of '79, '80, and '81 who generously shared their memories with us in gatherings at Fort Leavenworth, Kansas, and Columbia, Maryland, and in telephone interviews across the country—we are deeply indebted. And our very sincere and heartfelt thanks to Maj. Christine Bowers, who facilitated much of our research, and whose contributions to this project over the years have been immeasurable.

At Fort Lee, Virginia, thanks to Col. Joel Roberts (Ret), Col. Richard

Holley, Capt. Mary Ann O'Connor, 1st Sgt. Louis McNeill, 1st Sgt. Toni Ross, Sfc. Larry Worthy, Sfc. Jennifer McNeill, S.Sgt. Calvin Cooper, Sgt. Williams, Sp. 4c. Rosa, Jean Webber, and to the memory of CW3 Phillip Albert Zamora, one of the most professional officers and dedicated soldiers we have ever known.

A special word of thanks to Brig. Gen. Evelyn P. Foote (Ret), to Vicki Almquist, Director of the Women and the Military Project at WEAL, to the officers at DACOWITS, and to Col. Richard Entlich, Mrs. Sally Entlich, Lt. Col. Barbara Yost, Capt. Steve Koths, S.Sgt. Mike Enos, Pat Skinner, Pam Carter, and George Bromwell.

Finally, to our parents, family, and friends, whose love and support have sustained us through the writing of this book.

Captain Carol Barkalow,
Washington, D.C.

Andrea Raab,
New York City

To the class of '80

Contents

★

Author's Note

In addition to the information culled from my diaries (which I kept from July 1976 to May 1980) and my own recollections, this book is also based on interviews, beginning in February 1986 and ending in October 1989, with nearly sixty people. Because I wanted to include a broader scope of detail and reminiscence than was afforded merely by my own limited experience, particularly in discussing the years at West Point, I sent letters to all the women of the class of '80 whose whereabouts I could trace. Some women were willing—even eager—to be interviewed. A few were skeptical at first but overcame their reluctance and spoke candidly and movingly once given the opportunity. Some graciously declined the invitation, while others simply did not answer my letter. One woman wrote back a deeply felt letter of her own, explaining why she preferred not to summon up her painful memories of the past. I only hope that the impulses of those who have spoken will be understood by those who did not, as we have respectfully understood theirs.

All characters in this book are real; to protect their identities, the names of all current and former cadets, instructors, Tac officers, and active duty soldiers have been changed within the text, with the exception of the following, who either have granted permission to be identified, or whose involvement in the events described is a matter of public record: Gen. Frederick Kroesen (Ret); Gen. Andrew J. Goodpaster (Ret); Gen. Sidney B. Berry (Ret); Brig. Gen. Mildred Hedberg (Ret); Brig. Gen. Samuel W. Koster (Ret); Lt. Col. Jerome Adams; Maj. Christine Bowers; Capt. Andrea Hollen; Mrs. Caroline Gaspard; Dr. James A. Peterson; Charlotte Dimirack; Sara Myers.

For the sake of narrative continuity, my original diaries have been edited and/or amended, and some events presented in a slightly altered chronological sequence. I have attempted to create a factually accurate record of past events; any failings, however, are entirely my own responsibility. Further, it should be noted that the views expressed in this book are either my own or those of interviewees, and do not reflect the official policy or position of the Department of the Army, Department of Defense, or the U.S. Government.

A final note about the book's title. *In the Men's House* was inspired by a quote from Kate Millett's landmark book, *Sexual Politics*. Ms. Millett writes: "[In anthropology] the men's house [institution] is a fortress of patriarchal association and emotion. . . . While hunting, politics, religion, and commerce may play a role, sport and warfare are consistently the chief cement of men's house comradery."

With the possible exception of the NFL, the military is still America's leading men's house institution.

At a very early period she had
apprehended instinctively the dual life—
that outward existence which conforms,
the inward life which questions.

—Kate Chopin, *The Awakening* (1899)

IN THE
MEN'S
HOUSE

Prologue

★

Mountains end in a low curve. Trees in the distance stand like stubble on the back of a close-shaved neck; their branches throw shadows on the river.

Sharp cliffs of red granite form a natural bulwark along the road. Local architecture reveals the population's character in this region west of the Hudson River: simple cottages, taverns for family dining, car repair shops, and somber churches shape the landscape around Route 9W North—the approach to West Point. Scattered among humbler structures, Carpenter Gothic houses laced with scrollwork are sheltered from the highway by clusters of oak and maple trees, northern cedar and pine. Wildlife quietly but persistently preserves its place along 9W, too: among an abundance of leaves and rocks and twisted roots, in an occasional deer crossing, in a sudden rush of water from a high mountain spring.

Downtown Highland Falls, a nondescript main drag of motels, banks, pizza parlors, and souvenir shops, stands just beyond the reach of Thayer Gate—the entrance to the United States Military Academy. This checkpoint of no return, whose tollgate barrier allows access to authorized personnel and tourists alike, comes complete—in the manner of any military enclosure—with a turreted sentry tower and stone-faced MPs. With its pointed arches and iron-hinged wooden doors, this structure appears forbidding, but it is merely a token announcement of the grand, austere fortress that lies beyond.

In passing the front gate, it is critical to remember that one is not entering a college campus, one is entering a shrine. Every statue—every stone—is the physical embodiment of an ideal, for there is little that matters more than the physical to the thinking of a cadet. As if its values might be transmitted through osmosis, the Academy motto "Duty, Honor,

Country" is materialized everywhere here, from the highest to the lowest, from the stained glass above the altar of the Cadet Chapel to the polished face of a roadside water fountain. West Point is perhaps one of the few remaining places in late twentieth-century America built on the belief that outer images are sincerely expected to reflect inner truths. That they seldom do, and that the place lives on in spite of it, is both the miracle and the tragedy of the Academy. It is also a subject of this story.

Before I entered the Academy as a seventeen-year-old girl in the summer of 1976, West Point meant barely more to me than a high school guidance counselor's suggestion, a shimmering "opportunity" for the future, a college I could attend for free. At sixteen my dream was to become an Army officer, but I had no conception of real military life or the generations of men and women who had struggled through it. I was not alone in this. Few of my classmates—male or female—with the possible exception of those who had grown up in military families (and even they were in for some surprises), had a clear sense of the direction their immediate futures would take.

Ordinarily, such ignorance might have been expected of fifteen hundred civilian teenagers about to enter their plebe year. But 1976 was by no means ordinary for the United States Military Academy. Much more than a year of transition, 1976 became a year of critical self-scrutiny, one in which the Academy was called upon to redefine its very purpose and identity.

By 1976 West Point had not shaken from its boots the mud left behind by the Vietnam War. Even in its aftermath, the wounds bled. The Academy had been suffering from years of low morale caused by frustration and disappointment at the way the war was being conducted—thirty-three officers in eighteen months had resigned in a crisis of conscience—in addition to the growing civilian antipathy toward the military, and the less competitive (though technically qualified) caliber of applicants who were being accepted when recruiting was at an all-time low. An instructor from West Point's Department of Behavioral Science and Leadership, who taught psychology at the Academy during the war years, commented that from 1969 to 1971, the recruiting situation had gotten "so bad that we accepted the majority of applicants for a couple of years."

However, the most devastating challenge to the honor of the Academy occurred when the school's highest officer, Superintendent Brigadier General Samuel W. Koster, resigned his position over the investigation of his involvement in the cover-up of the My Lai massacre. Although General Koster left West Point in 1970, his fall from grace dealt a crushing blow to the spirit of the Military Academy, one whose effects would continue to be felt for years afterward.

Nineteen seventy-six saw the eruption of the infamous "Electrical Engineering 304 Cheating Incident," when in March a staggering number of cadets had violated the sacred West Point Honor Code ("A cadet will not lie, cheat, or steal, nor tolerate those who do") by either giving, receiving, or otherwise tolerating illegal help on a take-home exam. One hundred fifty-two cadets were implicated in these violations and the majority were separated from the Corps; in response, a class action suit was filed against the superintendent of the Academy and the Secretary of the Army for what some believed to be unjust dismissal. The former cadets maintained that the complex interpretations of what was and what was not considered against "honor" were contradictory and confusing. While some were guilty of cheating, other cadets had merely fallen into a legalistic trap. Contrary to the accusations brought, the opinion by U.S. District Judge Robert L. Carter held that the superintendent's action "was reasonable and did not entrench upon due process safeguards." His departure from the norm in this case of mass expulsion was deemed reasonable due to the number of cadets involved and the speed with which the actions had to be carried out. (The cadets were later granted the option of reapplying to the Academy the following year, and the judge dismissed the complaint on 4 February 1977.)

To avert further crisis, it was mutually agreed by the Academy's administration and the civilian government in the spring of 1976 that not only the honor system but also, in the words of the West Point Study Group, "all aspects of the Academy" needed a long, hard look. In-depth examinations were soon begun by three separate groups: the Borman Commission (a civilian-run investigative body chaired by Frank Borman, West Point, class of 1950, former astronaut and president of Eastern Airlines), the West Point Study Group (created to provide the Army's response to the Borman Report and comprised of Academy staffers, other military advisors, and selected civilian consultants), and the West Point Special Actions Group.

One faculty member recalls the unhappy period of intense and prolonged scrutiny when everyone felt that "people were watching over our shoulders, accusing us of doing something wrong." Perhaps nowhere was this defensive posture more evident than in the subtly urgent introduction to the West Point Study Group's final report, dated 27 July 1977, in which the authors of the document wasted no time dispelling any potential doubts by asserting up-front that they had found the United States Military Academy to be "basically a sound institution." However, they did admit that the Academy had "fallen victim to a number of problems," which they nevertheless believed, in true military spirit, could "be solved by prompt and vigorous action."

Before allowing themselves to proceed, as if the text that followed contained material too strong for sensitive readers, the authors then offered this qualification: *"The following report is inevitably problem oriented.* It makes no attempt to chronicle the many excellent aspects of West Point, and there *are* aspects of every part of the Academy which inspire admiration." (The footstamps of emphasis are entirely theirs.) Undeniably, the Academy believed itself to be under attack and felt compelled, once more, as it had at other times during its 174 years, to justify its very existence.

Into this atmosphere marched the first women ever to attend West Point.

The admission of women was opposed vociferously at first, but on 7 October 1975 President Gerald Ford signed into law the bill that would permit women to attend the nation's service academies, and members of the administration were forced, like any good soldiers, to abruptly reverse their negative position and follow orders. Of course, the vehemence with which the Academy's chief officers had previously voiced their opinions had already made an indelible impact on the impressionable young male minds of the Corps of Cadets. The damage was irreversible.

Despite the general belief that prior to 1976 the Academy had been a bastion of purely male influence, there were at least three other women, long before our arrival, who had already been granted a permanent home at West Point. They were, respectively, a goddess, a saint, and a folk heroine preserved in stone: Pallas Athena, Greek goddess of wisdom and war, whose helmet appears as a central symbol of the West Point crest; Joan of Arc, whose painted image in the Cadet Mess Hall gazes heavenward while cadets feed themselves below; and Revolutionary War heroine Margaret Corbin, whose statue stands within the grounds of the West Point Cemetery, just outside the Old Cadet Chapel, curiously hidden by a clump of trees.

These women warriors were our predecessors, however abstract. To the men, of course, they were welcome precisely because there was no longer anything real about them, nothing of flesh or blood to them at all. Naturally, we did not possess the same advantage. We were 119 *females* (as West Pointers clinically call women), whose dreaded arrival at the Academy one hot July morning was, by all accounts, anything but welcome.

WEST POINT

★

Plebe Year

1976–1977

★

My first memory of West Point is lunch—eating lunch in an enormous, drafty room with four thousand men. I was visiting at the time.

Just as I was swallowing my last forkful of blueberry pie, a tall cadet sitting across from me leaned over the table and said, "Excuse me, miss, but why do you want to come here?"

"Because," I said, putting my fork down, "I want to become the best army officer I can be."

"That's fine," he replied, "but couldn't you do it someplace else?"

7 July 1976. All incoming new cadets were instructed to report to Michie Stadium between seven and ten in the morning. I had heard that if you got there early the upperclassmen would be fresh and in relatively good moods, but if you arrived too close to ten o'clock they'd yell at you for being late. My father made a wrong turn after getting off the exit on the highway, delaying our arrival at the Academy by at least half an hour. I didn't speak to him again for the rest of the trip.

My mother, father, sister Janice, and I finally climbed onto the bleachers at Michie Stadium at the stroke of nine. At the base of the stairs, a senior cadet was speaking through a microphone to the gathered assembly. With unnerving calm, the young man told us what to expect that day. He did not, of course, tell us how we should expect to feel.

When he's through talking, I thought, I won't say good-bye, and I won't look back. I'll just go.

My mother reached over to kiss me, but I pulled back from her embrace. I waited a moment for the awkwardness to pass. I loved my mother, but I could not touch her. Not now, when it was taking all of my courage to leave. I walked away from my family and began to cry.

Soon I was stepping into one of the buses waiting to carry off the new inductees. Meanwhile, our families were being led away on a brisk tour of the Academy, which was intended to distract them from the sudden moment of separation, as much as to impress them with the institution's facilities and readiness.

"Hang in!" the colonel on stage told our mothers and fathers who had been rounded up for a special kind of parent-teacher conference at the end of their tour and seated inside the great auditorium.

"It's hard to explain Cadet Basic Training—it's called Beast Barracks—but it's not as demanding as you might think. Most new cadets form their opinions about Beast Barracks from mythology and hearsay. They don't really know what it is. In fact, Regular Army basic training is probably more physical than Beast Barracks at West Point, which tends to be more emotionally demanding. Above all, new cadets have to remember to keep a sense of humor."

Seemingly forgetting who he was talking to, the man continued, "Your kids are going to get depressed. We usually get about eight or nine suicide attempts the first year—cadets drink rifle oil, eat too many aspirins. So it's critical for the new cadets to feel that they're doing well. When they complain about how much they hate it here, don't take it to heart. The best thing you can do for them is listen. Just be a sounding board."

To my parents, his words must have conjured up images of three thousand fathers and mothers smiling impassively and nodding their heads as their children desperately poured out their tales of woe. Or a conspiracy of affirmation.

"Write to them," the officer urged. "Send encouraging letters and plenty of care packages. Try to get their friends to write to them, too.

"You know," he went on, "people with long-range goals tend to have trouble here. However, the exit interviews of people who leave indicate that even those cadets feel that they 'grew' during their time at West Point. We, at the Academy, believe that the cadets who do stay *want* tough, challenging experiences. We try to help them 'normalize' the stress they will encounter here. In exchange for all we ask of them, we know that West Point cadets are proud to belong to a very select, distinguished group."

.   .   .

24

While our parents were reaping praises for producing the country's next generation of leaders, the buses were systematically releasing us in front of Central Gymnasium for in-processing. There, we were stripped, examined, and fitted with new clothing—white T-shirts, black gym shorts, black kneesocks, and oxfords. Green and yellow tags were pinned to our shorts—the green ones were printed with long orderly lists of uniform pieces and other Army-issue items that we were to pick up at various checkpoints around the school; the yellow ones had our names and companies printed at the top, followed by another list of checkpoints that kept track of where we had been and where we still needed to go. "Cattle tags," remarked a girl in line behind me. The herded animal imagery seemed astute.

This was R-Day—Reception Day—a very dehumanizing experience, dominated completely by a godlike creature known to us only as "the Man in the Red Sash." The Man in the Red Sash was supposed to be this incredible, all-knowing being, but, as far as I could tell, the only reason he was considered all-knowing was that he had on that red sash. Every time we reported to him, he would grab hold of our tag—the little yellow tag that was pinned to our bizarre little shorts—while we stood there in our little black socks, feeling like kindergarteners.

Suddenly he would bark, "What's your name and where do you belong?"

Indifferent to the answer, he would look down at our tag and perhaps see that we needed a haircut. Now, he could have figured that out for himself just by looking at us, but he was totally dependent on what the tag told him. Even if we already had short hair when we got there, we'd probably be sent to the barber shop, anyway. So, we'd pick up our little green Army-issue bags and run off to the barber shop where dozens of cadets were lined up outside the door. While we stood there watching the line in front of us grow shorter and shorter, we could hear the menacing sound of scissors snipping and electric hair clippers buzzing, and chattering Italians who weren't speaking a word of English, but who were relentlessly cutting hair. We'd sit down in front of the barber with not a word passing between us until it was too late, and then suddenly realize, "Oh my God, this man is shaving my neck."

Hair regulations at the Academy were a special nightmare for female cadets. A woman's hair could be no longer than the bottom edge of her collar, and even at that length it was permitted to stick out only so far. Our hair was not supposed to protrude beyond the visor of our cadet hat, or further than an inch and a half from anywhere else. Male cadets, who customarily wore their hair shorn close to their heads, rarely had a problem upholding this regulation. Even after a woman's hair was cut, if it happened to be thick, sometimes there could be no taming it. Under no circumstances, however, would wild hair be tolerated. Often it seemed as though the Academy would sooner cut off our heads than permit us to walk around with bushy hair.

Because her hair was thick and indifferent to "regs," my classmate Julie Hawkins was forced to undergo seven haircuts over the course of the first two days. Every time they sent Julie to see the Man in the Red Sash, he ordered her to get another haircut. By the time the barbers were finished with her, the girl had whitewalls on both sides of her head. She later recalled, "After all that happened, my tactical officer [a West Point company's officer administrator, and disciplinarian] came to my room, put me at attention, and yelled at me for having my hair so short. Then he told me that under no circumstances was I to get another haircut unless I was given a direct order by him. So I just stood there *looking* at this man, and I wanted to scream, 'What's the matter with you? Do you think I *asked* for this?' "

Once we had completed our appointed rounds, we were sent to join our companies. As I was opening the door to the barracks, I suddenly heard an upperclassman's voice behind me.

"New cadet!"

I whirled around to face him.

"New cadet, what are you doing spazzing around?"

"I'm looking for my company, Sir. There's been a mistake. I was . . ."

"Miss! What are your four responses?"

I wildly searched my memory. Mercifully, I remembered the only four responses I'd be permitted to speak to my superiors during the whole first year of my new life.

"Yes, Sir. No, Sir. No excuse, Sir. Sir, I do not understand."

I was then commanded to report to the Man in the Red Sash, who was standing in the middle of a box marked in tape on the pavement. A second box was taped off in front of him. I approached timidly, stepping over the tape and into his box, clutching my bag. He spoke.

"Miss, did I tell you to step into my box?"

"No," I said.

"You mean, 'No, Sir.' Right?"

"No, Sir," I said.

26

I stepped out of his box.

"Step into my box!" he said.

I stepped back into his box.

"Drop it!" he said, referring to the bag.

I put down the bag.

"Pick it up!" he said.

I did so.

"Drop it!" he said, again.

I put down the bag once more.

"Pick it *up!*" he said, angrily.

I picked it up.

"Now, *drop it!*" he said.

This time, I dropped it. Mission accomplished.

The young man began to spout a rapid-fire stream of information which, he made clear, I would be required to recite verbatim upon command. At the time, I thought that the only things I would ever be able to remember were my four responses.

When the Man in the Red Sash was through with me, he instructed me to go to my room to drop off my bag, and then return to North Area to learn how to march with a thirty-inch step, how to "ping out"—walk at 120 paces per minute while hugging the walls and squaring every corner—and how to salute. About an hour later, I had learned these lessons satisfactorily, and was dismissed to the mess hall to be fed.

At the lunchtable, the table commandant offered me a few words of advice. "You'd better get your looks around now, Barkalow," he said, "because starting tonight you won't be looking at anything but your plate for a long, long time."

Cheerful.

So I got "my looks around," as he suggested. Thick wooden crossbeams on the ceiling were adorned with flowers, golden crosses, and crowns. Lamps of wrought iron with opaline glass shades, and a riot of flags representing every state hung suspended above our heads. A painted mural splashed rich colors across the south wall.

After considering the wall more carefully, I was startled to find among the depictions of history's greatest warriors the muralist's interpretation of Joan of Arc. There she stood in silver armor, alongside Richard the Lion Hearted and William the Conqueror, sword uplifted in one hand, helmet clasped in the other, red hair falling to her shoulders, with six knights kneeling in homage at her feet.

.   .   .

27

Lunch was followed by more drills in preparation for the afternoon's parade. It would be the first one in West Point's history that had ever been attempted on R-Day, or so I was told, and the first to include women.

At 1300—1:00 P.M. civilian time—I was sent back to the barracks to join my roommates. I was stopped once more—this time by the cadet first sergeant—because I was climbing the stairs incorrectly. He locked his eyes with mine and shouted into my face: *"Body against the wall, arms bent at ninety degrees, every corner squared. Is that understood?"*

"Yes, *Sir!*"

"Well it had better be, because Eighth Company is a 'strac' company and we won't take dirtballs like you."

"Yes, *Sir!*"

I discovered later that STRAC stood for "Straight, Tough, and Ready Around the Clock."

At last I found my room with my name and picture already mounted on a placard near the door, along with those of my two roommates, who were already inside. We didn't talk much as we unpacked, except to exchange basic information. Robin Bach, who had attended the United States Military Academy Preparatory School at Fort Monmouth, New Jersey, and obviously knew her way around a barracks room, sat at her desk dragging coolly on a cigarette. Our other roommate, Diane Yeager, was a novice fresh out of high school, like me. Robin had already claimed the sole single bed for herself—but we didn't have time to discuss sleeping arrangements; we had to dress for the afternoon parade. Diane and I decided to toss for the bunk bed. She got the top.

At 1530 hours, they brought us our trousers—light gray wool, with a black stripe down the side of each leg. The women's trousers differed from the men's in two ways: no back pockets (I guess they thought that our rear ends protruded far enough without them) and plastic, rather than metal, zippers. These "women's" trousers, however, did not represent the only problem we'd encounter with the female cadet uniforms. The design of the women's Full Dress uniforms also reflected the Academy's perception of our bodies. In contrast to the tailcoat worn by male cadets, our Full Dress coats were cut off at the waist for fear that our derrieres would appear too prominent during parades. Of course, the difference between the uniforms only accentuated what the Academy wanted us to conceal. It would be three years before the authorities relented and gave us coats with tails.

I struggled with the garment's cheap plastic zipper until I heard the cadre—the cadet chain of command—call us to assemble and then began

28

to hurry. Suddenly, my fingers slipped and I felt something snap. I looked down. The zipper was broken. The trousers were useless. At that precise moment, Cadet Russell, my twenty-one-year-old squad leader, walked in. He wanted to know if I were ready to go.

"New Cadet Barkalow, you're supposed to be downstairs. Your roommates have left without you. Why aren't you with them?"

I snapped to attention and saluted with one hand. With the other, I grabbed my fly.

"No excuse, Sir."

"At ease, Barkalow."

I dropped into the less formal "at ease" stance, positioning my free hand at rest behind my back. I kept my other hand where it was.

Cadet Russell circled around me once, then twice.

"Barkalow," he said, "will you please tell me what the hell is going on?"

"My zipper broke, Sir."

"New Cadet Barkalow," he asked, obviously resisting the urge to laugh, "do you really want to be in this parade?"

"Yes, *Sir!*"

"All right, then. Wait here. I'll be back in a minute."

When Cadet Russell returned, he was carrying a pair of gray trousers similar to the ones I had destroyed.

"These are mine, Barkalow. I think the length will be all right, but the waist is going to be a little big. Pull your belt tighter and hope no one notices. March *strac*, and they won't."

He was the first person to show an iota of kindness to me all day. I could have hugged him.

I ran outside to catch up with my company, which was standing neatly in formation in North Area. The band was already assembled on the Plain (the parade field flanked to the south and west by Eisenhower and MacArthur Barracks, and Washington Hall). I could hear the rum-ta-ta-tum of martial music. Everyone was skittish, waiting for the United States Military Academy Band to start playing, which was our cue to march out. The moment the band struck up, one member of the cadre marched before us and another one marched behind, calling cadence to keep us in step.

"Your left. Your left. Your left, right, left. Your military left. You're marching on your left."

Fifteen hundred pairs of feet began pounding across the Plain. I was in the last platoon of the last company, bringing up the rear.

Lining the sidewalks and streets, jammed into the reviewing stands, thousands of spectators had gathered to witness our transformation. In a few hours, fifteen hundred sons and daughters had been shorn, stripped, and re-created in the image of the perfect cadet. And in our half-formed state—one foot in the old life, the other in the new—we were more perfect than we would be again, unsullied, as we still were, by demerits, disobedience, and disenchantment.

As we passed in review, our faces shone with blessed ignorance. Our epaulets were straighter than a general's; our gloves were spotless white; our name tags were pinned to our shirts with fanatic precision. Only my pants looked awful. But they were staying up, and I was in the parade.

That night, as I lay in my bunk after Taps, I reached underneath my mattress for the diary my friend Grace had given me as a going-away present. I opened the book and wearily scribbled some notes. "What a day," I wrote, under a date that suddenly seemed too ordinary to mark everything that had transpired, "I have never been through anything like this in my life. *What a day.*"

The following week, *U.S. News and World Report* carried a picture of my platoon. In it I could see the bunched-up waist of Cadet Russell's pants on a tall, gawky beanhead who bore a vague resemblance to a girl I used to know.

Beast Barracks was like a deck of a thousand cards. We were tossed in and shuffled around, and only by some miracle of fate did we fall into place. Anonymity was our saving grace. We had names, but a common appearance. We adjusted without display. Tears were for the shower, for our letters, for our beds. In eight weeks we'd be trained, chewed up, and spit out either as civilians or as plebes. As with any rite of passage, we were robbed of our identities, only to have them restored to us in an entirely different form. We were expected to behave like robots—submerging our own personalities to fit in with the group. We marched the same way, dressed the same way, saluted the same way, and responded, "Yes, Sir. No, Sir. No excuse, Sir. Sir, I do not understand," with the same intonations. To the upperclassmen, we were beanheads, smacks, new cadets. Those were our titles. We were not even considered full members of the Corps until we survived the summer. As part of our initiation, we were forced to do and say ridiculous things. We were marched around a field carrying boxes of provisions, chanting "We are dumb, dumb knuckleheads." Some of us were assigned personal "poop"—invented by our squad leaders—that called attention to whatever surface characteristic they felt was the most grossly evident about us, alluding to our appearance, our attitude, or our performance. We'd recite this poop on demand:

"Sir, I'm the Madwoman of Borneo—I have more hair on my chest than you have on your head."

"Sir, I'm 125 pounds of twisted steel and sex appeal. The Lone Ranger would rather French kiss a rattlesnake than mess around with me."

Mine was: "Sir, I'm rough, tough, and full of stuff."

"Barkalow," my squad leader had told me, "whenever I say 'Gimme your poop,' you pop off with that." I considered it a compliment.

Eventually our squad leaders got to know us. But as females, we were always aware that they were still unsure about us, unsure about this "experiment," which is how they viewed our presence. In their eyes, we were society's guinea pigs, or society's freaks. Some of these men were either afraid to look at us or would engage in relentless hazing. We knew all of them were struggling with the change that had been thrust upon them, and though few of them handled it with grace, there were some men who tried to do their best in the situation. If they liked us, and if we seemed to be doing well—not falling behind during too many runs, not whimpering or complaining too much—they would sort of adopt us, like pets. Occasionally we'd even hear them bragging to their friends, *"My* women aren't wimps."

They took great pride in grooming us, and we were so grateful for their favor, our reaction was, "How can I let them down by getting a stress fracture?" If we injured ourselves or got sick, we would feel terribly guilty. Women suffered a lot of physical injuries in Beast Barracks, but there was a strong tendency to ignore them, to pretend they didn't exist. By the end of the summer, there were a few women who had nearly *destroyed* themselves trying to keep up physically, because they knew that they *had* to do it. They couldn't bear to think that their squad leader would be disappointed.

11 JUL 1976

The other day, some of us (new cadets) were down by the river playing softball. We were asking each other our first names, trying to get acquainted, when one of the upperclassmen piped in, "Do you all know what my *first name is?" We made a few guesses—all of them wrong—then he laughed and said, "My first name is 'Sir.'"*

Everything was all right today until after dinner.

For some reason, my name was not on the mass athletic sheet, so I didn't

31

know where the hell I was supposed to go. I got into trouble for being lost, and was also written up for an incorrect dress-off—my shirt wasn't tucked in properly. Then, as I was coming out of my room, I was stopped by two firsties [seniors]. When they had finished with me, I broke into tears. A third cadet, who had watched the whole thing, told me to come with him. He took me into his room and helped me calm down. He was very nice about it. I have to find out his name.

After I left the upperclassman's room I had to get a 4-C (Fourth Class Performance Report—little green forms on which our daily sins and possible achievements are recorded, and which are handed out by upperclassmen like toilet paper). I got the 4-C and broke down again. But the guy who gave it to me, stood by until I regained my composure. Then he said I had to report to Cadet Novak, who is in charge of the mass athletic sheet. Cadet Novak started in on me, too, and I broke down once more. Before I could go back to my room, I was instructed to report to Cadet Russell, my squad leader. He was real nice. He even told me that others had noticed I was in good military form. It was a definite lift. This has been the worst day so far. Please, God, help me. Drive on, Sir!

Two or three days after she arrived at West Point, my classmate Cathy Gordon finally allowed everything to sink in. For the first day or so, she'd kept a fairly positive and uncomplicated outlook, as her father, a career officer, had advised her to do. But soon she began to take cadet life very seriously, and that's when she started having problems. She was constantly tense and unable to sleep. Soon the uneasiness intruded into her days as well. Cathy got into the habit of clenching her jaw all the time, because she was terrified she might burst into nervous laughter whenever anyone gave her an order. She would walk around with a madwoman expression fixed on her face, until one day the cadet first sergeant looked at her and said, "Hey, Gordon, will you relax? You look like you're about to crack up."

Later, as she was practicing her public mask in the bathroom mirror, she said, "Fine. While I'm here, I'll live according to their rules, their law. I can do whatever they want me to do."

13 JUL 1976

Today PT [Physical Training] was tough. The calisthenics were exhausting, and I almost fell out of formation during the run. We had two classes in the morning, but had the afternoon off to prepare for an overnight in the field.

32

14 JUL 1976

Returned from our overnight at noon. I really didn't mind it. We ate C-rations. They were good! OD green [olive drab] cans filled with franks and beans, peanut butter and crackers, coffee, sugar, powdered cream, plastic-wrapped toilet paper, two pieces of gum, and "John Wayne Bars"—crunchy chocolate candies in the shape of silver dollars. I saved all of my John Wayne Bars and ate them at night in my tent.

This afternoon we played different kinds of games like tug-of-war, relay races carrying rifles and empty ammo magazines (the guys were carrying the guns' magazines between their teeth—the girls stuck them in their bras so they could run faster), and do-or-die. I was the only girl to play defense in do-or-die. One real big guy was pushing me around while I was trying to get his tag. I was damned if he was going to get past me. We were fighting, the guy was pushing me off, it was physical. He tried to make a run for it—like he was going to barrel me over—but I made a grab for his tag and got it! I think I earned a lot of respect from the upperclassmen and my class.

Reveille blared through the barracks every morning at 0500 hours. Forty-five minutes of calisthenics were followed by a two- to five-mile run in boots, and then we had fifteen minutes to fly from shower to formation before breakfast. Our summer days were filled with parade drills, weapons training, runs, and mass athletics—known affectionately among the upper-classmen as "Mass Ass." Weeknights brought screenings of "motivational" war movies and concerts of military music. Saturday nights were spent binging on junk food at Eisenhower Hall.

Most of Beast Barracks, however, was spent adjusting to postulancy in West Point's Fourth Class System. The Fourth Class System is a painstaking process by which leaders at West Point are not born but made. Plebes begin their Fourth Class Year in the West Point hierarchy (actually the first year at the Academy) ranked beneath "the superintendent's dog and the commandant's cat." From this lowly position they are subjected to a host of physical, mental, and emotional stresses designed either to eliminate them from the Corps or to make them worthy of further ascent. This is in keeping with the conventional wisdom that what doesn't kill people makes them stronger. If plebes can manage to raise themselves from the depths of the Fourth Class Year, they are rewarded for their efforts with the privilege of entering the Third Class Year (the second year at the Academy), and so goes the progression for two more years, until they graduate as second lieutenants in the Regular Army, where the process is begun all over again on the ladder's bottom rung.

The chief instrument of the Fourth Class System is discipline. Discipline is valuable, claims the system—no matter how absurd—because its purpose is to forcibly teach an individual to function under difficult conditions.

We used to have clothing formations, for example. Our squad leaders would call us into formation in the hall, then send us to our rooms with an order to change into our White-Over-Gray uniforms (white shirts over gray trousers), and report to them afterwards. They'd give us only one minute to dress, so we'd have to run back to our rooms, pull off all our clothes, scramble into White-Over-Gray and try to make ourselves appear perfectly neat, but we'd look half-assed anyway, and they would tell us we were unacceptable. Then they'd say, "Now we want you in Dress Gray." So we'd run back and change again. It was a complete mess, but they'd keep toying with us like this for as long as it amused them.

During the two months of Beast Barracks, and throughout the entire Fourth Class Year, we were the whetstones on which the upperclasses honed their leadership. Although nearly every waking moment of our lives was dictated and controlled, we would be taken to task for failing to do things we didn't know were required, or that we hadn't had time to learn, much less perform. Expectations were left deliberately vague. Punishments were not.

Nobody liked the Fourth Class System in the beginning, but most cadets will admit "it did build you up." On the other hand, if you wanted to see depression, all you had to do was look at a plebe. People were telling us all the time that we were not meeting their standards even though we were trying our hardest. It started to get to us psychologically, but there wasn't much we could do. Our roommates helped. Together, we would work out ways to alleviate the pressure. And a lot of people dropped out.

The ones who suffered the most were the ones who didn't know how to play the game. West Point is not a compassionate place. The Fourth Class System is administered almost like a game—and if an individual doesn't understand the rules, then he or she may be "encouraged" to leave.

One company, in particular, had a couple of "spazzoids" [screwups], and the upperclassmen were ineffective at getting rid of them. Principally, the sophomores would approach the plebes and say, "Look—you've got at least three beanheads in your company who are dirtbags, so you'd better get them out of here, or it's going to get a lot rougher for everyone."

It then became the mission of all the plebes in the company to force out their three "dirtbag" classmates. In other words, to make them quit. Of the three who had been targeted, the company succeeded in getting rid of two. The third one flunked out. Machiavellian by tradition, the upperclassmen wouldn't hesitate to turn our own classmates against one another. The rule was to target the stragglers in order to effect the end result, which was to get them out of the Corps.

In 1986 the Academy began to conduct an in-depth survey into the Fourth Class System, and reassess its effect on the class itself. West Point is currently trying to make its system a developmental one for leaders, instead of just a fraternity rite of passage. Since the early nineteenth century, New Cadet Summer has been characterized by pranks and practical jokes, but savage hazing was not an intrinsic part of the Academy's original idea of discipline. Violent hazing was introduced to West Point in the post–Civil War years, when war veterans began entering the Academy as plebes, and the younger, less experienced upperclass cadre felt that they had to resort to desperate means in order to enforce their authority. Physical hazing was tolerated in a variety of forms afterward, but by the late 1960s certain practices were outlawed—"bracing," for example, which compelled a plebe to walk with his chin tucked in so far that he made a perfectly straight line down the back of his neck, or forced a plebe to use his neck in the same position to sweat a nickel to the wall. Unofficially, though, the practice continued—in fact, it was still going on during my plebe year.

Now, instead of exemplifying this type of terrible hazing behavior, the Academy is teaching the upperclasses to develop the plebes' characters by treating them as they would a real platoon. A female graduate of the class of '86 who participated in the Academy's study of the Fourth Class System explains that West Point has since disallowed a lot of traditional rituals that were detrimental to their well-being, such as the deprivation of food at meals, screaming at them, and "Black Boxes"—in which plebes were made to wear black hoods, walk into a dark room with candles lit in each corner, and take part in extremely secretive ceremonies. The end of such hazing has generated a lot of flak, however. Old grads are saying, "You're never going to make a good cadet out of somebody who hasn't had a tough Fourth Class Year." But it doesn't seem farfetched to believe that plebes can be made tough without being destroyed. Pressure can be applied by inspiring plebes to do their best, which is not to be underestimated.

One of my former male classmates concurs. "The Fourth Class System has got to change," says Kevin Lang, now a captain in the Armor Branch.

"Those kids are treated in ways that we would never treat a soldier. If I had a lieutenant who treated one of my soldiers like the cadets treat a beanhead at West Point, he probably wouldn't live to tell the story. So why do it? Why give a cadet the impression that there is a place for that in the military? We can stress somebody—put him through Beast, Basic Training, the works—without hazing the hell out of him.

"When I was a company commander," he continues, "I had to spend weekends pulling my soldiers out of the damn jail, because they'd go across the street and beat the snot out of all the other soldiers in the Aviation Battalion. There was no lack of aggression among them. I mean, those guys would say, 'Well, we're not going to the field this weekend, so let's go beat up some other soldiers.' There's no need to haze someone to make him aggressive. The thing we need to do is tell him he's the best thing on earth, and to work his little rear end off until he thinks he can't stand it anymore. Then let him take one more step before we say, 'Hey, you've made it. See? It wasn't that tough.' So I have some fundamental complaints about the way the Fourth Class System is administered. There's no place for humiliation or degradation within the system. And yet there are cadets—little weenies—who go through West Point with a stick up their ass, and get their jollies out of picking on people. And we tolerate that."

According to the logic of the Fourth Class System, hazing was a necessary crucible for bringing would-be West Pointers up to speed. In its ideal form, hazing was specifically related to performing tasks, memorizing required information, and, most important, learning the time-management and self-disciplinary skills that would enable a potential officer to function in a high-stress military environment. Harassment was meant to be aimed only at those individuals who were not seen as meeting the "standard"— but never directed at their gender, religion or race. If misapplied, however, the Fourth Class System could be twisted into very cruel contortions. As with any draconian system entrusted to human hands, misapplications were inevitable.

Women, in particular, became a target group for special hazing, though certainly men were not exempt. The difference was, men had to prove themselves weak before they became subject to this kind of harassment; women had to prove themselves strong before they were spared it.

In one company, I'm told, the men had formed a secret committee that would target one female cadet a month and harass her until she quit, or just make her miserable while she was trying to stick it out. During Beast

Barracks, the upperclassmen would open their doors and have new cadets brace themselves with their arms outstretched horizontally across the doorway, their feet off the ground. This was known as the Iron Cross. Since few women possessed the necessary upper body strength to maintain such a position, they were often ordered to hang suspended from the clothing rod inside an upperclassman's closet for an unspecified period of time. This practice was called "hanging around," which, as with bracing, could only be carried out secretly. More common were the "legitimate" hazes when, technically, no rules had been broken. These were extremely tricky to police since the upperclassmen were careful to stay within the regulations, at the same time as they were pushing these hazes to unbearable limits.

Hazing was constant, emotional, mental. It was like a form of terrorism, because we never knew when it was coming and where it was coming from, whether the upperclassman walking behind us would leave us in peace or start making foul remarks about our mothers. The worst part of it was, we were completely defenseless, and there was nowhere to turn for recourse. We realized very quickly that we had to make it on our own.

"Turn and face the wall," an upperclassman would tell a female new cadet. "You're ugly."

Even the simplest social exchange could become an occasion for contempt. If a female new cadet passed an upperclassman in the hall and said, "Good morning, Sir," she might be greeted in return with cool civility. Then again, she might hear back, "Good morning, bitch." Or, "It was a good morning until you got here, whore."

One disgruntled fellow snuck into the women's locker room one night and discovered an anonymous way to express his feelings on the subject of women at the Academy. The next morning, my classmate found her bathing suit sticky with his opinion.

"In my naïveté," my classmate Denise Gavin now recalls, "I thought, 'They've passed a law, of course they'll welcome us.' The women in the class who were older and had seen a bit more of the world were probably more irritated and provoked by the upperclassmen's behavior, while I, with wide-eyed amazement, tended to absorb it and was more prone to respond by saying, 'Yes, Sir,' rather than 'Damn you.'"

Julie Hawkins used to get in trouble all the time for having a smile on her face—only a slight one—whenever she was being disciplined by the upperclassmen. These guys would actually stand around and argue about it, too: Was it a real smile, or was it just the way she looked?

It was as though they wanted to measure it.

And Julie would look them straight in the eye, and say, "Sir, I am not smiling."

Deep down, of course, she knew that she was. It was her little way of getting even, she said, a very minor thing, but it really seemed to bother them. They didn't want anybody smiling, especially a female new cadet.

Conversely, my classmate Lori Eller never changed expression at all. In fact, the upperclassmen in her company would try to make her crack a smile, but it would never work. It drove them crazy until finally one firstie bet a group of yearlings [sophomores] that they couldn't make her cry. Lori didn't know about this for nearly six weeks. After some particularly humiliating form of abuse, she would go into her room and yell, "What did I ever *do* to these guys?" Eventually, one of the other yearlings told her about the bet, and so they called the whole thing off. Sometimes it was the small rebellions that were the most effective.

25 JUL 1976

Sunday. I saw my parents today for the first time in three weeks. I can barely play the game anymore. My mother tried to ask me what was wrong. I asked her what she had brought me to eat. I'm getting tired of keeping up appearances. It's making me brutish.

"The first time my parents came to visit me," classmate Virginia Taylor recalls, "I got pulled back inside my room by an upperclassman. It was another hour and a half before I could meet them, because the guy who stopped me thought I was wearing makeup. He accused me of having rouge on my cheeks. The funny thing was, I never wore makeup; my cheeks were just naturally rosy. But this guy was certain I had put on some blush. So he ordered me to stay at attention while he phoned somebody to ask about makeup regulations. It was so stupid, because he didn't even know what 'blush' was called. He kept saying, 'You know, that red stuff they wear on their faces.'

Then, after hanging up the phone, he walked over to the sink, picked up a washcloth, and wet it. He came back to where I was standing, grabbed me by the back of the neck, and started scrubbing my cheeks—trying to get the 'red stuff' off. While he was doing this, he claimed over and over that I was lying to him. But I just kept repeating, 'No.'

When he was convinced my cheeks were clean, he threw down the washcloth and left the room. For a long time afterward I sat on my bed, holding my face in my hands. My cheeks were burning."

38

31 JUL 1976

Today, Saturday, we had two whole hours of privileges. Paul McClain and I went over to Ike Hall together. He bought me a chocolate milkshake and a sundae.

In the beginning, dating at West Point was rudimentary. It was strictly forbidden for plebes and upperclassmen to socialize; even many of our own male classmates were reluctant to talk to us, for fear of being hammered by the upperclassmen.

But even if one of them were brave enough to "date" one of us, all it meant was that maybe we'd actually talk to each other during a break in mass athletics, or maybe we'd go to church together, not necessarily for piety, mind you—church just happened to be one of the few places where male and female cadets could spend time in each other's company without being harassed for it. There were also rare moments when we'd be free to meet at the snack bar in Eisenhower Hall to drown our sorrows in ice cream.

Another barrier between the sexes was West Point's inflexible rule against PDA, Public Displays of Affection. Once, when my classmate Natalie Weston was holding hands at the movies with one of the bolder men in our class, trying to be inconspicuous, hiding their hands beneath the arms of their chairs, an upperclassman sitting behind them suddenly butted his head between them and barked, *"Miss, what's your name and your company?"* This meant that he was writing Natalie up for a punishment. "The way he carried on about it," she recalls, "I really got upset. I felt like the 'Scarlet Woman,' and then I thought, 'Wait a minute. I'm a college freshman, holding pinkies at a movie with a man my age.' I had to remind myself that there was nothing wrong with that."

A woman at West Point was judged not only for the inescapable fact of her sexuality but for how she projected it, and always according to what was deemed appropriate—however arbitrarily—by men. We seemed to be continually stuck in a tiresome stereotype—if we were not socializing heavily with male cadets, then it meant we must be lesbians. If we *were* socializing heavily with male cadets, then it meant we must be whores. The rumor mill at the Academy turned so thoroughly and well, that the slightest innuendo about a female cadet took only minutes to traverse the entire Corps.

Regulations were imposed to maintain modesty within the barracks.

39

Gone were the days when a male cadet could make a mad dash for the bathroom in his underwear, a minor freedom whose loss elicited a certain amount of cantankerous grumbling. And yet, despite the extra safeguards against impropriety, there were some strange contradictions. The Academy's practice of not installing locks on barracks room doors, for example, was a function of the Honor Code. (Cadets do not steal, therefore locks are considered an unnecessary precaution.) Consequently, a few women received nighttime visitations by male cadets who would creep through the empty halls after Taps. The majority of these visits, however, consisted of nothing more than an expectant face in the dark, peering through a crack in the door.

Some regulations stipulated that whenever a man and woman were in a room together, the door had to be left open, and, like an old Hollywood movie, if they were sitting on a bed together, each of them had to keep at least one foot resting on the floor. But such puritanical restrictions seemed almost pointless when I could still look through my window into the shadeless windows of the building next door, and see men walking around in their birthday suits.

3 AUG 1976

Our cadre is starting to treat us like human beings. They are always encouraging us. The days seem to be going by faster. We have only three more weeks of Beast Barracks. This morning we started running with our rifles. The men carry M-14's. The women run with M-16's because they're two pounds lighter. But we keep reminding ourselves that M-14's are really just for show; M-16's are what they use in combat.

8 AUG 1976

Today is Sunday. I wish I had time to write during the week. Thursday we left on an eight-mile hike that took about four hours. In the afternoon, we went through a gas chamber. The gas didn't feel too great on the eyes, but it was an interesting experience. We were handed a black rubber gas mask to pull over our heads and sent into this huge tent filled with CS gas, which is an irritant gas used in riot control. They wanted us to feel secure and protected in this chemical environment, but then they pointed to us and said, "Take off your masks." We were supposed to recite something—our names, or the alphabet—and most of us got only as far as "C" or "D" before we realized we were choking and couldn't breathe. Suddenly our eyes were watering and we were completely overcome. We felt totally helpless, and this was harmless gas! People rushed out of the tent coughing and sputter-

ing. The stuff smelled rotten; it burned our eyes and noses. We could even taste the bitter sulphur in our mouths, a taste that stayed with us for days.

Friday night we stayed up and cleaned! When we finished, our uniforms hung in our closets an even fist's distance apart. Books stood on their shelves in descending order. Drawers had been carefully arranged. Walls were bare, desks were clear. The sink had been scrubbed within an inch of its life. The room couldn't have been more spotless.

It rained Saturday, so we didn't have our thirty-minute run or Inspection in Ranks or a parade. But we did have room inspection that morning. Our Tacs gave us holy hell! They ripped everything apart—dragged our desks away from the walls, pulled the clothes out of our closets, messed up our beds—then calmly left. We were devastated. We had worked so hard. We all started swearing. I was so mad I was yelling—"How could they do this to us, those assholes!" Suddenly, there was banging on the door. Someone had heard me. It was our platoon leader, Cadet Fairbanks. He came into our room and, with a big grin on his face, said, "Barkalow, you are in deep shit. You are really in trouble now." Then he said he was going "to screw" us. He hates women.

9 AUG 1976

After breakfast Cadet Lyons came by and told me I had to see the Tac (Major Langhorn). Well, he chewed me out, saying I had a poor attitude and that I was trying to "get over" [meaning "get by with minimum effort."] I really got depressed about it. On my way out of his office, I passed Cadet Fairbanks in the hall and didn't say "Good afternoon, Sir" to him. He made me bring him a 4-C, and then ordered me to stand outside his room and repeat twenty-five times, "Good afternoon, Sir," to the wall.

12 AUG 1976

Thursday we had bayonet drills. . . .

Bayonet drills always seemed to be done in the heat of the day. The cadet instructor stood on a four-foot-high platform in fatigue pants, boots, and a T-shirt with the words Bayonet Committee and the image of a dagger emblazoned across his chest. My company was lined up in close formation on the Plain—ten rows of cadets, about eighteen per row, standing eight to ten inches apart—in full view of local passersby. We listened for commands from the instructor:

"Extend to the left, march!"

One hundred eighty new cadets moved an arm's length away from each other. The movements had to be quick and sharp, executed with precision. This was guerrilla theater and like Japanese Kabuki, it was performed with histrionic seriousness.

"Arms downward, move. Left, face."

One hundred eighty pairs of hands held out their weapons, with straight arms parallel to the ground. Protective plastic sheaths heightened the gravity of the exercise—these weapons were so deadly, we were never permitted to remove the green bayonet scabbards from their steel blades.

"Arms downward, move. Right, face."

We snapped back to the position of attention and executed a ninety-degree turn to the right.

"From front to rear, count off."

The shouts rolled upward through the ranks.

"Even numbers to the left, uncover!"

The even-numbered rows took one giant step to the left, giving us even more room to maneuver. The instructor issued the next command.

"Smash!"

I held my weapon at Port Arms—diagonally across my chest, with the barrel of the rifle close to my left shoulder. I stepped forward with my right foot, raising the butt of the weapon parallel to the ground and alongside my left ear, then smashing it forward as if I were hitting an opponent in the face.

"Slash!"

I stepped with my left foot this time, ripping the fixed bayonet diagonally through the chest of an imaginary body, then finishing off my enemy with rifle butt strokes to the head and groin.

The more vicious we appeared during these exercises, the more praise we received. All around me, people were growling and chanting: *"Kill! Kill!"* or, *"Blood makes the grass grow!"*

I chanted, too, without thinking.

Cadet Hart, an upperclassman, took note of my performance. He got in my face and yelled above the din:

"You think you're tough, new cadet?"

I thought he was taunting me, but then I saw his eyes.

"Yes, Sir!" I screamed, exhilarated.

"You think you've got what it takes?"

"Yes, Sir!" In his face.

"Damn!" Cadet Hart said to a firstie standing beside him. "This one's doing it like the guys."

·   ·   ·

42

The intensity, the sheer physicality of human assault training, was a blessed release from our taut daily routine. Most cadets found it exciting. Cathy Gordon got so caught up in it at one point, she psyched herself out and fell over, hyperventilating. (A lot of men did this, too.)

Some women, who were not athletically gifted, appreciated the bayonet exercise purely for pragmatic reasons. It was, for once, a game they could win. Lori Eller recalls, "The bayonet exercise was a real easy one for me, because all I had to do was carry on as though I enjoyed the stuff. It was a great opportunity. We'd just yell, 'Yeah! I want to kill somebody!' And the guys were like, 'Oh, wow!' because they expected us to be wimps. But I tell you, this was *easy*. I wasn't running, right? My neck wasn't against the wall. So, I thought, What do you want me to do? Scream? Drool? Okay. Just watch me—'*Yeah, blood!*'"

And yet, all this grunting and grimacing and belligerent behavior did not come easily to everyone. A few of our classmates were plagued by serious doubts about becoming paid killers, and they gradually set themselves apart from the group. One woman broke down before she even reached the assault course. Unlike most of us, she had deeply taken to heart the awareness that she was being taught the correct way to stab and bludgeon another human being to death. A member of the cadre pulled her aside and instructed her to treat the exercise as a game and to accept the cold-blooded chanting as merely a part of it. Still, she protested. I remember overhearing her say to him, "Sir, I just don't think I can do this. I don't think I can be so aggressive and maniacal about killing anyone." The cadet's final answer was chillingly direct: "That's because you're thinking, new cadet. Don't think. Do what I tell you."

By summer's end, under the determined tutelage of the upperclassmen, this woman had managed to overcome her squeamishness. So had most of the others who intended to remain at the Academy. According to the Report of the Admission of Women to the U.S. Military Academy (Project Athena: 1977), of the twelve different training exercises, bayonet training was ranked, third among men and fifth among women, as one of the most "motivating" exercises of Beast.

14 AUG 1976

It is Saturday evening, 1940 hours. Room inspection went really well, but I fell out of the run this morning. I am not in condition! I also had a dirty rifle during inspection ranks.

Our demerits came down on Wednesday evening. I had twenty-eight. If I'd been given one more demerit, I would have had to walk the Area.

When we walk off punishment tours on the Area, we bring our rifles over to the paved concrete lot behind MacArthur Barracks and spend two or three hours just zooming back and forth: forty-four steps, turn; forty-four steps, turn; forty-four steps, turn. And an upperclassman is always watching.

15 AUG 1976

We were in the field three days this week. We qualified on the M-16, firing from a prone, a standing, and a kneeling position. We also fired the M-60. I qualified as Marksman, which was the average score. Sharpshooter was better, and Expert was the best. Some women qualified as Expert. I was happy about that.

Friday morning—the thirteenth—was the last of our guerrilla drills. Saturday morning we had a thirty-minute run. Diane Yeager and I ran right next to each other, and we both made it together! It felt so good.

Later on Saturday, I had to go to the PX to buy a new pair of sneakers. When I came out of the store, a man stopped and talked to me for about twenty minutes. He was asking me how I liked West Point and what the training was like. It's weird—when I speak to civilians, only the good is brought out.

Tonight, Sunday night, wasn't so hot. I got hazed for half an hour by our platoon leader because Amy McWilliams (who lives one floor below) and I were caught talking to each other with our heads out our windows.

16 AUG 1976

Monday. We found out our academic year companies today. Mine is A-3. We live on the second floor of Eisenhower Barracks.

During Beast, when there are only new cadets and their cadre on post, there are eight companies. When the upperclasses come back in the fall, 4,417 cadets (the total authorized strength of the Corps) get shuffled into thirty-six companies, each consisting of approximately 125 people. Three companies make up a battalion, three battalions make up a regiment, and four regiments make up the entire brigade.

According to an Academy fact sheet, dated 5 October 1976, women had been assigned, in groups of eight, to the first company of each of West Point's twelve battalions for the first year, as a means of providing reinforcement and support. The following year, they'd also be assigned to the second company of each battalion, and so on, until women cadets were represented in each of the Academy's thirty-six companies at the end of three years.

As in Beast Barracks, men and women would be billeted during the academic year in the same barracks, on the same floors. Individual rooms would be single-sex, with the female cadets' rooms situated close to the women's bathrooms. With this small act of forethought the administration spared women excess hazing by making the trip to the latrine mercifully brief. They must have known that the moment female cadets left the sanctuaries of their rooms, they'd be dead meat. The vultures would descend upon them in a heartbeat.

17 AUG 1976

Tuesday was a pretty good day. I met my new roommate when we had our regular company formation. Her name is Michelle Mathews. Her father and my father work for the same corporation—only they live in Chicago and we live in New York. It's a strange coincidence.

25 AUG 1976

Today we moved to our regular company barracks. By some miracle I didn't get hazed at all. As I was walking back from formation this morning, a detail member stopped me and asked if I played basketball and if I was going to be on the women's team. My name seems to be getting around—I don't know if I like that.

We had to get our LCE (Load Carrying Equipment) together, for tomorrow is our great march to Lake Frederick.

26 AUG 1976

Beast Barracks is over! We got up at 5:00 A.M. to eat breakfast. Eighth Company finally moved out at about 8:30. Major Langhorn told me I would be carrying our guidon for part of the trek to Lake Frederick. Cadet Lyons said that the major didn't tell just anyone to carry the company flag. I think I've proven myself to him. I must keep driving on.

The march was kind of tough! We went up the ski slope (that was the hardest) and Bull Hill. We didn't reach Lake Frederick until almost 2:00 P.M. We ate C-rations when we arrived. It's great that I am in a tent by myself—I am really sick of having roommates.

28 AUG 1976

It's about 5:30 A.M. now, and we are eating breakfast. Yesterday we had orientation training with a compass in the morning and land training in the afternoon. Next we had pugil stick training. First they dressed us up in helmets with protective face guards, mouth guards, and gloves. Then they

45

handed us these four-foot-long pugil sticks with hard rubber cushions on either end. After two cadets were called into the middle of a big circle, an instructor would yell, "Go!"—and the contenders would have to block their opponent's moves. They kept smashing each other until somebody got knocked over. It was fantastic. I knocked Bach on her ass! I'd been waiting for that chance ever since I found out about pugil stick fighting. I knocked up Yeager pretty well, too. All my frustrations came out then. The human assault course should be neat. We do that on Monday.

Tonight I had guard duty with my classmate John Hogan—what a pain. We had shifts from 7:45 P.M. to 9:30 P.M. and from 1:30 A.M. to 3:30 A.M.! Cadet Lyons and Cadet Hart tried to attack us. We didn't get too much sleep.

30 AUG 1976

Today we went through the human assault course. Five different lanes were set up on the other side of a gully. We had to run down our lanes through the gully, climbing over barriers and meeting our opponents on the other side. "New cadet, can you hear me?" the instructors would yell. When we'd answer affirmatively, they'd say, "Parry left!" Or, "Perform a butt stroke to the head!" If a reaction wasn't quick enough or accurate, they'd say, "Lady, you're dead! I want you to do that again!" Liz Jenkins got halfway through the men's qualification course before they realized she was a woman and sent her over to the "women's" lane. She was mad, too, because she'd been doing well.

I thought the human assault course wasn't bad, except for the simulators (fake artillery rounds that burst and make the air thick and smoky like gunpowder) and the run back, which was very tiring. My lungs filled up with smoke and I kept coughing. CBS News and many other reporters were there watching us. It was kind of disturbing. All the guys were getting angry because, just like R-Day, the focus was on the women.

Press Day, Lake Frederick. The Academy had refused to allow any media to film us during our training because they had wanted us to concentrate on the training itself. So they set aside a Press Day when anybody who was anybody could come. And they certainly did—cameras, reporters, the whole nine yards. The entire day was designated for interviews. The scene reminded me of people flocking to a Macy's sale right after Christmas. There were camera crews *running!* And where did they run to? The women, of course. And did that sit well with the guys? Hell no.

Every reporter brought the same bag of questions:

"Why did you come to West Point?"

"How are you adapting?"

"How does it feel to be here with all these men?"

"Are you being discriminated against?"

Our answers would be equally pat:

"I wanted to be an officer, and this was the best place to go."

"We're not being discriminated against; some guys don't like us being here, but we expected that."

But my favorite question was, "Do you feel that you've lost your femininity?" As though femininity were an umbrella, or a hat. Some of the women said, when they wanted to feel more feminine, they'd put on makeup or a skirt. For me, femininity was not a matter of how I looked or what I wore, but how I felt that counted. Because no one could take that from me.

Soon, nearly everything we did came under scrutiny. Outside West Point, the press attention was overwhelming. Inside, it became an excuse for further divisiveness. When my classmate Fran Boyd was once quoted in the newspapers, men she didn't even know would come up to her and say, "You're Cadet Boyd, and you said such and such in the *New York Times,* and I don't agree." Officers would not return her salutes. Upperclassmen spat insults at her. Much of the backlash against the media attention was sour grapes on the men's part, but this time we understood their resentment—some women even felt it was justified. The possibility of coming to West Point had always existed for these guys. Many of them had been looking forward to it since they were kids. They had worked hard to get there. Yet the only thing people wanted to hear about was what the women were up to. And there wasn't a damn thing we could do about it.

The Public Affairs Office would refer reporters to women who were doing well at the Academy and would present a positive image. A few were outspoken—they'd comment frankly on the guys' immature behavior and how they felt we were being mistreated, statements for which all of us were held responsible. Some of us turned ourselves inside out trying to distance ourselves from those remarks, to prove that *we* weren't the ones who were deliberately trying to stand out. We'd sit around with our male classmates and bad-mouth those women, not to mention the press.

31 AUG 1976

Tuesday—the march home, eight miles. When we got to our new companies, I spazzed real good. I was asked "the Days," which meant that I had to stop whatever I was doing and recite, in perfect order, the number of days that remained between now and every single major event that would occur during the academic year. Needless to say, I screwed up.

My squad leader's name is Kaplan. He is short, skinny, and mean. *He made it clear to us that he isn't going to let any of the women "get over."*

Tuesday morning. We took down our tents, folded them into our rucksacks, packed up our gear, and formed up for the march back home. We marched to West Point by company. My company—8th Company—was the last to leave. By the time we started marching, it had gotten hot; we were carrying forty-pound packs on our backs, but we had to keep looking good. Even though we'd been in the field and had showered maybe once every few days, we knew our first impression on the upperclassmen would be important. We knew they had just returned to school and would be there, waiting.

People began to get excited as we approached the Academy, singing songs and calling out cadences.

> There's a yellow bird with a yellow bill,
> Sitting on a windowsill.
> I lured it in with a piece of bread,
> And then I *stamped* its little head.

When we said, *stamped*—everyone stamped heavily with their left foot. That one was real popular.

By the time we reached the gates of West Point we had goosebumps. Hundreds of people had lined the streets from Thayer Gate to the Plain, cheering as we marched in, company by company, past the giant statue of George Washington, up the gray stone steps, and into the shadows of the mess hall for our first meal back.

The room was a gigantic sea of faces. My stomach was in knots—I wanted to eat and get out of there as quickly as I could. The upperclassmen left us alone, but they were watching us.

After lunch, when the battalions were given the order to "Rise!," I ran back to the barracks. While the new cadets were bustling around, unpacking and cleaning their gear from Lake Frederick, the upperclassmen were putting their rooms in order, too. Most of the noise in the hallways came from upperclassmen greeting each other—until they'd spot one of us. And, of course, if we were doing anything remotely wrong—not walking fast

48

enough, not keeping our eyes straight ahead—they would stop and admonish us, *"You'd better quit spazzing around in this company, dirtball,"* to establish their supremacy at once.

I guess I must have been doing something wrong, or maybe my uniform wasn't straight, because a firstie cornered me and started drilling me on the Days.

The Days were so hard to memorize that people used to make up little calendars for themselves and carry them around. This time I made it until Christmas all right, but I messed up on One Hundredth Night—which was not a good night to mess up on, because that was the seniors' hundredth night until graduation. The cadet kept asking me the Days over and over, until my head was swimming with dates and days and I couldn't think straight anymore. At last, he gave up and commanded me to bring him a 4-C.

I knew what would happen next. I'd bring him the 4-C, and he'd write: "Poor performance; i.e., This new cadet did not know the Days."

Then he would give the 4-C to my squad leader—a little hard-nosed guy who couldn't stand it when anyone in his squad messed up. And I'd have to go see him, and recite them again. When I had performed to his satisfaction, he'd finally let me go.

That afternoon we began our drilling on the Plain, practicing our marching formations for the Acceptance Day Parade. The Acceptance Day Parade was the first major milestone in our lives as cadets, because it signified both our successful completion of Beast Barracks and our formal acceptance as official members of the Corps.

But the upperclassmen would haze us even during the parades. And we had better answer when they called, even though they'd tell us to shut up right afterward. They'd ask us to recite the Days or the Chain of Command (naming every key military officer from our own squad leader up to the president of the United States), or they'd maddeningly ask, "Who am I?"—which we'd then have to guess from the sound of their voices behind us, because we didn't dare turn our heads. During our Acceptance Day Parade, one particular upperclassman kept repeating my name, but I couldn't hear what else he was saying, so I didn't respond.

The cadet approached me later and said, "Hey, Barkalow, didn't you hear me calling you?"

"Yes, Sir," I replied.

"Why didn't you answer me, then?"

49

"No excuse, Sir," I said.
"You had better learn my voice, Miss!"
"Yes, Sir," I said.

3 SEPT 1976

Wednesday we had lots of drills—and lots of classes. It seemed that every time I got back to my room, I was leaving again for another formation.

Now we are busy getting ready for SAMI [Saturday A.M. Inspection] tomorrow, when the upperclassmen will come in and sweep their white gloves over everything. We've already Brassoed the doorknobs, scrubbed behind our desks, swept the floor—we've even scrubbed the lightbulbs. The beds look perfect—the folds in the sheets, the fluff of the pillows, the cuts in the corners. Rather than risk a wrinkle, we'll sleep on top of the covers.

During Saturday morning inspections, we'd stand at Parade Rest beside our beds—backs straight, heads and eyes forward with our feet shoulder-width apart, and our hands flat across our backs—right on top of left—elbows out. We weren't supposed to lock our knees in this position; it could cut off the circulation in our legs and make us pass out.

After all the rooms were inspected, our company would form up outside on the apron for the in-ranks inspection. When we'd stand at Parade Rest with our M-14 rifles, we'd hold our left hands behind our backs, and our rifles in our right, with their butts on the ground, angled out from our bodies at forty-five degrees. When we'd come back to attention, we'd snap everything back into place, like debutantes snapping their painted fans shut. The most likely reason for a cadet to acquire a demerit was for the rifle's condition. We never fired the damn thing, but somehow it was always dirty. We had to clean it at least once a week and Brasso all the little parts. The inside of the rifle chamber had to be lubricated and oiled, the spring taken apart and cleaned. We'd polish the stock with linseed oil, but we'd get demerits if the wood seemed too oily. We were never given bullets for these rifles, but there were no firing pins inside them, so we couldn't have fired them anyway. In Beast Barracks we'd carry rifles on runs, but during the academic year we'd use them only for inspections, marching in parades, and walking off punishment tours on the Area.

When the cadet inspector stepped in front of us, we'd lift up our rifles, pull back and open the chambers, and hold them there—a lock held them in place—which was the hardest thing for a woman to do, because the spring was so tight. To make this process easier for women, the Academy modified the hammer spring on the women's rifles by shortening the operating rod. Men were left to struggle with their rifles as they were.

Because in-ranks inspections took so long, we went from standing at strict attention to relaxing slightly into Parade Rest, and then snapping back to attention again—mainly so we wouldn't get too stiff in one position and fall over. But we had to be told to switch positions before we were ever allowed to move.

When it came to inspecting the plebes, the upperclassmen would snatch our rifles from us, which was always startling. We practiced and practiced to be ready for that moment, because to us, those guys were perfect. They were immaculate. Out of the corners of our eyes, we'd see them snatching other people's rifles, and knew that we'd better let go of ours as soon as they grabbed them because they'd get mad if we didn't perform exactly right. There was a whole ritual governing how they inspected the weapon. Very military, very precise. The cadet would gaze along the barrels, drawing them slowly in front of his face as if he were examining a fine cigar. Then he would swing them down, open up the butt plates, snap them back into place, then swing them up so he could inspect the underside of the weapons. This took about two minutes to perform, but it felt like an eternity. All the while we stood there, staring into the young man's breastplate because we couldn't move our eyes anywhere else. One upperclassman escorted the inspector on the right, and another flanked his left, recording our flaws.

At my first brigade inspection I was marked for "Oily Weapon" and "Rusty Weapon." No matter how perfect we were, they had to find something wrong. A fourth classman was never perfect, otherwise how could we improve? On the other hand, they did compliment us if we had good shoes or good brass. Then they'd give back the rifles with one hand, and we'd stand perfectly still until the trio moved on to the next cadet. Like mechanical dolls, we'd click the weapons shut, the bolts sliding forward, and bring them back down to our sides.

That day we got inspected twice, so we were standing out in the hot sun on the cement apron skirting the Plain for about two hours. There was a slight commotion; it turned out some guy over in Company B-3 had fainted. Meanwhile, we could see the weekend tourists lined up on the Plain's diagonal walk, and we could hear them hunting for women cadets. "Look, there's one!" they'd point and squeal. We fled to our rooms.

51

4 SEPT 1976

Saturday morning we attended an Honor lecture given by Cadet Fox. Some of the guys who had been found guilty of cheating in EE-304 had not finished with all the legalities, and are being allowed to stay and start classes.

In the wake of the 1976 cheating disaster, the Academy became more Honor-conscious than ever. When our class arrived, the administration seemed hell-bent on drilling the Honor Code into our heads. Living within the Code meant living beyond reproach, they told us, with no room whatsoever for mistakes. Telling the truth was the only possible solution.

We were not obligated to inform on classmates who merely broke regulations—at least not in the way that we were obligated to expose liars, cheats, and thieves. However, situational distinctions could be subtle and easy to confuse. In one instance, Cathy Gordon recalls, a cadet regimental commander violated regulations by going out drinking with a group of his buddies in downtown Highland Falls. Subsequently plagued by guilt, the cadet not only turned himself in but also everyone else who had accompanied him.

Consequently, the isolation and loneliness we felt, particularly as plebes, became augmented by a fear of sharing confidences. We were still very young, after all, going through a time in our lives when a lot of things were happening to us that we needed to talk about, but couldn't. In most cases, it wasn't other people's malice that we feared; it was their honor. We were reluctant to divulge anything too intimate, even to a close friend—hell, *especially* to a close friend—because by doing so we were placing both ourselves and our friends in potential peril. If our friends knew something secret about us, they were honor-bound to reveal it upon being asked. If an officer or upperclassman wanted to know, "Where is your roommate?" and we happened to know she was upstairs with her boyfriend, we could not say, "I don't know, Sir, maybe she's in the library."

Of course, if we walked into our friend's barracks room and saw her flagrantly breaking regulations by sitting there and drinking a beer, we could probably get away with saying, "Hi there, see you later," and walk out.

But if we walked down the hall and someone said, "Hey, did you know so-and-so was drinking a beer in her room?" and we said, "Really? Gee, I didn't know that," not only might our friend get into trouble, but by knowing and withholding such information we could get our asses kicked out, too.

So, exactly what is "honor" in West Point's view? According to the Code, an honorable cadet "does not lie, cheat, steal, nor tolerate those who do." The "nontoleration" clause is reported by cadets to be the hardest to uphold, but the concept seems endemic. There are, after all, many things which are not tolerated at the Academy. The fat ones, for example, or the stragglers, or the sensitives. One does not tolerate. And how is this state of nontoleration achieved? Is it possible to construct a human community completely free of weakness, frailty, failure, and regret?

As West Point has discovered, there are only two ways to do it. The first is by immediate excision—like a cancer—of those who fall from grace. There is no place at the Academy—at least not initially—for repentence. Once a cadet is pronounced guilty of an Honor violation, separation from the Corps—the worst of all possible punishments for individuals whose highest ideal is group cohesion—takes place swiftly and without prolonged debate.

The second, which is much less direct but equally useful, is by way of evasion. The Code, in practical effect, inspires obedience, not reverence. The commitment to truth is too often overshadowed by a fear of confrontation. "Don't tell me about things going wrong," becomes a pervasive attitude. "Don't put me in a position where I have to do something about it."

5 SEPT 1976

Last night was our first Plebe Hop. I wore my uniform skirt. I hate that thing! The hop was in Ike Hall—the first and last time it will be there. From now on, it will be in the gym. I had a good time dancing with guys I didn't even know. I got in after midnight. I was so tired, I just went to bed.

Mandatory good times are common in the military, and West Point was no exception. The Plebe Hop was the first time our whole class had come together for a party. No alcohol was served, but we could buy soda and milkshakes, sandwiches, and pizza. Tables were set up around a dance floor, and the Academy brought in a rock and roll band. This caused some unanticipated distress among certain members of the administration, who were reportedly perturbed by the sight of mirror-image couples dancing in short hair and dress gray trousers. A rule was subsequently passed declaring that women could attend all future hops in trousers, but they had to wear skirts if they wanted to dance. Some of us deliberately went to hops wearing trousers after that, so none of the men could dance with us. As it turned out, not many of them wanted to dance with us, anyway.

Unless we were permitted to take leave and go off post, our only option for at least three years was to stay in the social vacuum of Ike Hall. First Classmen had cars and privileges; we'd watch them leave for New York City to have a dinner and dancing date, or to see a show. There just wasn't that much diversity on post, and we rarely had regular college-type parties, so the social atmosphere was fairly strained. It seemed especially debilitating for the men, who needed exposure to women and normalized experiences with them. To remedy this, the Academy would bus in civilian women, which we called "the cattle call." We were very threatened by this, and acted very catty about it, too, because it pissed us off, especially since female plebes were forbidden to date upperclassmen, so the male plebes were our major resource. As we saw it, we had the potential for much better relationships with the men, since we were intelligent, athletic, and, most of all, we were going through the same thing they were. We *understood* it. But the male cadets would always make a big deal about the "real" women coming up for the hops. To us, these women who were brought in from nearby Ladycliff or Mount St. Mary's College, seemed as if they were merely an opportunity for the men to have a sexual release, and not necessarily a real relationship.

"I think it's a lonely world for these girls while they are here," said Mrs. Caroline Gaspard, the Academy's Cadet Hostess, "because they do want to be accepted as 'just one of the guys,' but they want to feel attractive, too. Before a dance the boys will always ask me, 'When are the girls coming up?' And I'll say, 'Dance with your classmates.' And they'll say, 'Oh, them. We see them all the time.' I feel sorry for our girls, because we do bring in civilians for the guys to dance with, but we don't bring in civilian guys for them. So, while they're here, some of these girls will simply resign themselves to not having boyfriends."

(According to a female graduate of the class of '86, the Academy did ask the women of her class if they wanted civilian men shipped in for the dances, and they responded with an emphatic "No" because "there would be superbacklash. We would rather go without," she said, "than have to withstand the crap we'd have to take from the male cadets if that happened.")

Women were lumped together at West Point with a disdain that was truly alarming. There was a definite streak of misogyny, however playful. We realized this when we began to notice that many of the female cadet

54

jokes we were hearing had been modeled on the Ladycliff jokes, because some women had reported hearing vicious jokes about the "Cliffies," too.

Female cadet jokes dealt with topics ranging from looks to love life, but the majority focused on weight:

"What's the difference between an elephant and a female cadet?"
"About five pounds, but you can force feed the elephant to make up the difference."
"What do you call a bunch of beanettes in a swimming pool?"
"Bay of Pigs."
And when the class of '81 came in:
"What do you call a female yearling and two plebes?"
"Pork and beans."

Of course, none of the men who told these jokes stopped to consider that all the cadets were then required to attend every meal, and normally consumed between five and six thousand calories a day. By our senior year, attendance at breakfast was made optional, and in subsequent years a nutritionist was brought in to supervise cadets' diets, and the caloric level of their meals was somewhat reduced.

Further, sometimes the only positive stimulus we could find in a day tended to be something sweet and fattening. Instead of smoking a cigarette or chewing on a piece of gum, some women would reach for a bag of M&M's. When they became overweight, it caused them to receive even more adverse criticism than usual, and so their sense of self-esteem would go right down the tubes.

To compound the problem, we had professors—majors and lieutenant colonels—who also told jokes about female cadets. One of the cadet clubs had a standing joke that there was a U.S. conspiracy to create an army made up entirely of women. So if the Russians beat us, we could say "So what? You beat an army of women!" They thought this was hysterically funny.

Perhaps the cruelest of the jokes, however, were the "pig pools"— contests to see which cadet could bring the fattest or ugliest woman to a dance, which, in my experience, was always a civilian. Each guy would chip in, and then they'd vote, and whoever had the ugliest date won a bagful of money. Sometimes we'd be sitting at the table laughing along with these guys, yet a part of us would be thinking, This is stupid, this is awful, this is mean. But we felt forced to be on their side, because we weren't one of those girls. We weren't in the bathroom with them, preening and primping and adjusting our little halter top dresses. We were in uniform.

Of course there were times when we'd hear one of these jokes and think that maybe we should have been more vocal against them. The overriding question was, Where do we expend our energy? We had to pick our arguments. In some cases we learned to suppress our anger, even outrage, when we figured it simply wasn't worth it.

Finally, word came down that anyone caught telling a female cadet joke would be punished, so no one dared to do it openly anymore. As a male graduate from the class of '87 remarked, "There will always be female cadet jokes, but the females are now protected by the institution." Perhaps it was preferable that the hostilities went underground, because it meant that at least some behavior modification had taken place, which was better than none at all.

Even so, it was exasperating, because every woman who entered the program had come in with a fairly positive self-image—she wouldn't have taken the leap unless she felt she could land with grace on the other side.

We had imagined West Point to be this potentially wonderful experience with superior people who were the models of society, but the harassment and chauvinism we encountered on a daily basis were demoralizing. Day after day we were essentially being told: "You're not desirable, you're not good." And just imagine the eye contact you have with a man when his whole expression tells you, "I hate your guts." Somehow we learned to overcome it. We put up incredible facades. And, yes, we became assertive, because that was how we survived.

On the other hand, some of the most aggressive and dynamic people I knew at West Point were also among the most insecure. A woman's self-esteem was extremely threatened there because, after all, she had left the civilian world where she usually wore makeup, had long hair, and boyfriends, and when she got to West Point, suddenly a man wouldn't look at her, wouldn't touch her. She was not considered desirable, either as a professional or a sexual partner, so, in a way, she had to re-create herself. Which a lot of women found difficult to do. We did progress. We did learn things about ourselves that we might never have learned otherwise. We became a lot braver than we used to be, and a lot tougher. But we still didn't know whether we were going to end up liking ourselves. We continued to pray that maybe, if we persevered and excelled, our performance would eventually speak for itself.

LABOR DAY—6 SEPT 1976

Melissa Patterson and I went to locate our classes. I just hope I can find them tomorrow. I am Brigade Minute Caller this week, which means I have to stand in the Brigade Staff hallway and announce the ten, five, four, three, and two-minute bells before formations. I will be lucky if I don't get hazed.

At dinner we found out who made the basketball team; thirteen girls were chosen, and I was one of them.

7 SEPT 1976

Today was our first day of classes. I had math and phys ed in the morning, Spanish and earth science in the afternoon. I know I will be tied down with homework every night. Basketball started today. We'll be working on the Nautilus machines. I did leg presses first—and felt sick afterward. Then we ran two miles. I thought I was going to throw up. Cadet Hunt is CCQ [Cadet in Charge of Quarters]. He asked me my first name, and now he usually calls me Carol (when firsties aren't around).

Tonight we had a scheduled rally. We dressed up in the craziest things we could find, and yelled "Rally!" down the hall. I couldn't believe all the different outfits people wore. Everyone was in Old South Area, and the cadet band played.

Rallies were held before football games to raise esprit de corps, especially early in the season, before we'd started to lose. At precisely ten minutes before Taps, we'd hear someone—right on schedule—run through the hallways calling for a "spontaneous" rally after Taps. The rallies were usually held in Old South Area. It was really the best place to have them, because we could climb out on the overhang between the first and second floors of the Old South Area barracks building, and a few dyed-in-the-wool daredevils could try to jump off the fifteen-foot clock tower onto the pavement below. People came dressed in the craziest outfits—togas with sabers, or Full Dress coats with shorts instead of trousers. The band would play Army fight songs, while the Rabble Rousers [West Point cheerleaders] would dance and lead cheers. Everyone threw water balloons, and rolls of toilet paper. At West Point I learned there was an art to getting a roll of toilet paper to unravel as it was thrown. Rallies gave us an added incentive to act crazy, because the more motivated we seemed, the better the upperclassmen liked it. Even our recreation was a performance.

9 SEPT 1976

David Murray (yearling) got into trouble today for being too friendly with me. It made me mad. There are other upperclassmen around here who BS with the male plebes, but once they talk to a female, it's assumed there must be something between them. It's so much easier for the guys to hide plebe-upperclass friendships, because two men are allowed to go into a room together and close the door. With men and women, the door always has to be open, so anyone can look.

9 OCT 1976

I got back from the Penn State game today. All last week I was up for getting out of here. Now it doesn't feel as if I've been gone. I have to fall back into the West Point routine, even though I don't want to. Right now I wish I could go home for good.

The Penn State game was our first trip off-post, the first time we met the outside world since becoming cadets.

It rained hard all weekend long. On Saturday night, I snuck off to Arby's for a roast beef sandwich with some friends. By the time we reached the restaurant our hair and clothes were drenched. When I got to the front of the line, the girl at the counter looked at me and said, "Can I help you, Sir?" Well, I had to leave immediately. "Come on," I said to my friend Steve, "let's get out of here." We walked outside together. The cold air hit me and I started to shake. I excused myself and ran back to the hotel. When I got there, I locked myself in the bathroom. I looked at myself in the mirror and cried. I felt so confused. Did I look like a man? What was West Point doing to me?

16 OCT 1976

Today I have a lot of mixed emotions. I don't know why. On Saturday, I went on a trip to Saratoga State Park with the Military Affairs Club. Some of my old friends from home had arranged to meet me in the Dunkin' Donuts parking lot there. Two carloads showed up—Amy came, and so did Kim, Karen, Oompa, Lisa, M.J., Coon, and Willy. Mitchell and Stephanie, too. I had a good time talking with everyone, but then I kind of wanted to go back to West Point. I think I missed it! It felt so strange. I wish I could have spent time with each of my friends, just talking with them the way I used to. I feel they are mine to watch over. But I also feel myself pulling away.

When I returned to West Point I went to Nancy's room and stayed there until 12:45 A.M.—fifteen minutes before Taps. We talked a lot. I wish we had nothing like Taps. I could have stayed there and talked all night. I miss having a close friend.

21 OCT 1976

I got yelled at tonight by Joe Dimitris—a cow [junior] in the company— because I messed up on minute calling. He knows nothing about good leadership and tact. He is going to find the Regular Army very hard.

28 OCT 1976

Classes are boring but I am not "D" (deficient) in anything yet.

As plebes, our time was not our own. Every minute was planned. A typical day went like this: Reveille, clean the room, make the beds, shower, dress, form up on the apron for breakfast, march into the mess hall, see that the upperclassmen's needs were attended to, sit ramrod straight in our chairs and eat, then head to our first class. If this happened to be math, we'd have to stand before the class, wipe the remaining cobwebs from our brains, brandish our pointers and declaim mathematical formulas at 7:30 in the morning with the proficiency of Pythagoras. If we'd miss a class without valid authorization, we'd have to walk the Area or be sentenced to sitting alone for hours in our rooms.

In between morning classes, we had duties to perform—either picking up or delivering bed linen, dry cleaning, and other laundry, or scribbling homework. After our second hour of classes we'd help distribute the mail (all the company mail must be sorted and delivered before lunch).

Once the various bells were sounded, and we had formed up on the apron and marched in to lunch, we would serve our betters their beverages, hastily eat our own food, serve the desserts, then attend two classes in the afternoon. When classes were finished, we'd have sports practice or meetings. I played basketball, so as soon as practice was over, I'd take a split-second shower, ping back to the barracks, and dress for dinner before the ten-minute bell. If, by some miracle, I had managed to find some spare time, I'd use it to accomplish whatever other duties I had been assigned, and then proceed to the mess hall for dinner. After dinner, we'd go back to our rooms at seven o'clock, and from seven to eight we'd be at the disposal of our squad leaders, if they needed to talk to us. If not, we'd be in the bathroom practicing pull-ups or frantically completing our unfinished duties for the day. At eight, we'd start our homework. And though it wasn't supposed to happen, upperclassmen would often take this opportunity to come around and haze us.

Taps were at eleven, but if there were going to be an inspection the next day, we'd often stay up past one in the morning, cleaning our rifles or our rooms. We'd have to fall asleep quickly, however, because at 5:00 A.M. the day would begin again.

31 OCT 1976

Halloween. Tonight a lot of the yearlings, and a few of the cows and firsties came around for candy. It was "boodle or brace"—give the upper-classmen candy or sweat a nickel to the wall. I wrote home for the first time since Beast. It was nice to just sit and write.

8 NOV 1976

It's Monday morning and I'm sick of this place. Michelle and I had another argument last night. She came in crying twice from doing pull-ups. I can't stand it when she cries. Right now I want to quit. I'm so frustrated here! I dread each new day, when I should be looking forward to it. And Michelle doesn't help matters at all.

[LATER]

Well, it has been quite a night. Michelle says she is going to resign. She's been bawling all night long, and I am getting a new roommate on Thursday morning.

Michelle and I handled stress differently. Whenever she got into trouble, or whenever something didn't go her way, she'd lie on her bed and cry, and I'd always have to listen to it. In the beginning I tried to offer support, but I was working hard to keep myself motivated, and it was becoming increasingly difficult to do that for the two of us. Her attitude had begun to affect me; it was wearing me down. One evening, it reached the limit.

Everybody had to practice pull-ups. Women only had to do a flexed arm hang from the pull-up bar, and we were judged by the number of seconds we could keep our chins above the bar. Practically every night the squad leaders would take their squads into the men's bathroom—where the pull-up bar was—to practice. On this particular evening, Michelle had come in twice from doing pull-ups, and she hadn't been able to do a single one. Each time she came back to our room, she began her nightly ritual of collapsing onto her bed in tears. The second time, I exploded.

"Michelle," I said, "this is ridiculous. I can't handle your crying anymore."

I was sitting on the sink, and Michelle was lying across her bed, and we both started yelling at each other. The next thing we knew, our squad leader was pounding on the door. He didn't wait for a "Come in," either—he just threw the door open. I had already kicked the door a few times and banged my fist on the sink—between that and the sound of Michelle's wailing, he must have thought I was hitting her.

We both jumped to attention when Cadet Fairbanks walked in.

"At ease," he said quickly. "As you were."

Michelle perched on the edge of her bed, and I slumped back onto the sink.

"Now," he said, "I want you both to tell me what has been going on here."

"Sir," I said, "my motivation level is low. I'm trying to help Cadet Mathews, but it's not working."

I had already spoken to Kerry Norman, another woman in my company, and she had agreed to switch rooms with Michelle, so I suggested the move to Cadet Fairbanks.

Fortunately, he was amenable. He understood that the world we lived in as plebes was as compressed as a golf ball. The moment something went wrong in our personal lives, it would instantly affect our academics, affect *everything,* in fact, and it would mess us up real fast.

10 NOV 1976

I got three demerits for wearing my sweater outside the company area. Cadet Daniels caught me. That guy is such an ass. Well, only thirty-seven more days until Christmas. I can't wait.

12 NOV 1976

Kerry looked out the window tonight and all of MacArthur barracks was formed up on the apron. Firetrucks stood in front of Washington Hall. Someone had pulled a fire alarm. It was rally night again, so we were yelling "Rally!" out the window and talking to the plebes in the room above us. All of a sudden, Kerry got hit with flying water—that's war! So we got glasses of water and tried to throw water back up at them. Of course, Cadet Evans yelled at us for making too much noise. But it was a kill—I'm in a much better frame of mind. Now that Michelle is out of my room, I have a clear feeling in my head.

17 NOV 1976

Basketball practice was good today—it was the last day I had to ping back for formation. We got to fall out at dinner because it was Steak Night. Steve Chapman and I were fooling around. He was at the next table, and

61

we played "looky"—stealing quick glances at each other, then looking away while trying not to laugh. For once everything here seems almost normal.

22 NOV 1976

We had a leadership evaluation meeting with our Tac in the company dayroom. We are going to fill out our peer evaluation reports next Monday. Cadet Harrington showed me his and Cadet Kaplan's evaluations of me. They both ranked me number one in the squad! Not all the women are so lucky. Somebody in Fran Boyd's squad wrote, "Cadet Boyd should be a schoolteacher, or a librarian."

It was apparent to most women at the Academy that the command structures could not fully support us. As Lieutenant Colonel Jerome Adams, formerly of West Point's Department of Behavioral Science and Leadership, now observes, "First we had to understand the problems; then we had to convince the decision makers that the chain of command wasn't going to solve them. So, by sharing information with the Naval and Air Force Academies, who, of course, were also going coed, we all agreed to try and assess, through paper-and-pencil measures, the feelings and attitudes of West Point men toward the rights, roles, and privileges of women in society and in the military. Questionnaires were administered to the male faculty and cadets early on in the integration process, to determine whether these men were egalitarian, progressive, or traditional in their beliefs. And they were *very* traditional. However, no one really cared what their attitudes were, what mattered was whether they acted according to standards of professional behavior. And those early studies clearly linked the men's subjective biases in professional judgment with their attitudinal beliefs. To the senior policy planners, this demonstrated that integration was not going to work 'on its own' over time, unless certain institutional priorities were set.

For example, after we documented the 'traditional' attitudes of the faculty and cadets, a laboratory experiment was conducted that artificially assigned half of the task groups to be led by male cadets and half to be led by females. All of the followers in the groups were men. Half of those followers had traditional attitudes and half were egalitarians. The nature of the task assigned to these groups was twofold—one was an expressive, narrative, command project and the other was a finite form of engineering drawing. When both tasks had been completed, and done well, we asked the female-led male groups with traditional attitudes, 'How do you account for your success outcome?' And they said things like, 'Well, the group was cohesive, we worked well together,' and so on. They did not recognize the influence of the female leader. When more pointed questions were asked, such as, 'What about Leader X?' They would respond, 'Oh, she was lucky.'

However, when we asked the same questions of the female-led traditional groups who *hadn't* done well, the cause was invariably linked to the female leader. So there was compelling evidence that the male cadets were allowing attitudinal biases to influence their judgments, even in the face of such an objective criterion as, 'Is this engineering task drawn correctly?'

We then presented the outcome of our experiment to the policy planners. We explained that these same kinds of biases were bound to impede the normal leadership development of women. And that was our initial framework. We went on to conduct a series of forty-two different leadership studies, charting the progress of our initial groups and those that followed, to determine what issues were coming up so we could target our interventions accordingly, though not very well, I must say, in the beginning.

The superintendent at the time, General Andrew Goodpaster, was a tremendously vocal advocate of the women when he came on board. He got all of the officers and senior noncommissioned officers together at the start of the year and said, 'Here are my organizational goals for the Academy.' He talked about excellence in academics and athletic success, and then he set aside time for a special discussion on the integration of women. He said—and he was referring to members of the staff and faculty as well as to the cadets—'Women are here at West Point, and they are here to stay. Anyone who cannot support that institutional goal can see me, and I will make arrangements for him to leave.' Which was a very strong statement for a general officer to make in an open forum, but we needed that kind of advocacy after the previous superintendent had already stated as a role model that women shouldn't be here. Even so, General Goodpaster's statement by itself was not enough. We then had to severely punish or extinguish the undesired behavior that unfortunately persisted. But the senior policy planners didn't have any clear strategy to determine what they ought to be doing next. In the formative years, the Academy was simply in a very reactive mode. 'Okay, here's a problem—now let's deal with it.' For instance, we had large numbers of male cadets making very disparaging remarks to female cadets, and someone had to say, 'That's not right, it will not be tolerated, and punishment will be swift.' Well, initially, the senior leadership said, 'Have the women report this problem through the chain of command, and we'll take action.' The chain of command, however, was often part of the problem. So, through trial and error procedures, the commandant at that time conducted special groups where he would bypass the chain of command by regularly consulting a number of female cadets, so he could have direct access to the problems they were experiencing. Well, that might have worked had there been a systematic way of gaining information. But the commandant just picked a few women arbitrarily. And their comments, of course, were not necessarily reflective of all the women. Consequently, there was some divisiveness within the class as to how the women's thoughts were being represented. Some women wanted simply to be cadets and not make waves, while others were more vocal—there had been a good deal of dissension in that regard. So bypassing the chain of command wasn't working either, because there wasn't any way to ensure that the women talking to the commandant were presenting balanced information on behalf of *all* the women. We then decided to set up an annual conference—every officer who was a lieutenant colonel or higher stopped work and went down to the Hotel Thayer for three days to discuss the circumstances that were impeding integration—whether in the classroom, on the athletic fields, in physical training, or barracks life. It became the only solution to the problem of making the senior activity directors and faculty department heads fully aware of the kinds of things that were usually found out through hearsay, and let them know to what degree these problems involved and affected *them,* as well as how they should be addressing the integration process."

None of us had imagined that integration would occur overnight, and we knew it couldn't be enforced by rules and regulations. We also knew that even if the administration set up an institutional framework, there was still a volatile chemistry at work within every cadet company, and tactical officers couldn't act as policemen twenty-four hours a day.

We had to learn to be our own psychiatrists. If we confided in anyone, we confided in our roommates, but even that wasn't always possible. Going for a run was one way to vent the tension. Taking a walk and looking at the Hudson River to try and calm down, was another. Had we been at the end of our own resources, we might have sought help from the Cadet Counseling Center or our sponsor [an officer who functions as a "big brother" or "big sister" for cadets] or from professors. But we were very reluctant to approach anyone, no matter how hurtful our experience. We thought that talking about our troubles would blow them too far out of proportion or that our vulnerability might be interpreted as weakness.

We did cautiously seek a certain amount of refuge within our own ranks, however. As plebes we were not permitted to speak in the latrine, but we could be "at ease" in there. So, of all places, the bathroom became our haven. We'd go way in the back by the showers and turn on the water so no one could hear us, and we'd gossip and cry and giggle like normal teenagers until we'd get to laughing so hard that an upperclassman would come banging on the door:

"Bam! Bam! Bam! You shut up in there! You beanheads get out in thirty seconds or we're coming in!"

We'd then zip through the back door before they could get us.

As Colonel Adams explained, General Andrew Goodpaster, who ultimately replaced General Berry as superintendent on 13 June 1977, was genuinely supportive of women, but his example was not always followed the way it should have been. An instructor, for example, might take it upon himself to go on a ten-minute tirade in class about how he thought the women on the basketball team were dykes. Or, as it happened in military science class, when the class had to write an essay, Liz Jenkins got a C, while a male classmate got an A-minus. When they compared their papers afterwards, and saw no appreciable difference in the quality of the two essays, Liz approached the instructor to ask why she had gotten such a low grade. His response was, "A woman shouldn't be doing well in tactics."

Major Christine Bowers, a former Academy Tac officer, recalls that at other times, "teachers would do something which could best be described as 'silhouetting.' They would deliberately flush the women out. In a law class of nine male cadets and one female, for example, after they'd been discussing some case, such as the 1961 *'Mapp v. Ohio,'* the teacher would turn to the lone female in the room and say, 'Now let's hear from the *woman's* point of view,' as if her point of view would necessarily differ. And so, the suggestion would be planted in the minds of the nine males who were sitting there that just because she was a female, she automatically had a different viewpoint."

Dr. James A. Peterson, then Associate Professor of West Point's Office of Physical Education and Officer-in-Charge of the Women's Basketball Team, observes, "The one thing I regret most about the entire integration process was our failure to educate the faculty. We educated and barraged the bejesus out of the cadets. We educated and barraged the bejesus out of the people in P.E. But what we really needed to do, with an almost equal level of intensity, was to get the whole damn West Point faculty together, one department at a time, and say, 'Hey, this is what this means.' But how do you correct prejudice? How do you correct ignorance? You can't change a two-hundred-year-old institution with a policy pill and, all of a sudden, make it work. I don't imagine that the admission of blacks was as traumatic to West Point as the admission of women. Even color barriers aren't quite as definitive, in my opinion, as the fact that cadets feel the presence of women lessens the value of the West Point experience, which somehow lessens *their* degree, or achievement. This is a physical place. So, graduating people who can only do fifteen push-ups, have fat asses, and generally are not good physical performers, is a very difficult thing for certain people in the system to accept."

Dr. Peterson was one of many instructors who expended a great deal of energy trying to keep things fair and right. There *were* men of character at the Academy, whose vision was sufficiently broad to reach beyond the limits of prejudice. Some of them were black cadets, who could draw upon their own experiences for analogy. Cathy Gordon remembers when one of our black male classmates stood up during a class on leadership and said, "I understand what these women are saying, you know? Because I've been through this, too," and when another confided, "I'm so glad you women are here, because you take some of the pressure off of me."

Dr. Peterson also recalls, "One of the nicer things that happened to the Academy with the admission of women was that their presence facilitated a great number of changes—in policy, in practices, in educational development—that should have been made years ago.

For instance, in our old summer training program we used to have rifle drills in the morning, instead of calisthenics. Well, a rifle drill is basically a worthless activity, but I couldn't convince people of that. I'd be talking to colonels and generals and they'd say, 'You mean you want to get rid of something that was part of the program when *I* was here? My God, this is the program that made *me*—why would you ever want to change that?'

And then we started issuing running shoes instead of having the Corps run in boots, because, goddamn it, I knew, and I kept telling them, that given their structure, if you run those women in boots—and those boots each weigh a couple of pounds—you're going to have an enormous number of stress fractures and shin splints. Sure enough, the first summer 29 percent of the women were severely injured. The next year we issued running shoes to the entire Corps for the first time *ever.*"

28 NOV 1976

It's Sunday—2:15 P.M. We got up at 4:20 on Saturday morning and left West Point for Philadelphia at 6:00. I slept on the bus all the way down.

We got to the football stadium at about 9:30. The march-on went fine, but the game was bad! Navy beat us 38–10.

We were released for the Army-Navy game and an evening's revelry. Denise Gavin met her parents for dinner that night, and when she rejoined her classmates, practically everyone was drunk. Visibly drunk. Puking in the bushes. Her mother was aghast. "Oh my God," she said, "you're not getting back on that bus with all those drunk men." She suddenly realized they were not all the boys next door. And as she watched Denise calmly board the bus and take her seat, she also realized that her daughter could handle herself among them. It came as a bit of a shock.

30 NOV 1976

We had basketball practice in our uniforms for about an hour today—my number is forty-four. Tomorrow is our first league game against Skidmore.

1 DEC 1976

We won! 73–48. It was fantastic—we didn't play all that great, but we beat them! I went against a girl who was five-ten, and I beat her in the jump. There were so many people there! The brass was everywhere. A lot of my company was at the game—that felt good. Even the Rabble Rousers were there. We had a press conference afterward in the locker room, then we ate dinner with the girls from Skidmore in the mess hall. I think they were really impressed. I was so proud to be a part of this place. Well, sixteen-and-a-butt days left before vacation!

I was scared to death before our first game. There had been so much speculation about it—could women cadets possibly muster a winning team? We held the game down in Central Gymnasium, which our team called "The Pit," because the room was so small, had no windows, and was always beastly hot. There was one wall for bleachers—a set less than ten tiers high ran the length of the court—and that afternoon, the stands were filled to capacity. Officers, instructors, and cadets—from firsties to plebes—had turned out in force. Even the commandant showed up to introduce our team and to wish us good luck. A swarm of reporters had come, too, and spent most of the game interviewing the spectators. We later read a quote given by one male cadet who'd been asked why he'd chosen to attend. His answer was straightforward. "Why did I come to this game? To see the freak show, of course."

My teammates and I had no idea how many others shared his attitude, but we were aware that there wasn't much clapping along the sidelines in the beginning. But we didn't permit ourselves to be distracted by their response to us, or lack of it. We were too engrossed in the game. Ours was not a tall team; our basic strategy was to run the other team to death. At five-foot-eight I was Army's tallest player and, as the team's center, I had to compete against a five-foot-ten beanpole from Skidmore in the opening jump. This girl was cocky; I could tell just by looking at her that she thought she had me beat. But when the ref tossed the ball in the air, I outjumped her, and tapped the ball into Cathy Gordon's hands. After that, it took us a couple of minutes to score the first two points. I remember the shot—it was a little lay-up over the front edge of the rim, and I was the one who put it in. The moment the ball swished through the hoop, the whole place suddenly came to life. To our delight and amazement, people actually started cheering. Riding on that wave of confidence, perhaps, our team went on to win the game.

Because I happened to be a scrappy player, one enthusiastic sports columnist from a local Highland Falls newspaper dubbed me "The Moxie Maid." Frankly, I think a lot of people were surprised. We had won for West Point, but we also had won for the women that day. The skeptics had come to see us fail, and saw us succeed instead. Unknown to us at the time, we were making it possible for the Academy to project a public impression of women cadets as an aggressive, hard-charging, all-American team, regardless of what was happening to us behind the fortress walls.

12 DEC 1976

I hurt my foot badly during our last game, so I had to go into Keller Army Hospital tonight. My squad leader brought me over. He was being real cool, too—asking how "our" team was doing. He told me there are guys on the battalion staff who call me "Dr. C." So many upperclassmen are proud of the women's basketball team—it feels really good to hear both the male and female cadets yelling "Defense! Defense!" with no Rabble Rousers leading them.

When the word got around that women cadets were playing gutsy basketball, the guys loved it. It was true—we played like brutes. What we lacked in talent, we made up for in heart. The gym was always packed for our games—standing room only. At last, here was one way to get a little positive attention for ourselves. We were playing a so-called man's sport, and we were doing well. Somehow that seemed to translate into the idea that we were women who were tough enough to take risks and make decisions. We wouldn't hesitate to take aggressive action, even if it meant we might be physically hurt. Women who took those kinds of chances, we learned, were the only women these men would ever trust in a leadership role.

Our coach was a nice guy named Richardson. I liked playing for him because he treated us like human beings, which was especially encouraging during plebe year, when nobody was treating us that way. He'd always greet us with a smile and say, "Hey, how are you doing today?" It was a very simple thing, but it made us feel less like robots. Basketball became such a refuge for us. For two hours or so, we could relax. But there was a downside, too. Going to practice made us late for dinner, so we'd have to sit in the mess hall at attention while everyone else was leaving. They would have already announced "Battalions rise!" and we'd still be there, eating as the upperclassmen shuffled past us, gruffly asking, "Miss—what are you doing? You're supposed to be gone."

We'd have to explain ourselves to each one.

"Sir, I've been at basketball practice. I'm authorized to stay late for dinner."

Of course, everybody who passed us had to stop and say something. It was too inviting—we were clear targets.

But, later on in the season, guys started coming over and sitting down next to me, saying, "Hey, I know you—you play basketball." I saw a change in the way the men treated me, and that made me feel good.

17 DEC 1976

Today is Friday—tomorrow I'll be home.

24 DEC 1976

I went to Mass tonight in my Full Dress Uniform. I was really proud to wear it—I know my parents were proud, too. My family had always gone to Midnight Mass before Christmas, where we'd sit unobtrusively in the back. This year our entrance created quite a stir, however, with my walking into the sanctuary in my gray woolen Full Dress coat and trousers, complete with black and gold embroidery on the jacket, and rows of gold buttons down the front and at each wrist (placed there in bygone days, I'm told, to discourage gentlemen soldiers from wiping their noses on their sleeves.)

Though mandatory chapel attendance was abolished in the mid-seventies, the ties between West Point and religion remain strong. The Cadet chapel

69

still dominates the Academy, both architecturally and spiritually. It stands on a hill, a cruciform-shaped building with a tall central tower, its massive walls pierced by rows of stained glass windows dedicated to famous biblical battles and the soldiers who led them. Carved above the chapel's entrance-way hangs a mighty stone replica of King Arthur's Excalibur.

To my knowledge, there was no direct attempt among the chaplains at West Point to debate pacifism as an alternative to the military ethic. Biblical passages about being a soldier and a defender, and putting on one's armor for the Lord, were frequently quoted. In the Academy's view, the soldier did have a place in the Bible, and God recognized the legitimacy of that role. West Point taught that Army officers could embrace religion, even though they might be called upon to kill in the line of duty.

In fact, some cadets looked to religion as a form of protection in the face of the harshness of Army life; particularly as plebes, these cadets took tremendous comfort in their belief that God cared for them and was watching over them—especially at those times when it seemed as if no one else did.

For others, religion at the Academy functioned as both a haven and a social outlet. Cadets joined the various chapel choirs (in part so they could leave post on group excursions) or they went to morning church services just to get out of the company area. Church was a calm, refreshing setting, where we could sit quietly, and uninterrupted. As plebes, however, we had to be pretty devoted to attend services. If we were pegged for missing morning formation because we'd skipped out to church, we'd be sure to get grief from the upperclassmen.

12 JAN 1977

It's been two and a half weeks since I've written in this diary. Vacation went by much too quickly. Our dinner tonight was mandatory, but now we get to sit "at ease" during every meal. Dr. P. gave us a lecture on weight control. It's funny, because all we ever do when we go to his house is eat. We had spaghetti there on Saturday night after the Princeton game.

1 FEB 1977

Steve and I got caught! Tuesday night after Taps we were called into my CO's room along with Michelle and David Murray. Steve and I had both signed out in the CO's book saying we were going to morning chapel, but when a note from Michelle to David was intercepted a few days later, mentioning a rendezvous among the four of us, our company commander put two and two together and summoned us to see him. The CO had

70

Michelle and me (the two plebes of the group) stand at attention against the wall. Then he grilled us, and we had to tell the truth.

Instead of getting written up, the four of us had to confess in front of the company, on Thursday night. I was really nervous telling everyone that I had been illegally "recognized" by Steve. I have decided—since I have no other choice—to cool it with him. As punishment, Steve and I are each sitting two weekends of room confinement.

A yearling (sophomore) and I had decided to risk a relationship, though we knew we'd have to be discreet. It was rumored that approximately 75 percent of the female plebes were dating upperclassman on the sly, which we called having "illegal friends." Cadets would sometimes go out for runs carrying blankets in their laundry bags, and meet each other clandestinely. One time, a classmate of mine recalls, a couple of cadets headed down to the newly painted stadium bleachers, and came back with stripes smeared across their backs.

All of this went strictly against regulations. Upperclassmen couldn't "recognize" plebes; they couldn't shake their hands, address them by their first names, or make any other gestures indicating a personal relationship, nor could they detain them for more than eight minutes at a time. Even these brief conversations could not concern anything apart from cadet business. Any plebe caught fraternizing with a member of the upperclasses was given a "frat charge." This resulted in both parties sitting long hours of room confinement, or walking the Area.

27 FEB 1977

I felt like quitting today—more than usual. Some days, during lunch formation, I have wanted to walk out of the formation and never come back. I get tired of putting up with all the hazing nonsense even more now. Sundays are the worst days around here. It means "tomorrow we start all over again." I don't even want to call my parents because of the rotten mood I'm in.

We lived our lives at the Academy on an emotional roller coaster. As friends of mine used to say, "If you see a West Point cadet who's very positive and upbeat all the time, he or she is either very well adjusted, or they're lying through their teeth."

West Point deliberately gave cadets too much to do in too little time. We found ourselves constantly having to prioritize; we were never given ample time to devote to any one task. So, instead of creating one extraordi-

71

nary product, we'd usually end up with a lot of mediocre ones, rarely achieving a true sense of satisfaction for our accomplishments. We could do a lot of things quickly and well, but didn't seem to excel at any one of them. A friend of mine at the Academy remarked that she knew plenty of men who felt very vulnerable because of this, and thought, I must be worthless; I can't seem to shine at anything.

Finding no other outlet, our anxieties sometimes expressed themselves in dreams, or patterns of disturbed nocturnal behavior. I can remember nights when I'd suddenly wake up and find myself standing in the middle of my room. My roommates would tell me that I'd been marching back and forth in my sleep. Pam Deitz remembers when she and her plebe year roommate would wake each other up by hollering, "Yes, Sir! No, Sir!" Sharon Davis got into the habit of grinding her teeth at night after one particular upperclassman had decided to take on hazing Sharon as his personal crusade. The noise and intensity of her teeth-grinding became proportional to the amount of hazing Sharon had received that day, so Sharon's roommate always knew when, and how hard, she'd been struck. "I guess McFarrell's really been on you again," she would say to Sharon, after an especially loud and restless night. Another one of my classmates, no longer in the army, says she is still haunted by her dreams of missing class, or being out of uniform.

But why not just leave the Academy if life there was so difficult? I was constantly evaluating my position. I'd speak to a number of people who were leaving, and most of them were glad to be getting out from under all the pressure, but a few also regretted not being able to see it through. We were, by nature, ambitious and competitive people. Most of us had been quite successful until then. And that was key—*until then.* None of us were quitters, and we'd certainly never been run out of anything. To graduate was one of our goals. It was our decision to be there, and it would be our decision to leave. The women cadets dug in their heels. We had to prove something to ourselves, and many of us felt it was important to demonstrate a special kind of fortitude to each other. Most of the women who stayed simply entrenched themselves, declaring, "No one is going to push me out." Others took an opposite tack and left the Academy, thinking, I'm better than this, I'm not going to stick around and be abused. Still others left because they simply didn't want to play the game anymore.

I thought quite a lot about dropping out, and came close several times, but the Academy can be a very hard place to leave. As they tell us in *Bugle Notes,* West Point's informational guidebook and so-called bible, "There is no place in the military profession for an excuse for failure." So, the administration did everything it could to talk us out of going; our parents tried to discourage us, and there was pressure from our classmates not to quit because they knew that if we walked out of there, they'd probably never see us again.

Finally, there was the pressure we had put on ourselves. I mean, we'd been on TV, our names had been in the papers, and everyone back home was saying, "These wonderful girls from *our* high school are going to West Point." It wouldn't be the same as dropping out of a regular college. Leaving West Point would have been a tremendous stigma. We also realized we'd be losing significant career opportunities, and in the face of that evaluation, our complaints would begin to seem very small.

But sometimes it took a true hero to be able to stand up and say, "I'm not going to take it anymore." There are moments when I think that the reason I didn't leave West Point was that I didn't have the courage. Now, however, I'm glad I didn't.

1 MAR 1977

Saturday. We lost our last game of the season against Immaculata's Junior Varsity. I would have done the team more good if I had sat out the whole game. Melissa got a concussion from ramming into Nancy, who got a bloody nose. Liz got cut under her eye. What a game! Afterwards we gave Coach Richardson a saber with his name engraved on it.

7 MAR 1977

Monday. I made a big mistake last night. I went to see my squad leader, Bear Jackson. I've been depressed for a long while now and have had serious thoughts of quitting. We spoke for a long time. I found out today that he told a few people what we talked about, and said that the reason I wanted to quit was to marry Steve! I couldn't believe it.

18 MAR 1977

It turns out that I am athletic sergeant for Plebe-Parent weekend—that's when the upperclasses go on spring break, and our parents are invited to spend the weekend watching us be little model cadets. Nancy is Battalion XO [Executive Officer, Second in Command], Cathy is Battalion S-3 [Operations Officer]. Cindy Owings is Battalion CO [Commander]. Athletic sergeant is one of the lowest positions there is. I kind of wish I had an important job. I want to be good!

28 MAR 1977

Saturday we got to fall out. It was weird. We looked like lost mice running through the halls. It felt so strange to be able to walk around normally.

On Monday, all of the women had an early dinner because of a manda-tory lecture. Revlon gave us a two-and-a-half-hour talk. They showed us all sorts of neat things to do with our faces—(yeah sure, real neat.*) I thought the meeting was a waste. We missed an hour and a half of our company party! And we were allowed to wear civilian clothes, too.*

All the women cadets were called to a mandatory meeting during Plebe-Parent weekend, in which professional makeup artists sat down with all their colors to teach us how to apply makeup, and we were mad. We wondered, Who the hell is making us do this?

It was as if the administration had made some ivory-tower decision, thinking, The female cadets aren't wearing makeup, they aren't wearing skirts, they don't look like women, therefore, we'll show them what to do and that'll fix all the problems. And yet, the administration seemed totally oblivious to why those problems existed in the first place. After all, we still had upperclassmen making us get our weekly haircuts.

One of my male classmates says he remembers the first time a female cadet stepped outside wearing a skirt with her uniform, instead of trousers. Not only did the guys give her a hard time, the women gave her grief, because no one else was doing it. Sometimes we would talk among our-selves at PT, and we'd ask each other, "Are you going to wear your skirt?"

"No."

"Are you going to wear your black beret?"

"Heck no."

But this girl wore that black beret, she wore the skirt, she wore the little black go-go boots, and *boom,* she was hammered by eight or nine upper-classmen, because it was a skirt. It was probably the first skirt that had ever been seen in a cadet formation.

So when it came to the makeup class, the Academy's intentions might have been good, but once again it felt as if we were dealing with people who wouldn't treat us with reality in mind. We felt as though they just wanted to keep us their made-up little girls. I mean, we weren't twelve—we were seventeen and eighteen years old. Some of us already owned all the makeup in the world, but we'd bought it on our own. So we decided to make a complete mockery of the makeup class. While the makeup artists circulated through the room, checking on our progress, some of us took the blush, and the powder, and the lipstick, and started war-painting our faces. They didn't make us do it again.

2 APR 1977

We had a lecture last week with General Berry—all the women will be shuffled next year. Women will be in every company. This summer, during Cadet Field Training at Camp Buckner, all the women will be put under one roof. We also found out, at the Supe's lecture, that the third and fourth classes will not be allowed to attend this year's graduation ceremonies. Instead, we'll be out at Buckner, doing something "worthwhile," I'm sure.

10 APR 1977

Plebe-Parent Weekend. On Friday night, Nancy's family and my family went out to dinner together at a Japanese restaurant. It was fantastic—they cooked our food right at the table. I wore civilian clothes—my yellow pantsuit. It felt so good to be normal again, even if only for a little while.

The Saturday night banquet was great. Robin helped me put on some makeup. I think our Dress Mess looked nicer than any of the other girls' dresses. I was very proud to be wearing that uniform.

15 APR 1977

It's Friday night. I'm in the hospital now because I have mono. I came in on Wednesday. I have had a continuous headache since Monday afternoon.

18 APR 1977

Monday. I've been out of the hospital since Saturday. My joints are still swollen and sore. While I was in the hospital, I met an upperclassman named Bob, who ended up asking me out for a date a year in advance. We talked for the longest time on Friday night. It got so late, the head nurse had to tell us to go to sleep. On Saturday morning, Steve came to visit me, and who should walk in but the Tac. Now Steve and I have to appear before the regimental board—a board of three officers from our regiment who will hear our case, and decide our punishment. Meanwhile, there are some nice rumors going around about me—that I am dating an officer, that I bawled out a yearling because he called me by my first name . . .

75

30 APR 1977

11:26 P.M. Saturday. My slug [punishment] came down last Monday. I got a 20 and 10 [twenty demerits and ten hours of disciplinary tours on the Area]. So did Steve.

The disciplinary award report said: "Delinquency: Fourth class woman cadet fraternizing with upperclassman; i.e., while hospitalized, visiting on a one-to-one basis with upperclassman who had no professional or official reason for visit. Aggravated by the fact that the cadet was previously counseled about apparent personal relationship developing between herself and same upperclassman."

I walked off some of my hours on Friday afternoon—what a suck. I also walked today for about an hour and a half. It was my first time walking the Area.

That spring I got very, very sick. I was in the hospital and Steve came to visit me. Major Phillips, our company tactical officer, happened to walk in, so we were both given a frat charge. It had been nearly three months since we last "dated," and the visit was completely innocent. As an upperclassman, however, Steve had no "legitimate" reason to visit me—he wasn't in my chain of command—and because we had been caught fraternizing before, the Tac assumed we were still involved. But this time, no one even bothered to ask. We both got punished, and Steve had all of his privileges taken away.

After that incident, Steve and I barely spoke to one another again—we were too scared. The next year, he was shuffled out of my company, so time and distance kept us apart. Over the summer, he was off in training, and I was at Camp Buckner, where I started seeing Michael.

12 MAY 1977

Nancy and I went running this morning. We both have to take the OC [Obstacle Course] tomorrow. Please, God, give Nancy some confidence. I know she can make it. Make her believe that she can.

13 MAY 1977

Friday the 13th—a lucky day for me. I had to run the OC today. I must have had God on my side, because I ran it in three minutes and fifteen seconds. Of all the women, I had the fastest time.

The Obstacle Course was run once a year by each class in the east gym. We could always tell when it was coming, because the course was set up two weeks prior and there were people in there practicing on it day and night.

The course consisted of low-crawling for about ten yards beneath simulated barbed wire, jumping over a pommel horse, swinging ourselves onto a ledge six feet off the ground (women had the most trouble with this part, because it required a lot of upper body strength), jumping from the ledge over a fence onto a jungle gym, then swinging down to the floor, jumping through a suspended tire, handwalking through two sets of parallel bars, bounding over a six-foot wall, traversing (while dangling from) a long, horizontal ladder, then climbing six feet up a rope until we reached an elevated track that circled the gym, after which we had to run once around the track carrying a leather medicine ball, a second time holding a wooden bowling pin, and three-quarters around one last time to the finish.

Because running the course made us nauseated, there was a big barrel provided at the end, where cadets could vomit. And I thought, How accommodating, after six people already had thrown up in there, I was next.

At dinner formation it was obvious who had run the OC that day, because they couldn't stop gasping and coughing. The test took only about three and a half minutes to complete, but it knocked everyone out. It was worse than running in boots.

17 MAY 1977

Today we found out our Buckner companies. I'm in 5th Company—so are Melissa, Kim, Natalie, Jan, Alison, and some others. Nancy is in Eighth Company with Leslie and Robin Bach. Fifth Company is right near everything—including the women's barracks—so we won't have far to go for formations. I have Trux as my XO first detail. Just my luck.

Trux was Michael Truxel—a little Napoleon if there ever was one. He was a fierce type—a hard charger—and then I found out his middle name was Francis, and he hated that. It was so unmacho.

My plebe year encounters with Michael were all bad. Any time he could find something wrong with me, he did. He'd stop me in the hall and say, "Barkalow, you'd better shape up. I don't like your appearance, and I don't like your attitude. Your hair is too long, and your shoes look like *shit.*" Or he'd haze me incessantly. He'd order me to do the "eight-count gaze around"—making me stand at attention and look up, then straight ahead, then shift my head and eyes to the right, then straight ahead, then

77

down, then straight ahead, then to the left, then straight ahead—and he'd insist that I repeat these rotations one hundred times in a row, until I got dizzy. Or he'd abruptly ask, "How is the cow?"

And I'd have to give the spiel: "Sir, she walks, she talks, she's full of chalk, the lacteal fluid extracted from the female of the bovine species is highly prolific to the *nth* degree."

There was no limit to the number of times a plebe could be hazed. Sometimes Michael would just keep hazing me until I made a mistake, and then he'd punish me.

So when I heard he was going to be my XO at Camp Buckner, I was worried. I later learned that Michael—like many upperclassmen who'd felt a certain amount of inner conflict over their budding attraction to the hated (and forbidden) female plebes—had a rather unmilitary motive for disciplining me so much—he was attracted to me. It was just one more topsy-turvy thing about the Academy, and not a very good precedent for future relationships, I must say, because if a male upperclassman liked a female plebe, the only way he could legitimately express his feelings for her was to make her miserable.

24 MAY 1977

I came back from leave this weekend to find myself in the rotten position of Head Mail Carrier. I was in charge of distributing the mail and newspapers to the entire company, and those papers are heavy—*especially on Sundays! It was my first "Head" job this year, and this is the last week for plebe duties. I understand that Truxel "suggested" I get it.*

On Sunday night, Robin and I were so bored that we took our rain hat covers—the clear ones—and put them over our white cadet hats, then put on sunglasses and sat around hoping the OC would come in and find us.

That night also began the traditional "spin the spurs" on Sedgwick's monument to "go pro" [proficient in academics].

During term end exams, those cadets who felt they might need a little extra luck in order to pass would dress up in Full Dress Gray, and on the midnight before the first exam they'd run out to Trophy Point to spin the moveable metal spurs that were set into the stone of Sedgwick's monument. The tradition said that good luck would come to those who spun the spurs and made it back to their rooms without having the OC catch them. Some OCs were hardasses who'd write up the cadets they'd catch; others would just make them drop and do a few push-ups. Everyone knew it was going to happen, so on the designated night, we'd all crowd into the cadet rooms on the Plain side to cheer on those brave, "deficient" souls who were out there trying to grab themselves some good luck.

31 MAY 1977

This week, I'm Head Minute Caller. That's going to be a real suck, with all the parades, and all the coming and going to Camp Buckner. Well, seven-and-a-butt until summer leave.

1 JUNE 1977

It never fails. Someone here can always ruin your day. Some guy stopped me and told me to quit gazing around. I felt like telling him to go to hell. I have a feeling that when Recognition Day comes this week, we're going to see a change in a lot of the cadets' attitudes because that's the day we officially become upperclassmen.

Ironically, just as I was beginning to feel hopeful, I read an article in the June 1977 issue of *WomenSports* magazine by journalist Candace Lyle Hogan, which, among other observations, documented her impressions of the prejudice that she witnessed on her visit to the Academy during our plebe year. She wrote: "When, in early February, the Academy offered as one of its free films *Hearts and Minds,* the documentary on American military involvement in Vietnam, the audience of upperclassmen seemed receptive, even though they were warned by an officer before the film began that it was 'a biased political statement to be viewed skeptically.' The only occasions in the movie that brought outright hoots and jeering laughter were those involving women. . . . The men began giggling strangely when the camera lingered on the stoic faces of two old Vietnamese sisters bereft of family and home by American bombs and poison gas. When an officer (and returned POW) said, 'If it's a choice between the gooks and a hundred women climbing down your back, then you think maybe the gooks aren't so bad,' the men exploded into their loudest cheers and clapping of the evening."

5 JUNE 1977

Friday morning we had a parade for the alumni. For most of them, it was their first time back since women have come to the Academy. Some of the old grads were great—they came up to us and wanted to talk. Others wanted no part of us—they turned around and walked in the opposite direction when they saw us coming. Anyway, with all these people around, we are going through another phase of being stared at.

A former Academy instructor and retired colonel, a 1956 grad himself, once talked about the adjustments West Point's older graduates had been making toward accepting West Point women into their cherished long gray line.

"The alumni are getting less crusty about the gals," the colonel remarked, "and I'm talking about alumni from the twenties, thirties, and forties. I was standing outside, when one of them came up to me and said, 'Come on, Colonel, tell me what you really think about the gals being here at West Point.'

"And I said, 'Tell you what, Sir. The second best thing that happened to West Point in the nineteen-seventies was voluntary chapel.' I didn't dare ask him what the first thing was.

"Then I said, 'Look, Sir, you're going to be here all day. Why don't you talk to some of them?'

"He came back later that afternoon.

" 'Colonel,' he said, 'you know, you've really got some good-looking girls going here.'

"And I said, 'Well, Sir, why not? We've had good-looking guys here for years.'

"I was being flippant, but then I said, 'Seriously, Sir, go out to your good high schools, find a gal who has somewhere between 1250 and 1350 on her SAT scores, see if she's playing a varsity sport; if she's also in some extracurricular activities, she's probably pretty good-looking, too, so why shouldn't she be at West Point?'

"He thought about that for a minute and said,

" 'Yeah, I guess you're right.

" 'We do take in a good breed of animal.' "

Yearling Year

1977–1978

I'm home now. This has been an unforgettable week. Tuesday morning we were transported from Camp Buckner to West Point for lunch and then the Recognition Parade. I was Head Minute Caller this week and decided to do something different. We called the minutes normally except for the last—at the two-minute bell, all the plebes lined up against the wall outside the CO's room and said: "Sir, there are two minutes until assembly for Graduation Day parade formation. If you don't know the uniform by now, your shit's weak. Don't forget your lights, don't forget to tie your shoes. This is the last time I'll have to call you 'Sir.' Two minutes, Sir." Then we all ran to formation.

While I was calling minutes, a yearling came up and smashed my breastplate—boy, did that hurt. Out in ranks, a firstie inscribed "W.P. [West Point] 1977" on my waistplate. Then I got my shoes destroyed—cut to ribbons by sabers. All of the firsties left the formation and we passed in review in front of them. Everyone shook my hand. It was kind of neat to be recognized—by some.

The Recognition Day Parade was like being metamorphosed in slow motion. Before the parade, we were beanheads, smacks. After the parade, we were everybody's friend, sort of. The Fourth Classmen of each company would line up facing the upperclassmen; our first names were written in magic marker on the underside of one of our crossbelts. An upperclassman would then walk by and turn each of them over, one by one, so our elder companymates could greet us by name for the first time. The firsties came over to shake hands, then the cows, and finally, the yearlings.

This year, in some of the companies, a few upperclassmen refused to walk through the Recognition line. Others would go down the line shaking hands, but when they approached a female cadet, they'd stand directly in front of her with their arms stiff at their sides. Theirs was perhaps the more sincere gesture. These guys had been giving us so much grief for so long—were we now supposed to be happy when they shook our hands? Now *we* wanted to be the ones to say no. Lori Eller said it was insane having some guy who had openly despised her for a year suddenly walk up, shake her hand, and say, "Hi there, Lori." All she could do was stand there and think, Oh, so now you call me 'Lori' instead of 'douche bag'?

6 JULY 1977

Today is R-Day for the class of '81. Our class got back yesterday from summer leave. My feelings about returning are very complicated. I want to be here, and it's nice to see everyone again, but I could have stayed away a bit longer. Other people say they feel the same. We are all closer to each other now in a very different way. It's the way it has to be—we need each other to survive.

With the arrival of the new Fourth Class in the summer of 1977, the women of my class were confronted with the task of administering what little authority we had over a younger version of ourselves. I, for one, tried to make it my policy to use hazing as a means to correct plebes, not to harass them. Most of my female classmates behaved in similar fashion, but there were dissenting opinions. Others, once free of the shackles of the Fourth Class System, flatly refused to participate in hazing of any kind. In another group there were some very enthusiastic female participants, a number of whom went overboard harassing younger women—ordering them to do rapid-fire changes of uniform, summoning them into their rooms for questioning like Grand Inquisitors, grilling them relentlessly on their memorization of trivia. A few of these women claimed they needed to be demonstrably tougher on female plebes so no one could accuse them of showing favoritism. I believe these women suspected—and rightly so— that our newly acquired upperclass status did not unanimously assure our position within the Corps. Even as the ranks of women cadets gradually swelled from one classful to two, many of us remained in separate camps. At best, we observed each other from a distance—across a divide of diffidence, misunderstanding, and fear.

82

From the beginning, there was a wedge between our class and those who came later. Some of the younger women seemed to regard us with awe, because they knew we had broken the ice and made their lives a little easier. At the same time, we were still the Amazons, the guinea pig class, the weirdos. The new girls coming in fresh off the street didn't see themselves that way. They were not icebreakers, they were part of a "normal" class. They felt that they belonged.

"I had my first encounter with a woman from the class of '80," recalls class of '81 graduate Traci Reid, "when I passed her in the stairwell, braced against the wall. I thought, *Hey, great, this is the first time I've seen a female upperclassman.* She took one look at me and snapped, 'Get a dress-off!' "

"My female classmates did not look up to the class of '80 women as mentors," said Traci. "Our perception was that the female cadet jokes were not really about us, they were about them. All through Beast Barracks we were told how rotten and terrible and ugly the class of '80 women were. It was hammered into us from the first day—'Don't do what the class of '80 did. Don't call attention to yourself. Those women all got fat during plebe year. They just wanted media attention.' Naturally, the women in my class didn't identify with them. Our attitude was, 'Hey, don't worry. *We're* not going to be like that.'

"My classmates and I still feel that the men and women from our class bonded together well, that there was not a lot of hostility between us. But we felt, and I know *I* always felt, that the class of '80 men disliked their women. And the feedback we were getting from the Academy seemed to confirm that. In lectures or in surveys, all the statistics seemed to point to the women in our class as being better than the class of '80. So there may have been something close to resentment between the two classes of women. The upperclassmen, especially, were trying to get us to hate our predecessors. But, of course, we didn't hate them. We just said, 'Fine. We'll take all their hard lessons learned.' "

9 JULY 1977

Right now I'm at Camp Buckner sitting CCQ—what a bore. For the last two days my company has been scrounging around in the woods. Thursday morning we went to the same land navigation site that we went to last year at Lake Frederick. My buddy "Ranger Ed" and I did all right—we got sixty out of seventy points. In the afternoon I walked back from Lake Frederick to Camp Fun-in-the-Sun. We ate an early dinner that night, because we were scheduled for instruction in "Night Navigation." Ed and I had a tough time. I was pace-man and (literally) ran into a few trees.

83

Right near the end, I fell off a small cliff. I killed my shin and cut up my hand. I also lost one of my contact lenses. We didn't get back to Buckner until 12:30 A.M. I was exhausted.

The next morning we didn't have to run—thank God—so I went to sick call after breakfast to get something for my leg. We left for our Land Navigation III course at 0730, and spent the next two and a half hours searching all over the woods for twenty marked bags. Ed and I found twelve.

Monday morning we had guerrilla drills and a two-mile run at a 7:45 pace [seven minutes and forty-five seconds per mile]. Boy, was I hurting after that. We fired a lot of weapons on Monday—the LAW (a heat rocket launcher), the TOW (a tube-launched, optically tracked, wire-guided missile launcher), the M-203 grenade launcher, and the AK47 rifle. Then we had a tank class, which I thought was very interesting.

Mike Truxel is getting on my nerves. I don't understand his game. I'm thinking of confronting him with a few questions. Now that I'm an upperclassman, too, we're on slightly more equal footing. At least I don't have to call him "Sir" anymore.

12 JULY 1977

We have been at Camp Buckner for a week. This morning we had a three-mile run up Engineer Hill. For the first time, the cadences for the runs were being called, uncontrolled, by our classmates. And out came all the sexist company cadences that had been outlawed when we were plebes:

> If all of the ladies were bricks in a pile,
> and I were a mortar, I'd lay them in style.

I actually made it up the hill. I didn't think I would, but when Mike said he'd kick my ass, I decided that I didn't need any trouble from him.

Today we learned how to put together the 81-mm mortar—a small cannonlike weapon that can fire thirty rounds per minute at targets nearly forty-six hundred meters away.

Dr. P. came out last night and talked with us a while. He said the women cadets were doing fine.

It was summer. We'd been released from the compressed and tedious routine of shuttling back and forth between barracks and classroom, and were living more or less like primitives (or so we imagined) in the field. Made bold by freedom and their new status as upperclassmen, the men of my class emerged from the humiliating ordeal of plebehood by reasserting their masculinity through rituals and war games in which intellectual achievements held little or no sway. Instead, juvenile boasts of sexual prowess (as exhibited by the sudden increase in formerly prohibited "dirty" cadences) and contests of physical strength reemerged as the primary measures of leadership and success. Except where training requirements mandated their participation, women once again found themselves implicitly excluded from the male group.

Our exclusion took an explicit form as well. Rather than commission expensive alterations to the men's billets, the Academy had decided to house all the women separately for the summer. About eighty of us were stuffed like tuna into two little Quonset huts, with tin roofs and corrugated metal walls. A row of tiny windows and a screen door admitted the only breeze. Some female cadets objected to being wrenched from their regular companies and banished to "women's" housing, but I considered it a blessing. At last, we could talk.

As plebes, women barely had the opportunity to confide in each other. We would eat, room, and study with the same three or four women in our company. And these became the only people we knew in the whole world with whom we could share our West Point experience. Buckner changed all that. The pressure was still unrelenting. Whether we were leading patrols or doing mortar crew drills, women felt continuously obliged to prove we wouldn't melt in the rain or wither in the heat. Some women, even if they made the runs, would come back to the barracks and cry because it was so stressful. We'd see women bursting into tears every night as they walked through the barracks door. Buckner was a definite breakthrough, however, because we finally began to talk to each other at length. We found out that we weren't the only ones who were having these problems, which was a tremendous source of relief. I wouldn't say that our sudden physical proximity brought us much closer as a *group*—we were still trying desperately to fit in, and fitting in meant not making too much of women's "solidarity"—but at least we were able to commiserate among ourselves, and to draw strength from our individual efforts to survive.

14 JULY 1977

Yesterday morning we had a two-and-a-half-mile run at a 7:45 pace. I fell out. I tried to catch up—and I did once, but then I got the dry heaves. I feel really bad that I dropped out, especially since many of the other women in our company dropped out, too.

This morning we went through a Claymore antipersonnel mine class and also a grenade course in which we each got to throw two live grenades. It was a very strange feeling.

We had the afternoon off, so I went back to West Point. It felt so odd to have the new cadets salute me.

15 JULY 1977

Today we had windsprints and grass drills. We also had NBC [nuclear, biological, and chemical warfare] training. At least I didn't fall asleep.

I took notes during the lecture.
Chemical:
Cloud—
—inhaled,
—on the skin;
Nerve gas—
—incapacitating agent;
What it causes—
—vomiting
—blistering
—choking
—bleeding
Advantages—
—covers large areas,
—penetrates,
—little property damage.
Biological:
Used in past—not today;
danger—more;
purpose—to kill, injure, or disable the enemy,
his animals, or his crops.
Nuclear:
Hiroshima,
Nagasaki;
Effects—
Thermal,
1st,
2nd;
Blast—
air,

ground;
Radiation,
Fallout.

20 JULY 1977

Something really weird has been happening to me lately. All year this guy has hazed me and suddenly I have a strong feeling for him—and he seems to feel the same way. I approached him one day and asked him directly: "Mike, are you interested in me? Do you want to go out with me?" He stammered a little, but that broke the ice. Then we started meeting every evening after dinner, down by the lake. I can't say for sure if I love Mike, but I've been feeling awfully strange when I'm near him. It seems to get worse every time I see him. When I'm away from him, he's all I think about. I don't want to tell him how I feel—I did that with Steve, and things didn't work out. I like Mike because he isn't a puppy I can lead around on a leash like some of the other guys I've dated.

21 JULY 1977

This week we had communications training—we learned how to put field phones, a switchboard, and PRC-77 radios into action. We also learned how to make a field-expedient wire antenna, and how to operate a remote set. Thursday morning we learned how to fire out with the M-102 105-mm howitzer.

After lunch I went back to "Woo Poo" [West Point] with Mike—he had to get his stitches taken out, and I had an eye appointment. While I was there, I passed by a new cadet who didn't salute me. I was going to say something to him but didn't. That won't happen again. I will stop anyone next time.

Saturday we left for Fort Knox, Kentucky. That night, everyone went out. Mike and I did a lot of talking and even some dancing. He walked me back to our billets, but no kiss—not yet.

26 JULY 1977

On Sunday night, Mike walked me back to my barracks, and he kissed me. The only problem was, we got caught for PDA. We had to go see the Tac and tell him why we did it. Then we both had to do a detail—I spent a few hours picking up trash in the woods.

27 JULY 1977

Today is Wednesday. Last night I went to the Officers' Club to tell everyone we weren't going to have PT this morning, and ran into Mike. I walked back to the barracks by myself, and all the way there I kept singing the song, "I Think I Love You." I felt so warm and funny inside.

This morning we played "kill the tank"—I was a gunner and a driver.

"Kill the tank" was an exercise where we would line up five tanks on one trail, and five more tanks a few miles away on another trail, and then all the tanks would drive toward each other and have a war. One of the tanks in the exercise ended up with an all-woman crew. As far as I knew, this had never happened anywhere else. When the instructors realized they'd put four women together in one tank, the men started conferring with each other, and said, "What are we going to do? We can't have an all-woman tank."

"So we argued with them," recalled Julie Hawkins, who was one of the four, "and insisted, 'Why not? Let us go. This is not a male-female thing. We can do it.' But the guys were real leery about it, as if they didn't think we were competent enough—even though the sergeant would be going with us. Finally, they said, 'Let 'em try.' And we won! Everybody else was dead, we were still alive, and we were just screaming—going crazy, yelling and cheering over the tank's mike.

Meanwhile, the old armor sergeant was no longer wringing his hands, saying, 'Oh my God, I can't believe this.' I mean, the guy had been in the army maybe twelve years, and he'd probably never seen a woman anywhere near his post, let alone four of them manning his tank. Now, all of a sudden, he was walking around like Studley Dudley. There was a ceremony to announce the names of the winners and the winning crew was presented with a little toy tank. To think that this time the winning crew was four women! It was great."

28 JULY 1977

Tonight Mike picked me up at about 7:30. We went to a little place that sells ice cream and hamburgers, then to a bar where we could slow dance. He started to walk me home, and we were right in the middle of a kiss when a car drove by. It's awful when you can't show your feelings without being scared someone will see you. Mike and I walked all the way back to my barracks tonight and then shook hands. It's so sad.

29 JULY 1977

Right now it's 2345 hours. In less than five hours we will be in formation, getting ready to leave this place.

This morning, at about 1:35, two male enlisted soldiers tried to break into the women's billets—they succeeded and were run out. One guy crawled through a girl's window; the other climbed through another window into an empty room. People were screaming for a long time—no one wanted to go back to bed. I went to sleep in Katie's room for the night.

I wish I weren't so insecure and scared all the time.

31 JULY 1977

Today is Sunday, the last day of July. We had to get ready for Infantry-Recondo training. It rained, so everyone was cold and in bad moods. I was freezing and so glad to get back to Buckner. Wednesday was our last night in garrison for a week. We are all psyched up for Recondo.

Recondo was three days and three nights of continuous Infantry training and patrolling, when we taxed ourselves beyond our limits. As serious as it was, there remained a "Peter Pan" quality to the experience. It seemed like the ultimate little-boy's fantasy. For three whole days we lived without bathing, went on maneuvers in the woods, played hide-and-seek, shot blanks at each other, and made a whole lot of noise. We learned how to navigate using a compass and how to feed ourselves off the land. A few guys from the 82d Airborne Division were even flown up from Fort Bragg, North Carolina, to act as our "aggressors"—playing military "Fridays" to our "Robinson Crusoes."

5 AUG 1977

Thursday morning we went out to set up our bivouac area. We began our mountaineering in the afternoon—climbed down twenty-five foot cliffs and did the suspension traverse. We then walked about two and a half miles to the Recondo site: The Pits, we called it, and believe me it was. The ground was covered with sawdust, and after two hours, so were we. We got back to our tents at 9:30 P.M. I was exhausted and went straight to bed. It sure didn't feel too good, though, sleeping on a couple of tree roots.

Friday morning we returned to the mountaineering site. We had to free-climb a seventy-two-foot cliff and then rappel ourselves off of it, which scared me to death. On the way up I started to fall a few times. I thought I would never make it to the top. But when it was my turn to jump, it was one of the greatest feelings I've ever had in my life, looking over my shoulder, shouting, "On rappel!" and then bounding—and walking—down the side of a cliff.

Friday night was Survival Night. It began with the sergeant telling us we could find several kinds of foods (and a few kinds of snakes) in our immediate area. It ended with Connie Duncan biting the head off a live chicken—that, we were told, was the Recondo way! I made it perfectly clear that I would make the stew, but the others could kill and clean the chickens. Needless to say, I went to bed a little hungry.

By the second day of Recondo, I was so filthy that if I pulled on my hair, it would stay in the direction I pulled it. I had camouflage paint and charcoal rubbed all over my face, neck, and hands, and since my hair is blond they made me put charcoal in my hair, too. The only items of clothing I could change were my socks. I started to smell so bad, I just ripped off my underwear and left them in the woods. I didn't want anything that close to my skin after I hadn't bathed for a couple of days.

On Survival Night, the guys from Special Forces told each squad that we'd have to forage for our food, but they did give us a head start—a few potatoes, carrots, and celery to stew with three live chickens, which we were required to kill and eat. They taught us that there was an art to killing chickens. First, they said, we had to massage them, so they would relax and the meat wouldn't be tough. We got those chickens so relaxed, we just tucked their tiny feathered heads underneath their wings and snapped their necks. However, at least one of my female classmates decided the neck-snapping method wasn't a tough enough test for a true "Recondo." She preferred to bite one of the chickens' heads off instead.

According to a former female Tac officer, the Academy switched to using rabbits for a while, in place of chickens, and the cadets called it "bunny baseball." They'd name the creatures Thumper and Tweety and Dusty and Sneezy, but they'd forget that pretty soon they were going to be eating them. They were required to kill them by bashing their heads against a tree. But the cadets were so afraid of hitting the rabbit too hard—maybe they were afraid of decapitating it—that often someone had to step in with a baseball bat to make sure the rabbit was dead. Of course, the men were squealing through most of this, too; they didn't like it any better than the women did. So it was a difficult night for everyone—man, woman, and beast.

(Though the "Survival Dinner" was still a part of Cadet Field Training as of 1986, a female Tac officer who is currently at the Academy states that it has since been discontinued.)

8 AUG 1977

Saturday morning, I failed the run by a lousy twenty-three seconds. I was pretty upset. We had two more hours of hand-to-hand combat in the

Pits after that, and I was in no mood to do anything, especially not the Pits. When our fun-time rolling around in the sawdust was over, we marched back to the bivouac site for lunch, then went on a practice patrol until 2400. It is harder than I thought to walk in the dark and keep quiet. On our first patrol, it seemed as if we hiked all over creation. On our second, we stayed up until 0100 hours, then lay on the ground and attempted to sleep until 0400.

0400 came quickly. We moved out on our first graded patrol at 0500. I was freezing—I never realized summer mornings could be that cold. While we were on the perimeter—our line of defense—I fell asleep. The sergeant woke me up by saying, "Miss, you are now the patrol leader." I had to get us to a site for a partisan linkup. But first we had to conquer two huge mountains—the guys carrying the M-60 and the radio must have been hurting. We reached our destination at 1230 hours and set up security. Joey was there and he looked at my feet. They hurt so bad, I thought I was running a blister factory.

I sat up most of that night, securing the rucksacks with Ron Hicks. Managing the stress of all this was supremely important—functioning without sleep was supposed to approximate the conditions of war. I tried to stay awake by chewing some of Ron's tobacco, but I accidentally swallowed some, and it almost made me sick.

By the third day of Recondo, I was dead tired. My buddy and I (we always traveled with buddies) would walk for miles with our squad, then we'd choose somewhere to stop for the night. We'd set up a perimeter, maintaining 50 percent security at all times—one of us would sleep for an hour while the other kept a vigil. Then we'd switch. If cadets learned anything at West Point, it was teamwork. "Cooperate and graduate" was our motto. Fraternity was the bond we were supposed to develop, despite our equally powerful drive toward competition.

11 AUG 1977

Monday night was the worst night of my life. We attempted to climb Hill 1431 in the dark. What a mistake. People all around me were falling and hurting themselves. Finally, we were allowed to turn on our flashlights, but we got lost, anyway. The sergeant eventually gave up on the exercise; we just kept looking for the road.

Tuesday night we must have walked four miles. Every time we stopped for a rest, one minute later we'd hear snoring up and down the line. I was so tired that if someone fell or got hurt, all I could do was laugh. Being out in the woods, hiking around with virtually no sleep for three days, is one of the weirdest feelings I have ever had. I'd be sitting on the perimeter, and I'd swear I could see these little bearded men about twelve inches high running back and forth between the trees. But I wasn't the only one beginning to hallucinate—I saw one of the guys in my company walk up to a tree and try to talk into a telephone.

After we had set up our perimeter late Tuesday night, a cadet positioned fifteen feet away from me got jumped. I didn't think the soldiers from the 82d Airborne, who were helping us with our training, were supposed to do that. I had also heard that there were two civilian men running through the woods in fatigues, carrying loaded weapons. I became so frightened, I couldn't even blink my eyes. Thank God the trucks picked us up at 0500.

We got back to Buckner at 0600 and had breakfast down near the Infantry shack. I must admit we were a sight. We looked terrible—and smelled worse.

Immediately after breakfast we marched over to White Oak Island to complete the Recondo confidence course. I had to run about three hundred yards around the island carrying a heavy iron pulley, yelling, "Recondo! Recondo!" Then I had to ask permission to negotiate the suspension traverse—more commonly known as the "slide for life." Imagine climbing a sixty-foot tower, attaching a pulley to a rope strung over a lake, and sliding down that rope while raising your legs in the air and shouting "Recondo!" before dropping into the water. It felt as though I were flying. And then, while still soaking wet, I had to climb a tall ladder and walk across a long balance beam, only six inches wide, poised thirty feet in the air. To get down, I had to swing over the water on another rope—head first. At a certain point I was supposed to ask for permission to drop, and salute in the process, but I didn't quite make it. While changing my grip to get to the hang position, I fell in. As I waded to shore, I saw the sergeant sitting there, waiting for me to salute and say I had successfully completed the course. Well, I couldn't say that because I had fallen off the rope, so he told me I owed him ten push-ups on his red rock—which just happened to be in the water.

30 AUG 1977

Here it is, the end of August, and we are back at Woo Poo for Reorgy Week [the transition week between summer training and the academic year]. It's hard to believe that Camp Buckner, the so-called "best summer of my life," is over. Our last two days of training at Buckner consisted of learning how to build real bridges, and then blowing up smaller models. We *also had the fun of watching the plebes make their long march out to Lake Frederick on the 24th.*

We moved back to West Point on the 28th, and I met my squad leader—I'm his assistant this year. I have five plebes in my squad. Hearing them say, "Good morning, Ma'am," makes me want to turn around and see who's behind me. I still feel they can't possibly be talking to me. I can barely get used to not having to walk against the walls.

14 SEPT 1977

Wednesday, after lunch. I just finished a letter to my parents, and I'm sitting here wondering what my friends from high school are doing—if they're happy where they are, and, mostly, what typical college life is like. I found out last night that Cindy Owings is quitting. I guess she just doesn't like it here. Nancy heard about it, too—I was afraid it might put a few ideas about leaving into her head, but it didn't.

I really like this place. I think it suits me. Sometimes it can get a little heavy and depressing, but that's normal. I wouldn't trade West Point for anywhere else.

16 SEPT 1977

I hate this place right now. After lunch I found out that I'm on the Area because I was late to dinner formation last Wednesday. At West Point, one minute everything is good and you feel great; the next minute something can go wrong and it can keep getting worse. I'm supposed to go to Lieutenant Kincade's for dinner tonight—well, my Tac, Captain Hill, just told me I can't go. I am so upset I could quit. Now I have to call Lieutenant Kincade and tell her about it. But I'm afraid if I talk to her, I'll start crying. Even though it helps me to get upset, I hate holding in my emotions and frustrations all the time and then having them suddenly blow up and go out of control.

I think I'll go polish my shoes.

25 SEPT 1977

Mike knocked on my door a little while ago, as I was about to sit down and write. He certainly had a few things to say to me. He has begun to act so badly: treating me like a plebe, constantly inspecting my room, insisting that I be better than everyone else in the company because I'm his girlfriend. I don't know if I can feel the same way about him anymore. I think he wants me to be perfect. I've been trying to tell him that I don't think we should continue to see each other while he is company commander, and boy, did that hurt him. But we are both still cadets, and I don't want anymore trouble. I struggled enough to make it through plebe year—my first priority now is to graduate.

The commitment of a woman at West Point to make a career for herself occasionally led to some rather discouraged male cadets. In my class, we were dealing with very tradition-minded men, at least 40 percent of whom agreed in one Academy survey that "A woman's activities are best confined to the home."

What was so jarring, then, was their discovery upon entering the Academy that they'd entered an environment where old forms didn't apply. West Point was a place where men and women were first drawn together, not socially, but professionally. We discovered, gradually, if our personalities meshed, if we had similar beliefs, and from there the socializing flowed.

I knew for some time that Mike was finding me tough to handle, because I was straightforward about my rights as a person. Women at the Academy were caught in a peculiar bind: Being in the minority often put us in the position of having to take a back seat to the male cadets; at the same time we had to come on strong and stand up for ourselves. Of my class, which by the beginning of yearling year had dwindled from its original strength of 1,485 to 1,143, only eighty-six women remained, so naturally we had to keep a low profile. We didn't dare make ourselves stand out because the first noticeable thing we did would be picked apart. Some men had trouble dealing with us first as peers or colleagues, and then, if we were given rank, as authority figures. It came as no surprise that many of them were threatened by that; they were offended when a female was in authority. We always had to remember that we were dual-roled. Even in the simplest cases of etiquette, we knew we were not to wait for doors to be opened for us; we were not to take a man's arm if we were in—or out of—uniform. We had to carry an air of independence, and we had to let people know, just by looking at us, that we were professional women, something that should seem to come naturally.

Unfortunately it didn't come naturally to everyone, and Mike Truxel was one man who could never quite get used to the new order. We were always fighting—he'd want to open doors for me, and I'd have to remind him, 'Mike, I can do that for myself.' When he was made company commander, our problems became more serious. Now he had real power and the line between his demands on me as a girlfriend and as a subordinate under his command began to blur. He expected much more from me than my other classmates. He said I needed to set the example for them, to be better than they were. He wanted to see my uniform, my room, and my shoes always spit-shined. Well, no one is *that* perfect. But he would say, "Carol, you've got to do better than this. You've just got to do it."

And I would say, "Mike, please, let me be a normal yearling. I've spent an entire year in prison, and now I'm finally getting a little freedom. Come on."

There were hundreds of rules and regulations—every time I walked out the door I was probably doing something wrong. We had to wear our scarves this way and our gloves that way, and some people would get so wrapped up in the game, they'd forget what the rules were supposed to be *about*. They'd forget that the game itself was not important. It was learning to "lead by example," to work together and support each other. "Duty, Honor, Country." A cadet will not lie, cheat, or steal. That's what we were supposed to be learning, not how to put on a scarf. But Mike remained insistent. I knew he was trying to prove to me and others that dating him didn't give me any special privileges, that I had to be as strac as everyone else, actually more so. And yet, I also knew that I couldn't possibly live up to his expectations. I couldn't walk that line any more.

13 OCT 1977

It's been a few weeks since I've written in here. The days are going by quickly. Mike and I are getting along much better now. Tempers have cooled, and we've agreed to remain friends.

3 NOV 1977

On Wednesday night, I invited Lieutenant Rorabaugh to dinner in the mess hall, although I have to admit that I'm kind of afraid of her. She is such a strac officer, that I am very conscious about my actions and my appearance whenever she's around.

It was fairly easy to anticipate that in the early years of women's integration at West Point, contact with female officers was going to be hard to come by. To fill the gap, a new position was created within West Point's chain of command. Before our arrival, four women were brought in by the Academy to be SATOs—Special Assistants to Tactical Officers. The SATOs were intended as role models for women cadets and advisors to the male tactical officers on "women's issues." However, no doubt because of their auxiliary status, the SATOs were relatively ineffective. Once Beast Barracks was over, it was recommended that their positions not be reinstated. Instead, it was magnanimously suggested that women be made full-fledged tactical officers. And so they were—all two of them.

There were other female officers on post, but just a scattered handful. Colonel Mildred Hedberg (now a retired general) was Chief of Staff of the U.S. Corps of Cadets when we were at the Academy, but we saw her only at official functions. We knew Colonel Hedberg had begun her military career in the pre-integrated Army—in the Women's Army Corps—and we wondered sometimes how her early experiences compared with ours as cadets. Unfortunately, she was too high-ranking and remote for her presence to have any impact on our daily lives. There were also a number of women academic instructors, sports coaches, and phys ed instructors, but many of them were civilians.

Lieutenant Kim Rorabaugh was one of the few military females at West Point I knew personally. A hard-core Army officer, she was five feet seven and muscular, with freckles and strawberry blond hair. Lieutenant Rorabaugh had a dog named Smaj, which was short for sergeant major. That's how gung-ho Army she was. We rarely, if ever, got to see her human side. West Point officers often remained aloof from cadets, but this was particularly true of women officers—especially with regard to women cadets—to avoid accusations of showing favoritism, or, even worse, charges of fraternization. There was more than a touch of paranoia about such charges at the Academy. At practically every moment you had to stop and check your behavior—was it correct? Given half a chance, almost anything could, and would, be taken for impropriety.

Although it never occurred to many of us until much later, the most disturbing thing about all this was that we really needed contact with women officers. We needed their experience, their advice and their example. We needed to be able to talk to them without suspicion or fear. We needed their empathy and their concern. We needed to be brought up the way men at the Academy had been brought up by their own for almost two hundred years.

According to one female phys ed instructor, the P.E. department had been hoping for a "Farrah Fawcett" instructor. They wanted a bionic woman who could perform every physical skill in the world, who could equal the strength of Arnold Schwarzenegger, but who also looked like Farrah Fawcett, to establish the idea that "One doesn't have to look like a lady wrestler to be physically fit." Well, neither she nor any of the other women instructors who came to the Academy quite matched that idealized conception. Lieutenant Rorabaugh taught close-quarters combat, that is, hand-to-hand combat. "When the men walked into my class," she said, "I could see their faces drop, and I knew they were thinking, 'Sheesh, a woman instructor.' So, of course, my assistant instructor and I put on quite a show, to prove that we were confident in what we were teaching—and were able to demonstrate it. After their first lesson, I rarely had any problems with them. If you are a woman officer at the Academy, you have to maintain a talent, and you have to be a professional. You cannot get away with mediocrity."

This intense pressure to prove competence and meet military standards extended to all women at the Academy, cadets and officers alike. A female tactical officer once told me, "I had a big fracas with my women cadets over haircuts. They were having them done at marginal level, and I didn't think that was good enough. Their hair was too long. And they'd say, 'But when I bend over and pull as tightly as I can, my hair still doesn't touch the bottom of my collar.' And I'd say, 'You're missing the point. The old lady doesn't like your haircut. That's all that matters.' I spent a lot of time trying to tell them that it was inappropriate for them to cling to marginal standards, because they would not be able to do so as officers, and whether they liked it or not, their upholding of standards would have to exceed the men's. The truth was, their haircut would be noticed long before any man's. And in the Army, you can live and die by your haircut and weight. They are truly insignificant things when you think about other leadership components, but they are visual, and end up being applied unfairly to women. So I said, 'You can continue to cling to your marginal haircuts and take crap from me for the next month or so, but I will get you, one way or the other, or you can shrug your shoulders and say, 'There's no sense playing hardball; we're getting her torqued off, so let's get well within the safety standards and not have to deal with it anymore.' Fortunately, all of them decided not to torque off the old lady."

4 NOV 1977

Tonight at dinner, Megan Price was telling some war stories—it seems that her squad leader in Beast had a few problems showing the women how to fold their underwear. When he went over to inspect her roommate's closet, he found her bra dangling from a hanger. What a time that must have been. Whenever something like this happens, though, I've noticed that the guys are usually the ones who are the most embarrassed.

I remember the first time we tried to figure out how to fold a bra correctly. It was not that hard, but we'd watch some of the upperclassmen spend six minutes doing it. We'd have to step in and say, "Hey, Sir, relax. It's just one cup inside the other." But they'd be freaking out. "Can I touch this? What's going to happen when I touch this?" The upperclassmen would be furious with Julie Hawkins because her roommate's drawer was so nice and neat, while Julie's seemed so crammed with stuff. It took them weeks to figure out it was because her bras were bigger.

Sometimes, from the way they carried on, you'd think these guys never had mothers. Or sisters. Or girlfriends. They behaved almost as if we were the first women they'd ever seen.

With things like menstruation, unless a woman had severe cramps, she simply had to grit her teeth and go on with whatever she was supposed to be doing. It was often the case that a woman would get so wrapped up in her day that she'd be minutes away from when she'd have to change her tampon, and sometimes she would miss the moment. Consequently, the laundry was coming up with a high number of stains on uniform pants. The Academy actually distributed a bulletin, noting this problem, among all the companies. The note said, in effect, "Women, if you have to change your tampon, just get up and leave class." Now, there was simply no getting up and leaving a West Point class—you'd get punished if you were caught falling asleep in your seat, let alone having the audacity to get up and walk out. It would have been a highly conspicuous thing for any woman to do. So when we got the note, some of us laughed, but many of us thought, How dare you tell us to change our tampons? It's none of your damn business.

Of course, some of us never had to face that problem, because we had stopped menstruating altogether. It was frightening, but it was also one less thing to worry about. Women were reluctant to visit any of the Academy's gynecologists—one of them was a fat little man with a black moustache who doubled as the officer representative to the hockey team and used to talk intensely about the games while we were getting our Pap smears—but those who had stopped menstruating and did go to see a doctor were issued birth control pills, which usually started things flowing again. Extremely high physical and emotional stress seemed the most likely cause for the interruptions of our monthly cycles, but nobody really knew for sure—the body of medical knowledge on the subject wasn't large enough at the time. I think the only data the Academy had were on female Olympic athletes, whose bodies had evidently undergone similar changes. We knew they were very worried about us not having our periods. I think they were secretly terrified that they were turning us into men. At any rate, it gave the Academy the topic for its next questionnaire.

The day the Menstruation Questionnaire arrived, we took one look at it and thought, Oh Lord, what next? On top of everything else we had to do, it was just too embarrassing making ourselves the menstruation experts of North America. But we dutifully answered all the questions.

How heavy was your last period?
Was it painful?
Was it fun?
How many days since the last one?
And it was real easy for those of us who wrote, "Well, about 365. . . ."

26 NOV 1977

Army vs. Navy, 1977. We were so cold at the football game that we had to put newspaper in our shoes to keep our feet from freezing. Final score: Navy 14; Army 17. For the first time in five years, we won.

8 FEB 1978

I got a letter from a friend today who asked, "Why the Army?" She said she couldn't imagine joining up because she was too independent. How can I tell her that I am very independent, and that independence is a state of mind? That's the trouble with so many cadets—they lose themselves in the system. As long as you can stay in touch with who you really are inside, you'll have no problems with West Point. I'm keeping my individuality.

A lot of times the only thing that will get someone through West Point is the thought: I have a mother and a father who love me, and brothers and sisters and friends. Cadets mustn't let the Academy take their foundation away from them.

14 FEB 1978

Today is Valentine's Day. Mike came by for a while. He's really down. He doesn't like being a CO anymore. I can understand that. The COs are responsible for everybody's problems. It's a hard job with few rewards. Mike has to spend most of his time counseling people who are in trouble. He also has to keep up with his own academics. Mike likes the power of command, but I think he now realizes that it doesn't give him the freedom the other seniors have. As company commander, he is never allowed to let down his guard. Still, he says, he's not going to quit.

99

21 FEB 1978

The cannon was just fired. That means it's 4:30 P.M.—Retreat. I love watching them take down the flag, and seeing everything and everyone in this place stop.

After dinner tonight, a bunch of women are supposed to have a meeting with the commandant—another one of our periodic bitch sessions, I guess.

A well-meaning group called the Corbin Seminar—named for Captain Margaret "Molly" Corbin of Revolutionary War fame—sprang up as an outgrowth of the Cadet Counseling Center. It was intended as a place where both male and female cadets could go to discuss women's issues, and where women could find institutionally approved solidarity and support. We were encouraged to attend meetings, lectures, special events. But not many dared to do so—it was too high-profile, too risky. They'd announce the meetings over the PA system during dinner, which would be immediately met with hisses and boos from the male cadets. Naturally, no one was going to go after that. The main stigma attached to the Corbin Seminar was that it was a "women's group." We were always made to feel bad about wanting to group together with other women. The first hurdle for men seemed to be accepting that women could do the same things they did. Once they got over that, their attitude was, "Okay, you women can do what we do, but then that means you're one of us. As long as you blend in, you're okay. But don't stand out as a separate group." There could be no unity without uniformity.

28 FEB 1978

My stupid-ass platoon leader wrote me up this week for being late to dinner formation, and for wearing civilian clothes in the latrine during Saturday inspection. I hear he's becoming an MP—hell, I wouldn't follow him to the bathroom. One time he wrote me up for a punishment because my long overcoat was missing from my closet. He didn't even consider that I might be wearing it. What a nerd.

I talked to Mike tonight for half an hour. He told me he has to decide tomorrow where he wants to go for his first assignment. I always knew he would have to leave and go somewhere far away, but suddenly it's become very real.

2 MAR 1978

I talked to Mike again last night. He has decided to go to Fort Carson, Colorado, for three years.

21 MAR 1978

Tuesday was officially the first day of spring. So, what do we wear? Our thin gray jackets—no more winter uniforms—it doesn't matter how cold it is. "After all, it's spring now," they say.

11 APR 1978

Almost three weeks have elapsed since I've written in here, which shows just how boring this place can be. The most interesting day was last Friday, when several of us took a "stroll"—a two-hour walk on the Area for yet another violation. The Area birds played tag most of the time.

12 APR 1978

We've heard rumors that they're taking away some of our privileges next year. I wish I knew which hat they pulled these decisions out of. Instead of giving us increased responsibilities, they're babying us even more. Some cadets won't be able to handle themselves when they get out of here because of this. Why don't they just open up their eyes.

"In the academic arena," says an instructor from the Department of Behavioral Science and Leadership, "I think we may go too far in structuring our courses. We tell cadets, 'Read this, this, and this, and here's what's important.' But then they are commissioned and when they get there, no one tells them, 'Read *this* tonight, lieutenant.' They've got to figure out for themselves which field manuals they're supposed to be reading. A lot of West Point graduates assume that somebody's going to tell them what to do, so when they go into the field, they screw up. Academically, we think we're promoting inquiry, questioning, and critical thinking, but we also know that the cadets are living in a military environment where a high degree of conformity is expected and where they are taught to obey and do exactly what they are told. A cadet cannot simply wake up one morning and decide, 'Hey, I don't feel like wearing a gray shirt today.' And while instructors may be teaching literature or psychology, many of them are also wearing military uniforms, so the cadets must respond to them, too, in a hierarchical way. That's got to be a difficult place to grow up in."

101

13 APR 1978

Megan Price is definitely leaving the Academy after term end exams. I think she'll be much happier somewhere else, although she would have made an outstanding officer.

One morning, very early, Megan Price came downstairs into our room, curled herself into a quivering ball in one corner, and began to cry. Through convulsive sobs she blurted out that something had happened to her. One moment she'd been asleep, she said, her voice cracking, and the next, she'd been awakened by the touch of a man's hand between her legs.

We'd heard vague stories before about male cadets sneaking into women's rooms at night, but no one had ever dared to report it. Megan did. It was a while, after that, before we heard anything more about what was happening to her—all we knew was that she had been moved to another company. Then the rumors started flying—that Megan had consented, that she had "asked for it," and then called it sexual assault, but we knew that wasn't so. She was terrified when my roommate and I saw her that morning: She was shaking all over. She had been violated. She hadn't consented to or encouraged a thing.

To set the story straight, and to provide an open forum where female cadets could discuss their feelings about what had happened to Megan without fear of male backlash or disapproval, two of the male officers associated with the Corbin Seminar called a meeting. About thirty women attended, including Megan. When people started asking her questions, we watched her expression change from the friendly, outgoing one we knew, to that of a meek and frightened little girl. All she said was, "I'm not supposed to talk about it."

When the case was tried, the only thing that could be proved conclusively was that the cadet had entered Megan's room "unauthorized." It was, therefore, resolved that the young man would be allowed to graduate from the Academy, but he wouldn't receive his Army commission. Some male cadets still blamed Megan. They said she'd made an issue out of nothing. One of them said, "Well, is she pregnant?" And when the answer was, "No," he said, "So, what's the big deal?" His attitude was, "Oh, come on, buck up. Be a man about it." And he was not alone in his opinion.

Two of my female classmates went to see the commandant to protest how easily the cadet had been let off. They thought it was an absolute outrage that not only was he being allowed to graduate, but that he also had been excused from his five-year obligation to serve in the Army. The commandant maintained that the Academy had given the young man a severe punishment—his dream of being an Army officer was shattered. Maybe. But the way we saw it, the cadet had received a free college education without having to pay anything back.

Many of us felt that what happened to Megan Price was an important turning point for women at the Academy. We hoped the administration was beginning to understand our situation, what had been happening to us all along. Everything wasn't running as smoothly, perhaps, as the surface seemed to indicate.

Throughout plebe year, we had known that we were in for a rough show. But our expectation was that once the first year was over, things would improve. By the second year, however, although the men couldn't harass us in terms of plebe nonsense anymore, they found other ways to do it. Some men would refuse to greet us or any of the male cadets who dared to date or even befriend us; they'd fill page after page of slug sheets with demerits for "Dust on shoes" or "Closed drawer during inspection," or any piddly offense they could dream up. We'd be continually ranked at the bottom of the class for leadership, and were regularly the subjects of vicious rumors that they'd spread behind our backs.

One of my female classmates said that, at a terrible cost for Megan, the incident was almost cathartic for the rest of us, because it got a lot of people talking about what constituted provocation, and whether women were a demoralizing factor at the Academy. Out came the hostility that male cadets were feeling: "It would be so much easier to run things here without you." The fact that everyone was finally speaking openly was helpful, in a bizarre kind of way.

Megan decided to leave West Point (she never returned after spring break), and in the wake of her departure new rules were conceived. Women were not allowed to sleep alone anymore. Even if we had to go to another company to do it, we had to sleep on an old World War II-type Army cot in someone else's room whenever our roommate was away for the night. It annoyed us that *we* were the ones who had to be inconvenienced; we felt it should have been the male cadets' responsibility to simply behave themselves. So we'd make fun of the rule. For instance, there was only one cot per company, and it was kept behind the door in one of the women's rooms. One company pinned a little note on theirs that read, "Sir, this is an anti-attack cot." Somehow, it never occurred to anyone to solve the problem by putting locks on the barracks room doors. Some said the Academy wouldn't do that for fear of what could take place on the other side.

.   .   .

In 1986 a female cadet said that sexual harassment had not stopped occurring within the barracks, most of it emanating from drunks. "They go after a plebe or yearling female who is easily intimidated, doesn't want to make waves, and will usually keep quiet about it. It's not rampant, however, and women here are taught two years of self-defense, so, theoretically, they should be able to handle themselves, even if they're disturbed while asleep. Administratively, they've established an informal sexual harassment representative within each company who acts as an intermediary for anyone who has been victimized, but who may not feel comfortable reporting the incident to a male squad leader. However, some of the representatives are also male, which is essential since the problem is both a male and a female one. Certainly men should be involved in the policing of their own ranks. These days, if men are found guilty of this type of sexual assault, they are kicked out of the Academy. Others say no, but in my experience, women are rarely castigated by their companies for speaking out. In fact, companies have become more supportive. That's a big change from when I was a plebe, and I'm sure from when the class of '80 women were plebes, because then a woman usually shut up and took it. She did not mess with that male bond. But now most of the men want to get those jerks out of here, because they don't belong with us."

20 APR 1978

Today in history class we had a discussion on the function—the ultimate function—of the Army. My "P" [professor] claims it is to kill. I say it's to keep the peace, that if our influence is strong enough throughout the world, we won't have to fight. Maybe that's an idealist's view. I just hope our country never has to go to war. I realize I'm being trained to lead "killers," to command when they will kill or will not kill, and it makes me feel cold.

Could I kill anyone? I think, yes—if my life, or the life of one of my subordinates or superiors, were in danger. To defend, but that is all. When I remember Beast Barracks and the bayonet drills—how they kept telling us to yell things that would motivate us, like, "Blood makes the grass grow!" Those words seem so inhuman. A few people got upset because they stressed the word "Kill!" so much. I was just playing the game and didn't think about what I was saying. I doubt that many of us considered what those words really meant.

A friend of mine from the class of '86 remarked that she was always interested in writing a paper on what female-designed weapons would look like. Or, she wondered, would women even create weapons? Because most weapons are, of course, very phallic—think of guns and tubes and cannons—all that projection and assertiveness and dominance is quintessentially tied to what men perceive to be their primary function. "I don't know if women would choose to deal with war in quite the same way," she said. "We might have terrific negotiating tables. Or, I had a literature instructor at the Academy who said that women probably wouldn't have weapons, they'd just tear each other to shreds."

My classmate, Captain Paula Stafford, disagrees that war, and the methods of waging it, are in any way gender-specific. "People always say, oh gosh, if only the world were run by women, we wouldn't have nuclear war because women would find a better solution, but I don't think that's true. The women who reached those positions of decision-making power would hold the same values and run things the same way that men have, and nothing would change. After all, if I were a general, and had a chest full of medals, don't you think I'd be proud? And walk around like a stuffed turkey, just like all the men do? I would."

22 APR 1978

Over the next four months, everyone in my class will be deciding whether or not to stay and finish at West Point (and incur their five-year commitment to serve in the Army).

I must say, the thought of quitting has certainly run through my mind—I think often about the ease of attending a regular college. Sometimes I have to stop and ask myself, What am I doing here? Is it really worth it? I know that the guys think about similar things, but the feelings are so different. Men have graduated from West Point before—women haven't. Everyone seems to be holding his breath, waiting to see how we'll do. It's such a big deal when a woman quits—though, of course, to those men who don't want us here, the attitude is simply, "Yeah! One more gone."

Within the cadets' inner circle existed a system of enforcement—we'd sense who would survive and who would not. Those who were weak would be hounded and hunted, pushed to the limit to see how much they could stand before they broke down and quit. Among the women, the drive toward perfection was consuming, not only for oneself, but for everyone. West Point is a bell jar, and when you entered the gates and signed your name on the dotted line you relinquished a lot of control and personal privacy. The tiniest infraction by one woman reflected on us all. It would spur any number of men to comment, "Look at that one. I told you

105

females don't belong here." Flawed men were glossed over as exceptions. So were stellar women. In the minds of these men, one "bad" woman would obliterate twenty "good" ones. Yet, as talents emerged, they inscribed their own futures. A woman who could make the runs, who could pitch a tent, who could fire a rifle well, who didn't snivel or cry, this woman would earn friendship and support. But if a woman was incompetent we would destroy her—even quicker than the men would—because she threatened all of us.

Some women felt that the most compassionate thing we could do for a female who couldn't cut it at West Point was to help her to leave. Not to "help" her in a negative way, but to say, "Look, these are the realities of this place. You're a valuable person; if you stay here you're going to end up hurting yourself."

There was one girl in Beast Barracks who got the worst hazing of any of us. She was *physically* hazed. I remember one time a gang of guys grabbed her. They shut her up inside a metal locker and then started pounding on it. The poor girl was terrified. She was reduced to a trembling nothing; by the end of the summer she quit. When she gave up, one of our female classmates said, "She didn't have what it takes."

Most of us couldn't tolerate weakness. "If a woman cadet couldn't do a pull-up, I didn't have much respect for her," says Paula Stafford. "I think that's rather narrow-minded now; I have reformed my views very much since then. But, at the time, it was a big deal. It really was."

Admittedly, we weren't highly comforting friends to women who were struggling. Everyone's image was linked somehow. In fact, there were times when we'd cringe at the performance of a less capable female classmate. We'd think, To hell with unity; I'm a member of my platoon. There was constant tension between showing solidarity with female classmates and wanting to be one of the group. As Lori Eller said, "Sometimes, you just wanted to belong. For crying out loud, you just wanted to *belong.*"

We weren't always hostile toward those women who couldn't keep up—but we would snap at them or make caustic comments. We knew we were living according to an intensely competitive system governed by a stopwatch. We'd distance ourselves from any woman who wasn't performing up to par. We'd damn her with silence by refusing to defend her against a male classmate's negative observations. Because, factually, the men's assessments of the women were generally true—yes, the woman did fall out of X number of runs. If the men were saying something slanderous, we might have said something in her behalf, but if it were related to performance, we wouldn't. We didn't want to get into the issue of performance indicators; we just didn't want to open up that wound.

24 APR 1978

This summer, it turns out, I'll be in Georgia, at Jump School. All those going Airborne had a meeting in South Area tonight—they told us what our training would be like. I don't think it will be too hard. We run with women and do our PT with women. That's good, in a way, because I think I'd be inclined to give up more easily if guys were around than if I were only with girls. If a guy beats you, it's one thing, but if another girl beats you—let's just say there is a lot of peer pressure to keep up.

After the meeting, a bunch of us were walking back to the barracks and discussing how many women were leaving the Academy. It's very disheartening.

25 APR 1978

The slug sheet came down today, and my name was on it. The Tac wrote me up for "Very poor posture" and for "Chewing gum." Why is there so much Mickey Mouse nonsense around here? I thought I liked to be noticed—now I'm tired of having people watch every move I make. I feel like I'm always in someone's little spotlight, always being observed under someone's microscope. A lot of people get fed up with it. I know I do, but I try to look at it from a different perspective. I try to see it as the means to an end.

30 APR 1978

Sunday. Took a shower and called my parents. Well, after all is said and done, I'm not quitting. The cut-off point for cadets to leave the Academy without incurring a five-year army service obligation comes this September, when we attend our first class of cow year. I know my Mom and Dad will feel much better when I go to my first class next fall.

3 MAY 1978

What a suck of a day—everyone going Airborne had to meet the standards on the APFT [Army Physical Fitness Test]. I did great on everything—then came the situps. The minimum needed to pass is thirty-two. I did exactly thirty and a half. I just couldn't come up anymore. It felt like my stomach muscles had frozen. Well, I wasn't about to come back and do it again the next day, so I waited five minutes and tried again. The second time I did thirty-three.

107

Yesterday I had a meeting with my Tac, and he gave me some good poop on how I should improve my behavior. I want to be good, but I need people to help me. I know I have to make an extra effort to spend time with the guys in my company, but because of the prevailing attitudes at West Point, I feel a tighter bond between myself and the other women in the Corps. Maybe the Tac doesn't realize this yet, but women aren't exactly popular around here.

23 MAY 1978

This is the last page in this book. Here's my summer schedule: Drill Cadet Program—Leave—Airborne School. The class of '80 has made it through their second year. Just over a thousand yearlings remain—seventy-nine women among them. Every day friends of mine are leaving for good. It's getting harder to say good-bye.

Cow Year

1978–1979

★

A bit of folklore.

"In the old days at the Academy," recalls one retired colonel, "plebes didn't have Christmas leave, or an initial yearling summer leave either. Instead they had one long sixty-day leave right before cow year, while the seniors and sophomores took care of training the new incoming plebes. The reason for this was, that shorter excursions were impractical, since there weren't any airplanes in those days, so the Academy would get those yearlings out of here and tell them to forget about West Point for two whole months. Legend has it that when the plebes complained about summer training, the upperclassmen would look at them and threaten, 'You think we're giving it to you bad? Just wait till the cows come home,' which is how the second classmen came to be known as 'cows.'

Back in 1976, one of the big worries at West Point was—and this just shows how ridiculous things can be sometimes—'What's going to happen when the class of '80 becomes second classmen? Those girls are simply not going to like being called 'cows.' And the Academy sweated that thing out—whether or not to order people not to call the girls 'cows.' But if you go out and ask a second class girl, 'What class are you in?' She'll say, 'Oh, I'm a cow,' without giving it a second thought."

11 JUNE 1978

It's Sunday, and I am sitting in a small two-man room, which I share with Cathy Gordon, at Fort Jackson, South Carolina. We arrived here at 6:30 on Thursday night for the Drill Cadet Program, whose purpose is to offer cadets a taste of real Army life from an enlisted soldier's point of view. On Friday I met my drill sergeant, my CO, and my field first sergeant. In the afternoon, we had orientation at the Drill Sergeant School. I was made an assistant drill sergeant and for the next four weeks, will assist in physical training, rifle marksmanship training, drill, and first aid instruction for about fifty basic trainees. Then, once my summer leave is over, I am sched-uled to fly down to Airborne School on Friday morning, 4 August, at 0335 (A.M.).

Thinking back to the Academy's Drill Cadet Program at Fort Jackson, South Carolina, I recall what an ego trip it was. I was assigned to an all-male platoon and had a direct impact on their daily lives for four weeks—half of their basic training.

One of my jobs was to wake up the soldiers in the morning. The men lived in a bay on the second floor of the enlisted barracks, and, using the platoon's drill sergeant as my example, I would scream at them from downstairs over the speaker system: "You've got five minutes to get your butts out of bed and dressed—and then I'm coming up!"

Sometimes I'd go upstairs early, just to give them an extra haze. As I'd walk past the open bay on my way to the platoon office, I'd catch the guys scrambling around in their underwear. I'd call out, "You'd better get it together. I don't want to see any of those ugly bodies!"

One extremely hot afternoon, we were coming back from the rifle range, on a forced march, and I was really pushing them hard. One of the guys kept complaining that he couldn't keep up. I took his rifle from him, and a few of his buddies grabbed his knapsack. Still, we had to prod him. Another guy got heat cramps, and we had to evac him to the hospital. I fondly remember that summer session as my first professional "test."

5 AUG 1978

Fort Benning, Georgia. Saturday morning. My training company is the 44th, but I live in the 43d company area. It's air conditioned, thank God. I can't believe how humid it is down here. All the West Point cadets had a three-mile run this morning, which we were required to complete in twenty-seven minutes. I made it in exactly twenty-seven minutes.

7 AUG 1978

Monday. Training began today. Wake up at 0400. We had inspection at 0530 and formation at 0605. By the afternoon, we had started in the Pits. We learned how to "Stand up, hook up, shuffle to the door, jump on out, and count to four"—just like the song goes.

Tuesday was our first full day. We were inspected by our cadre, the Black

Cats, then ran two miles and did calisthenics in the Pits. We did about two hundred push-ups, too. Man, you get sawdust in places you never thought you'd have sawdust. We looked like breaded eggplant—purplish green, with crumbs all over. Every hour, depending on the weather, we ran through showers to cool our bodies, which felt great. Later we learned how to do left and right PLF's [Parachute Landing Falls]. We practiced until we could do them in our sleep. They're very hard, and hurt if we don't land correctly. I landed on my neck twice.

Wednesday we jumped off the thirty-four-foot tower. If we're not careful, we get Airborne hickeys—huge purple bruises from the parachute risers pinching our necks as we go out the tower door. I got a few of those.

Thursday we had a two-and-a-half-mile run, then spent most of the day jumping off the tower. I qualified, so luckily I don't have to do it anymore.

Friday we had our three-mile run. That night, Kerry and I went to the NCO Club. Some of the men were making catcalls at us, and Kerry got upset. I told her not to worry about it. We have more important things to think about—like getting ready for Tower Week.

TOWER WEEK 1978

The first day we ran three miles. It wasn't that bad, but then we got into the Pits. They killed us in there for almost an hour. Our platoon did mass exits from the thirty-four-foot tower—that was neat. On C-141 airplanes, I'm told, all you have to do is walk out. Yeah, sure.

On Tuesday, Wednesday, and Thursday we each jumped off the 250-foot tower—twice. They say the floating feeling is the same as jumping out of a plane. I qualified on both jumps, although I landed harder the first time and really felt it in my calves. After that, I knew the only thing between me and jumping out of an aircraft was the four-and-a-half-mile run on Friday.

The week finally ended with a malfunction class—what to do if something goes wrong. I don't want to think about that right now.

When we finished our training, the lieutenant in the group gave us a cake with "Congratulations Whiskeys" written on it. ["Whiskeys"—phonetic spelling for "W"—in this case, meaning women]. We sat up in one of the rooms together that night, ate cake, and sang our fool heads off.

21 AUG 1978

Monday. What a day. We had classes all morning, then picked up our parachutes and reserve chutes and prepared them for donning in the shed. At all times—that is, except when we had the parachutes on our backs—we were supposed to move at double time. One of the sergeants—Sergeant

Lewis—was a character. He loved to hit hard [keep the pressure on], and yell loud.

I was in the first set of sticks [a group of people dropped from a plane in a single pass over the drop zone] on the C-141, which boarded at about 1330. (Our drop was scheduled for 1400.) I was also the first person to board the plane, and, consequently, the last person to leave. I was glad the C-141 was cold inside, because I was more than a little nervous and my stomach wasn't settled. Kerry was my stick leader, so she had to jump first. Our stick was the last to go, but just hearing the jump command for the other sticks set my heart beating faster. Suddenly it was our turn. "Six minutes!" the jumpmaster called. "Get ready outboard personnel! Staaaand up! Hook up! (We hooked up our static lines so our chutes would automatically open when we jumped out.) Check static lines! Check equipment! Sound off for equipment check! Okay—one minute, thirty seconds, standby, go!"

It is very dramatic when they open the doors on the C-141. This is not what happens to the average commercial airline customer. The C-141 plane is usually dark inside, but who needs light anyway? There aren't any stewardesses passing out peanuts or handing around the "barf can," which we passed along from person to person, so that everyone could get a chance to throw up in it. If there's more than one person who needs it at the same time, well, somebody has to miss a turn.

The rides are fairly noisy because these planes are not insulated like commercial passenger planes. Of course, it gets even noisier when the doors are opened and the air screams through the cabin. The light is sudden and brilliant (unless it's a night jump), so it's a very intense moment. To add to the impact, the jump is made almost immediately. The green light goes on, the jumpmaster yells *"GO!"* and that always comes as a big shock. Standing there, waiting to jump, one's legs no longer know the meaning of support. Mine were shaking.

I hesitated a little before I "walked" out, so I wouldn't get near any of the other jumpers. The jumpmaster sergeant fixed me with a look and said, *"Barkalow, are you afraid?"*

"No, Sir!" I gulped, praying for the light to turn green before he pulled me forward and I puked all over him.

"You see this size thirteen boot?" he yelled.

"Yes, Sir!"

"Well," he said, *"it's going to be up your ass if you don't get out that door. You'd better not hesitate!"*

I jumped.

112

A rush of wind sucked me out of the plane and turned me on my side. I counted one, one thousand; two, one thousand—then felt the tug of the chute. I glanced up and saw the canopy billowing over my head—no malfunctions, thank goodness.

When I looked down, the ground and the people on it seemed unbearably far away. It was perfectly quiet. I had to remind myself to pull my risers in the opposite direction of the wind drift. One hundred feet before I hit the ground, I prepared to land. I don't remember, frankly, which two risers I pulled to direct the chute, or which PLF I did. When I touched ground, however, I just lay there on the Drop Zone for a few moments with a huge grin on my face. Then I got up, collapsed my canopy, and fell into it. As I removed my harness, I began to tremble.

People were all smiles running off the Drop Zone and climbing onto the trucks, hanging over the sides and yelling *"Airborne!"*

We had one night jump after that—or rather, twenty-seven of us had night jumps. We were all loaded into planes and ready to go, but only one stick was dropped—right into a swamp. Eileen Simmons, who was deathly afraid of heights, got caught in a pine tree thirty feet up. They told her to hit her reserve, let it drop down, and then crawl out of the chute harness, but she started yelling back at them—"Fuck yooooouuuuu!" Somebody said they could hear her screaming two miles away.

There were no more night jumps for our group after that. Personally, I didn't care. The old joke really did apply to me—I could say all my jumps were night jumps; when I jumped, I closed my eyes.

25 AUG 1978

Our final jump was on Thursday morning. The only thing I did wrong was the landing. I landed: heels, back, head. But by that time, I just wanted to stand up and double-time it off the Drop Zone, which was one of the reasons they ran us during the last week of training—to make sure we didn't have any injuries, because people tried to hide them. After getting through that far, we didn't want to get recycled and have to do it all over again.

After everyone had finished, they bussed us immediately to the graduation site. It felt incredible when the man pinned those wings on my shirt. That night I went to bed with two heat packs on my back, but I was Airborne qualified.

11 OCT 1978

This semester I'm taking an elective course with Major Ken Rucker called "Women in America." It's a discussion class that deals with Ameri-

can trends about accepted modes of action for women. We have heated discussions in almost every class. I'm enjoying it more than I thought I would. I even do all my homework for it.

No one lectures women at West Point on their history anymore. A recent female graduate says, "I hardly know anything about women in the military—they didn't teach us about it at the Academy, isn't that interesting? We took an entire year of military history and there wasn't a single mention of the Women's Army Corps. Women's history was taught in some courses, but they were all electives. The information was not included in general knowledge courses, so very few cadets were exposed to it. And it's something both males and females should know, because it's a part of the institution to which we're dedicating our lives. If the men were taught the history of the WASPS, for example—the female pilots in World War II—and what kind of role they played; if they knew that American military women were at Bataan and Corregidor, or that they were deployed overseas to Italy and North Africa, following closely in support of the fighting men, they might back off a bit. But we were only taught about the Infantry and Armor leaders and how wonderful and brave and courageous they were. And so my entire course of study has taught me, by implication, that I'm not an entity in this Army."

When asked about this, one senior officer and former instructor at the Academy said, "The reason that cadets are not better educated on the history of women in the services is basically because it's no longer necessary. Not in great detail, anyway. In fact, if we did it too much, the men would say, 'Hey, you're forcing this thing down my throat.' I think most men acknowledge that women have always played a role in the American Army since the Revolutionary War. At least *I* do. But we don't want too much forced down our throats. We need room for it, but not too much. We need just a little bit."

One of my female classmates responds: "Oh, bullshit—it's been pushed down their throats to *accept*—if I hear that word one more time I think I'll puke—to *accept* women, *accept* women. People don't accept anything until they can value the contribution it makes. Unless that can be done, no one is ever going to 'accept' them. The fact is, the Army would fall apart without women. We couldn't maintain our force structure; we could not do our jobs. *This* is what has to be gotten across to people, not merely the idea that 'women are equal, too, so you've got to accept us.' "

NOVEMBER 1978

The following is a letter I wrote to a guy who is upset at the standards for Airborne School:

Dear Editor,

I'd like to respond to the letter written in the last issue of the Pointer *by Mr. "Name Withheld," concerning his complaints about women in Airborne School. I, myself, am Airborne qualified and am very proud of it. Mr. "Name Withheld" expresses his heartburn because of the difference between the standards for men and women in the two-mile run.*

First, the women in the two Airborne classes this summer ran behind the men by only one minute, and kept virtually the same pace. Second, the pace and the platoon we ran with (all women) was not by choice. It was the cadre's decision. Third, the purpose of running at Airborne School is not to make people good runners. It is to build up the muscles in the legs so they can absorb the shock of a parachute landing, thereby minimizing the chances of getting hurt.

Both men and women got dirty in the sawdust pits, leapt out of the same thirty-four-foot towers, and suffered on the suspended harness for the same period of time. We wore the same parachutes, jumped out of the same airplanes, and landed on the same field.

Running took up only thirty minutes of the entire day. After the run was over, we had to concentrate on the graded portions of the training because, if we did not pass, we would not make it to Jump Week.

In Airborne III one female cadet dropped out, not because she could not make the runs, but because she broke her kneecap.

If given the chance, women will perform, but it will take people like Mr. "Name Withheld" to grow up and deal with us on a professional level.

Thank you,
Carol Barkalow

16 DEC 1978

We finished our Christmas basketball tournament. I'm not starting anymore—and I'm playing less and less. I talked to Coach Martin about it. He gave me the party line—"Keep practicing." But I know what's going on. Coach Gillette and I got along fine in the beginning, but now the new girls have more talent. Dr. Peterson went out recruiting women—a better crop of athletes—from different high schools. And when that happened, I know I began to lose confidence in myself athletically. Gillette still treats us like plebes—very authoritarian, and impatient—hell, we get that all day, we don't need it from our coach. So I am a mouth and a pain to him—and he knows he can get the same results from someone else. It goes in a circle—when I'm not playing as much, I lose confidence and play worse.

One time he yelled at me—"Barkalow, your defense sucks! Keep your eye on the ball!"—and I got so mad I heaved a chair into the wall. I was trying my hardest. Maybe I want athletics at West Point to be an outlet, not a competition. Maybe I just want a release. Of course, I am competitive, but not to the point of destructiveness. It's not as though I have to win at all costs. I love basketball and will play my heart out, but it doesn't have to be a hassle. If the rest of my life were calmer, maybe I could keep a real sharp competitive edge. With the way things are, however, it's just too overwhelming.

21 JAN 1979

I am now a squad leader. I have four plebes, four yearlings, one cow, and two firsties. I'm keeping a notebook so I can properly evaluate all the persons in my squad.

I've decided that I must maintain my academics this semester. I'll be taking juice [electrical engineering], thermo [thermofluid dynamics], and philosophy—better known as "drugs," because it has the effect of a sedative. I've also volunteered for the Bayonet Committee this summer. I think I can project a good image for women who don't feel they can get into it.

We spent the first part of our philosophy course talking about ethical theory. The second part of the term we talked about war, which meant taking ethical theory and applying it to the military. The instructor did not ask us—"What would *you* do in this situation?"—to which everybody would have had an opinion and one approach would've been as good as another, and could've been justified. Nor did we learn—*"This is the Army position."* Instead, we were asked, "What is it that *constitutes* an ethical theory, and what are some of the classic ones?" So then when we started thinking, "I won't cheat, lie, or steal," the question became, *"Why* won't I do those things?" Which was a very difficult question to answer, but that's how the Academy handled the study of ethical philosophy. We studied Kant's theory—that there is an absolute somewhere, and what human beings try to do is recognize it. We also studied Mill's theory—that whatever is best for mankind at large, in the long run, is the right thing to do. Both of those philosophies fit into the military ethic.

"When they first taught us philosophy," Lori Eller recalls, "it was by

116

rote. It was very funny, too. The instructors tried to teach it almost like math, I thought. I guess somebody must have said it would be good to get a dialogue going between the Platonist view of the world and the Aristotelian view of the world. Well, we got together a group of cadets to talk about these two views—the Aristotelian, where real is what you can touch, see, hear, smell, and taste. And the Platonic, where real is the image of the real, that is, the ideal. The shadow in the cave, so to speak. And I thought that was interesting. But everybody in the class was thinking, 'Have you lost your mind?' *Including* the instructor. West Pointers are very concrete."

Fran Boyd agrees. "My educational background was scientific in nature," she said. "I tended to stay away from the social sciences. My own thought process was more objective anyway, and the Academy supported that way of thinking. It was part of the reason I stayed. I was more conservative—I came from a structured home environment where there wasn't much room for diverse opinions. I didn't really like the 'soft stuff'—sociology, history, literature."

Andrea Hollen, the highest academically ranked woman in the class of '80, and the only member of my class to be awarded a Rhodes Scholarship, observes, "The rote, black-and-white way of looking at the world wasn't part of my educational experience at the Academy. However, when I arrived in England I quickly took a course in Marxian economics. None of that had been given at West Point. I did not understand the word 'imperialist' when I hit Oxford. Students there called me a 'militarist capitalist imperialist,' and I didn't know what they were talking about. But then, at West Point, we were exposed to less radical political analysis. The view there was that the power structures in our society were basically benign, if not downright benevolent."

5 FEB 1979

We had a sexual awareness lecture for the Second Class tonight, and I was so embarrassed by the ignorance and lack of respect that was shown, I tried to walk out. Captain Hoffman stopped me from leaving. Still, he was very disappointed in our class.

Then, the other night, as I was walking back from dinner, I heard one of the yearlings in my company refer to one of his female classmates as bitch. *I told him he'd better refrain from using that language about female cadets. I got so mad. I know I'm really sensitive about this issue, but we have been stepped on for too long, and I won't let it happen anymore.*

117

27 FEB 1979

I am sitting at my desk, listening to "I Am Woman" by Helen Reddy. I have made a vow to myself that on the night before graduation—27 May 1980—that song will be heard throughout the Corps of Cadets at midnight.

As one of a series of lectures, the Academy brought in an "equal opportunity" consultant to conduct sensitization workshops to make people uncomfortably aware of their own sexism and racism.

We were called into the auditorium, and this man walked on stage and said, "I'm not the real speaker, I'm not the guy who's scheduled to speak, but the Academy called me at the last minute, and I'm going to tell you how it is: Women have no business being anywhere near the military."

At which point the male cadets gave him a standing ovation. They were screaming, "Yay!" and he just went on and on. All the women were dying a million deaths. He triggered everything the men were feeling, and they gave him tremendous support. Finally he got in too deep, so he switched over and started talking about blacks.

"And you know," he said, "anybody who tells you that a black person is genetically capable of handling the kinds of intellectual challenges that a white can, doesn't know what he's talking about."

Then the room began to get quiet. A few people still cheered, but it got real quiet. Everyone started to fidget and murmur, then the guy switched back to talking about women, and the men were cheering again. He'd go back and forth, talking about Jews and Hispanics, then turning back to the subject of women because the guys loved it.

Eventually I heard someone say, "I think it's a joke." But my classmate Gail Lewis stormed the stage and two officers had to restrain her. One of them was holding her by the arm. And when Gail got upset, you could tell the men's attitude was, see, there's another example of those hysterical women. She was yelling, waving her fist in the air, and some guys were laughing at her. And yet we all felt the same way; even when we realized it was a joke, it was still horrible.

At last the man owned up to who he was, and why he had come. He told us that we had been participants in a controlled exercise designed to raise our consciousness. When he finally left the stage, we were divided into groups to have discussions in different classrooms.

Mostly, however, there was only one woman per group, so we each had to defend our position alone, and some of the guys were saying things like, "Well, I knew he was joking all along. I just went with it." Lori Eller says

118

she distinctly remembers one of our male classmates saying, "I understand your objection to all the crap he said about blacks, but when he was talking about women, he was telling the truth!"

The whole thing had backfired. It really divided the class. When one guy stood up and tried to defend the women, another one of my classmates recalls that a few of the other guys immediately challenged his masculinity. They said he obviously had homosexual tendencies.

I heard later that the consultant told our superiors that he had never seen any crowd have such a violent reaction or such incredible hostility toward women in his life.

Part of the irony of our experience was that the women who went to West Point became feminists in deed, even if they rejected feminism in name. We were aggressive, independent, and ambitious; we were not radicals, we weren't challenging authority—but we were fighting inequity. We were not rejecting the military tradition, we wanted to live under its influence, its structure and discipline.

A former female tactical officer at the Academy explained, "Some women may go to West Point for feminist gains and ambitions, but many are there because they're the sons their fathers never had. Others have deep patriotic feelings and believe this is the best way they can go about discharging their civic obligation. I'd be inclined to think that most of these women are culturally, and politically, conservative. You probably won't find that many real political liberals among them."

"It takes a very motivated and very conservative woman to come here," echoed a former male instructor in the American history department. "These women are not what I would call—and it's an overused term—'feminists.' They're not here for any kind of 'women's liberation.' They're here because they want to be West Pointers; they want the opportunities West Point has to offer."

My classmate Denise Gavin, however, now readily admits she is a feminist. She said one of her most formative experiences occurred in 1980 when, in the flurry of press attention after graduation, she didn't handle one of the interviews gracefully, mumbling something about how "feminism wasn't my primary motivator," which became the cause of great concern to one feminist activist who wrote a scathing letter to her.

"And then I realized I had to wake up," Denise said, "because I *was* a spokesperson. I did have to formulate ideas on feminism."

A 1986 female graduate adds (and I agree), "Just because you're not a bra-burner doesn't mean you're conservative. Maybe women don't necessarily come to West Point to prove something and to dominate, but we

119

certainly aren't doing the traditional thing. Hell, no. I mean, people have got to be kidding themselves if they think women here are doing the traditional thing. They've never had to stand in our shoes and tell some man who may be our date or may be interested in us, what we do for a living. No, we are not traditional women. We might hold some traditional values, but by simple virtue of our coming here, we are breaking roles."

"I remember the very first day at West Point," my classmate Leslie Berger says, "this short, good-looking guy stopped me in the hall at the top of the stairs. He looked up at me, and said, 'Are you a feminist?' And I was thinking, '*Am* I a feminist?' You know, I was trying to process this. Well, aah, I don't know. Maybe? I'm not sure. At the time I didn't feel like a feminist, though I sure as hell was one by the time I left."

15 MAR 1979

I thought spring might finally be here, when the temperature climbed into the fifties, but this morning winter seems nearer. I came back upstairs and was talking to Sarah Andrews. She is mad about an incident that happened down at Ike Hall with some of her male classmates. It seems they'd been drinking a bit, and their mouths got loud, and they started voicing their opinions about women. Sarah ended up getting hit with some beer.

1 MAY 1979

Yesterday I found out something that made me very sad. Pam Deitz is resigning. She is probably the most respected female cadet in the Corps. It was such a shock to everyone. It's too bad when someone so good can't be kept here. The Army needs good women officers.

I'm having problems inside my head. What do I want? I don't know. I get tired of being a token sometimes. I think maybe that's how Pam felt, too.

Pam Deitz was a model cadet. One of seven women in our class to enter West Point from the Academy prep school, she was highly unusual for having won the respect of our male and female classmates alike. Pam was a little older and more experienced than most of us, having been prior enlisted, and appeared to be quite dedicated to the Army as a way of life. Extra consideration was taken by the Academy to monitor her military and academic progress, once the administration realized she was a woman who could fit their criteria as a leader. Pam was in good physical shape; she was easy to get along with, and had a knack for being persuasive without

120

coming across as abrasive or offensive. Had she remained at West Point, she almost certainly would have been appointed to a high position on the cadet brigade staff in our senior year. But Pam realized, three-quarters through her education, that the Academy was no longer where she wanted to be. This came as a great surprise to the Corps, especially since the period during which cadets could leave the Academy without incurring a five-year army service obligation had already passed. Pam was released from her obligation as a special case, which made her departure a source of controversy, as well as consternation, for everyone.

Pam explains: "Plebe year started out so well for me—it was an honor being appointed to the cadet regimental staff during Plebe-Parent weekend. Then, one day I heard someone say, 'There goes the token on regimental staff for first regiment.' I really thought I had worked pretty hard, and I felt my company knew that, too. Maybe I was naive, but I thought I deserved my position. I was on a high, and yet it took only one isolated remark to shoot down everything. I didn't even know who had said it, but it made me very angry.

"Later, the summer between junior and senior year, the Academy was selecting cadets for leadership positions, and I was chosen as the Executive Officer to the King of Beast, which was desirable, because if I did well in that slot it meant I'd get a good position during senior year. But that was the turning point. I'd been doing a lot of politicking, and it had started to make me uncomfortable. I realized I didn't want to turn myself into a chameleon, telling people only what they wanted to hear, regardless of what I thought or felt. I ended up leaving the Academy before I actually took charge.

"Initially playing the game had been exciting, because it was competitive. The Academy's selection of me was part of the process; I knew that if I went with the flow, and didn't get into too much trouble, I'd do fine. The key to survival was staying busy and working hard, which was easy. Keeping the right profile also had something to do with it. I did things that were approved of. I chose the 'right' jobs over the summers. I pushed the right buttons. 'Professionalism' was a buzz word back then, and I always presented myself as a professional.

"Then it hit me, all of a sudden, that I didn't want to be the enforcer of a system whose values I didn't hold anymore. It must have been an unconscious decision, because it just hit me one day between classes. I never went to my second class.

"The first question my Tac officer asked me when I resigned was, "Are you pregnant?" I wanted to slap him. Instead, I decided to beat him at his own game by spreading phony rumors about me before I left. 'I'm pregnant.' 'I'm gay.' The expressions I encountered were priceless."

I'm on Library Guard right now. It's not that bad—although when civilians walk by I feel as if I'm on display. The generals' wives from all the Academies just came in for a tour. I wonder if they enjoy putting on airs and entertaining as much as they do. I don't think I could be an Army wife. There are too many things I want to do for myself.

We have about twenty days left until the class of '79 graduates, and I take summer leave. I'm on the Recondo Committee this summer—in the Pits again. Meanwhile, the firsties are anxious to get out, the cows are looking to take over the Corps, the yearlings finally will be getting into some leadership roles, and the plebes—they'll become people once more.

We wore sabers at dinner formation tonight and had our first lesson in saber manuals. It sure feels excellent *to draw them.*

After dinner, the Second Class had a lecture at Ike Hall with the commandant. He talked about Pam Deitz quitting and got many of the women upset.

I remember the momentous "call into the auditorium," which I thought was very significant. The commandant of cadets brought our whole class together to respond to Pam's leaving, and to dispel the rumors we'd been hearing. What we didn't expect was how he would malign her.

He said that she was running from responsibility, that sometimes people will run from the line of duty. And then he started to ramble a bit. Finally he said, "You know, all I can figure out is that she was afraid to succeed. This was her chance to do it, and that's why she left." He said the Academy had been wrong about Pam Deitz. They'd been wrong to put her in a responsible position. He went a little overboard, but he must have been infuriated at her leaving; I think he felt that he had really stuck his neck out to bring her up.

Pam Deitz and Liz Jenkins had been bunkmates at prep school. When Pam left the Academy, she spent some time at Liz's parents house. After the commandant's lecture, Liz was prepared to stand up and have a face-off with him at the end of the session, but he didn't even stay to take questions. He said he was going home to watch a ball game that was on television. When Liz walked by his house afterward, she saw the blue light of the television set flickering in the upper bedroom. So she returned to her barracks and sat down and wrote him a letter about his remarks. She hand-delivered it to his office the next day and was summoned individually to speak with him. But Liz wasn't the only one who'd protested. Some of the men did, too. The commandant tried to explain himself, to diminish the impact of the remarks he had made. He also wanted information about Pam, because he wanted her to come back. Liz said he had pressured her Tac officer to find out from her where Pam was. But Liz kept Pam's confidence. She called her parents and told them not to divulge Pam's whereabouts if anyone called.

Eventually Pam did return to see the superintendant, who made one last attempt to woo her back. She made it clear, however, that her decision was final.

"I thought that the people up at West Point would be the cream of the crop," Pam said, "so it surprised me when they didn't live up to my expectations. A lot of us regarded the Academy as a magical place. I had to believe that, too; otherwise, when I saw people there who weren't all that wonderful, I'd think that maybe *I* wasn't so hot after all. As my friend Liz Jenkins once said, 'You love West Point, even when you hate it— because you want to believe. You don't want to give up your best fantasy.' "

Firstie Year

1979–1980

24 JUN 1979

I came here on Sunday, to Camp Buckner, with four other cadets from the Recondo Committee. We met the Special Forces soldiers from Fort Devens, Massachusetts, who are going to be working with us in the Pits. These guys are experts in hand-to-hand combat. I think they had some preconceptions about women, but I dispelled their thoughts when we were learning our throws and defenses.

28 JUNE 1979

My body is rebelling. Yesterday morning in PT we did exercises and ran two miles. No one was expecting that. I made it most of the way but fell out near the end. It made me feel like shit. We arrived at our site and then had forty-five minutes of more exercises. Afterward we went through different throws. My body is bruised all over. The sergeant major who is teaching us doesn't get tired, because he doesn't ever do anything.

2 JULY 1979

The class of '83 came in. I went back to West Point to be a tour guide for the parents of new cadets. Now I know what my parents did the day I arrived. Allen Killian and I walked up near North Area and watched the new cadets in action. It brought back so many memories. But I know we moved out faster than they did. The Academy is instituting a new policy this summer called "Positive Leadership"—the upperclassmen are supposed to try to motivate, rather than intimidate, the new cadets. The cadre isn't allowed to yell at them anymore. How long is that going to last, I wonder?

19 JULY 1979

This morning, I really goofed up. I sent the first half of 2d Company down the wrong route for the Enduro Run—a two-and-a-half-mile run carrying a full pack, rifle, and gear. God, what a stupid thing to do. Now my nickname is Wrong-way Barkalow.

Being the only female around here all day long is okay most of the time, but it can also be hard. Sometimes I want to feel like one of the guys, but other times I don't. I wish there were another female out here I could talk to—someone who was going through the same things I am, having the same feelings.

17 AUG 1979

I am presently writing to the sounds of drumming and Donna Summer. I'm back at school—it's been three days already. It's great to see black firstie brass on all of us. I am 4th Platoon sergeant this detail.

The rest of Recondo went like clockwork. Many days were hot, one Recondo almost died of heatstroke, and the last two days, it rained.

I feel the way I always do at the beginning of a semester—that I'm going to try to do well. And yet, it always ends up that I'm pulling things out [just getting by.]

I am not too fond of our CO—rather, he is not too fond of me, or of any other women at the Academy. I'm glad we have no plebe women in our company because I know I'd be going crazy feeling that they were being treated unfairly. I just want to do my job and be treated like a professional.

I thought I would have only one roommate this semester, so I was somewhat surprised to find myself in a room with both Kerry and Michelle. But I've decided I can get along with anyone *this year.*

As a plebe, I believed that only one type of person belonged at West Point—the hard core, show-no-emotion type—which was what I had endeavored to become. My last year, however, I realized that of the sixty-two women in my class who remained, out of 119 who entered, each of us had fought her own dragons—including Michelle Mathews. Plebe year, Michelle and I had our differences, and the rigidity of the cadet environment was not always conducive to solving them. But by the time we roomed together senior year, I had grown to respect Michelle for her determination under pressure. If I, one of the so-called tough ones, was having such a hard time, how much more difficult must the experience have been for her, who nevertheless persevered—and learned to fight back.

That realization bred a greater tolerance in me, enabling us to live together in harmony the second time around.

20 AUG 1979

Tonight, Monday, we had a basketball meeting. Our athletic director wants to (and did), change our team's name from the "Sugar Smacks" to "Army Women's Basketball." He thinks Sugar Smacks is a "kid's" name— not serious enough. I wish he would let us call our team what we want. Everyone identifies with the Sugar Smacks. We named the team when we started it plebe year—we were the first female "smacks" (plebes) and the name just seemed to fit. Nancy and I really wanted to keep our original name. We wanted to leave it behind us as a memory of our class.

10 SEPT 1979

We've been going through the end of Hurricane David. Trees have gone down, and there have been rock slides on the mountain. Two of my classmates have been in car accidents. One died. He was drunk, and his car went off the road on the Palisades. The other drove off Storm King Mountain; his poor girlfriend is worse off than he is.

The firsties had a meeting with the commandant tonight after dinner. He talked about the two accidents. Maybe now people will stop and think before they drink and drive. Probably not, though. All of us were sad about what happened, but life goes on.

19 SEPT 1979

Everyone's talking about branches. I have no idea which branch to choose. I get a queasy feeling when I think about next year. I am looking forward to being out on my own so much, sometimes it hurts just thinking about it.

When my class was graduated from West Point, the branches available to us were Infantry, Armor (Tanks), Engineers, Field Artillery, Air Defense Artillery, Chemical Corps, Military Intelligence, Military Police, Signal (Communication), Ordnance (Maintenance), Quartermaster (Supplies), and Transportation. Neither male nor female cadets had the option, as they do now, to enter the non-combat related human service oriented branches such as the Adjutant General Corps, the Finance Corps, or the Medical Service Corps (the Medical Corps administrators and suppliers).

Because of the Army's Combat Exclusion Policy, women were not

7 July 1976. Reception Day
(R-Day). One of my female
classmates learns the "four
responses" from the imperious
Man in the Red Sash.

Photo credit: U.S. Army

Practicing chin-ups
during weight training.
Fall 1976.

Photo credit: U.S. Army

Plebe math class—preparing to "take boards."
I'm the only woman in the room. Can you tell? Winter 1977.

Photo credit: U.S. Army

Leading the senior enlisted National
Guard soldiers at Bethany Beach,
Delaware. They'd never seen female
cadets before. Summer 1979.

Photo credit: U.S. Army

Throwing a slightly startled National
Guard lieutenant over my shoulder
during a self-defense demonstration.
Summer 1979.

Photo credit: U.S. Army

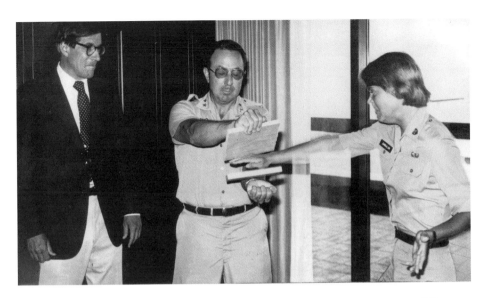

Breaking boards in Governor Pierre du Pont's office, Delaware, August 1979.
Major General F. Ianni is holding the boards.

Photo credit: U.S. Army

The Army Women's Basketball Team in Dress Gray, late fall 1979.
Our team captain salutes one of the few female officers at the Academy.
I'm standing at the far left, first row.

Photo credit: U.S. Army

From the Airborne School yearbook
at Fort Benning, Georgia. To become
Airborne qualified, I had to jump 1,250
feet—five times. August 1978.

Photo credit: U.S. Army

My yearbook entry in the
"Howitzer," 1980.

Photo credit: U.S. Army

CAROL ANNE BARKALOW   A-3
Laurel, Maryland   Sergeant

Most people found Carol sharply dressed, rockin'
to music, sitting con, or on leave. Confident in
people and her own abilities, she faced each day
with tremendous energy, always determined to
achieve her final goal. Carol — an understanding
friend, with time for those who needed it.

The women of West Point's class of '80. Fifty-seven of us
gathered at Trophy Point Monument. A male classmate took the picture.
I'm second from the right, top row. 12 September 1979.

Photo credit: Author's collection

"The Dragon" and I inspect my platoon at Delta Battery,
West Germany.

Photo credit: U.S. Army

Being promoted from second
lieutenant to first lieutenant. The colonel
pinned the first lieutenant's bar to my
collar, right before he kissed me.
November 1981.

Photo credit: U.S. Army

Victory photo from the
Roanoke Valley Women's
Bodybuilding Competition. It ran in
Fort Lee's post newspaper and
almost cost me my command. May
1986.

Photo credit: U.S. Army

Exchanging gifts with the
commander from a nearby French *Kaserne*,
after our soldiers beat theirs
in a running race.

Photo credit: U.S. Army

Taking command of the
57th Transportation Company,
Fort Lee, Virginia. 1 August
1986.

Photo credit: Author's collection

One of a commander's most
important jobs—re-upping
soldiers. This Transportation
Corps soldier chose to reenlist
in the motor pool while standing
on a 2½ ton truck. Summer
1987.

Photo credit: U.S. Army

permitted to select positions in either the Armor or Infantry branches, although at least one of my female classmates tried. In December 1979, Paula Stafford wrote a letter to the Secretary of the Army requesting an individual exception to Army policy, and outlining the "personally compelling" reasons for her unusual request. In the letter, Paula cited her physical qualifications (phys ed grades which placed her among the top half of the men in our class), her successful completion of the academy's demanding Jungle Operations Training Course, and her attraction to the Infantry branch based on its "physical demands, increased chances for field work, and opportunities to conduct small unit tactics."

Perhaps, too, Paula recognized the career significance of serving in the Infantry, as did World War II General of the Army Omar N. Bradley, who, in his second volume of memoirs, entitled *A General's Life,* wrote: ". . . we in the Infantry soon learned that it is in that branch more than any other that a soldier learns the art of leadership and command and, ultimately, has the best chance of reaching the topmost positions."

Paula's appeal received a response, but not the one she wanted. While explaining that the Combat Exclusion Policy was not based on a determination that individual women soldiers do not possess either the strength or skill to engage in close combat, and acknowledging that women certainly might be captured or engaged in combat by enemy forces in the case of general armed conflict, the Army nevertheless held firm in its policy, claiming simply that it was in the best interests of national security.

Paula joined the Ordnance Corps, where instead of leading soldiers into combat, she'd be confined to repairing their equipment.

28 SEPT 1979

At about 2:30 this morning, I woke up to hear someone banging on the door. Michelle heard it, too. After talking about it for ten minutes, I decided to check it out. I stepped out of bed, right into a puddle of water. Someone had RF'ed [rat-fucked] us. I knew then that something had to be leaning against the door. When I opened it, sure enough a trash can filled with water emptied into our room and all over the hall floor. We got up this morning and found a note that implicated B-3. Those bastards. I wish they'd just leave us alone.

11 OCT 1979

Two hundred twenty-nine days until graduation. I feel like a plebe again, counting the days till Recognition Day.

25 OCT 1979

9:00 A.M., Friday. This weekend I'm doing something I've never done before, and frankly I don't know why I'm doing it. A few of the women cadets talked me into joining them at a convent in Newburgh (New York) on a religious retreat. It's being sponsored by the Catholic Chapel at West Point, and it's called TEC—Teens Encounter in Christ. Nine members of the basketball team will be there. I'm going into it mellow, just taking in all that comes. I'm nervous.

[NEWBURGH, NEW YORK]

Ideals. Whose are the best?

It's Friday night, and I'm here at the convent. We've met our groups— there are eight girls in mine. Our group is named SOAP—Sunshine On All People. It's pretty good. One of the girls just gave a talk on Ideals, but I found my mind wandering to different things. The people here keep saying stuff like, "That's beautiful." I can't get into it. Also, the clapping bothers me. We do it constantly. And we can't wear watches, so we don't know what time it is.

I know I'm prejudging the people at the discussion table—I've already formed an impression about each one. I seem to be doing that all the time.

After the talk, we had to make a poster on what we thought about Ideals. Each group had a good poster, but this clapping is driving me crazy! What next?

My adult leader is speaking—Sister Deborah Morgan. Her talk is on friendship. It's my most important subject, I think, though I'm beginning to wonder. Now she's talking about the Bible and God and His letter to us. I want to look at the clock behind me—but I won't. I don't know anything about the Bible. She says the rainbow shows us God's promise that he'll never destroy the world with water. She has trouble looking straight at people. I wonder how many times she's been on a TEC retreat.

My mind is starting to fix itself on where I am and I'm trying hard not to anticipate anything. I know I believe in God—I just don't know if I can hear about Him all weekend.

People are listening, but do they hear what she's saying? Someone's sleeping at the table—or is she concentrating? I find myself putting my head down. Maybe it's an excuse to write.

Another talk. On the Paschal Mystery, the Dying, Rising, and Going Forth of Jesus. Father Mark is talking about dying—the deeper the pain, the deeper the joy. I don't know—maybe I look at things differently. When my brother was killed in a car accident, it was painful to me because it hurt my parents the worst. I know God said it was time for him—I accept that—but I don't see the joy in the pain. My parents sure weren't joyful. Father Mark said there's something deep within us that wants to come out, and many of us don't know what that is.

I would rather be someplace else.

"Our journey is a life made up to Be, and to roam on in the arms of He."

I try to picture myself on Saturday night. Am I going to change? What's going to happen? Another discussion. Can this whole weekend be just a bunch of meetings and discussions? I guess I'm anticipating again. I found out the clock behind me doesn't work! My watch is in my pocket.

Our group came up with a heart as our central symbol; the theme is our journeys toward it. I thought my journey was straightforward, until I got to the heart, and it was broken. That's where I am now. I'm mixed up, and everyone here is saying that God is the answer, through God we'll find our answer. I haven't said anything yet. I'm thinking lots of things. But when do you say things?

Beth got up to talk. She looks as if she's teaching a class. She doesn't seem to be getting into it. I'm one to talk—I'm not into it either. Or maybe I am, but I just haven't let anyone else know it. Sitting here, I'm looking at different people and realizing how critical of them I am.

Luke 15:11–32 The Prodigal Son

"Reach up as far as you can and God will reach down the rest of the way."

Father Scott is now talking.

"The way you feel has nothing to do with how close you are to Jesus. Jesus loves you just the way you are." Does he? Then why do people change, or why do people think others should change? He talks about eyes. You can see so much through people's eyes. I'm getting tired. I wonder what those girls in the kitchen are doing. I hated going to confession. He's right—penance is threatening. Saying three Hail Marys was merely an action with no aftereffects. I knew I would sin again. It didn't mean anything to me. So how can God forgive me? Is that why I'm here this weekend?

The importance of being touched by the love of God. The Act of Contrition. I said it on my way up to Communion as though it were a plebe duty.

On a little sheet of paper we each wrote down the things that are keeping us away from God. We put them in a basket and Father Scott is going to burn them so they will leave us, and then we'll be closer to God—wow. I'm writing by firelight now. Everyone is silent. Our burdens seem to be burning. Are they really? Is burning them in this basket going to rid us of these burdens? After going through the death comes life—when to die . . . and how? I don't understand what's going on! I also can't see anything. Smoke has filled the room. Father Scott and Father Mark have gone down to the chapel. We're singing songs—I like this one: "Sing Alleluia to the Lord." Some people seem to be lost in the music. What am I doing here? I'll stop writing for a while and just listen—no thinking.

A few people came back from the chapel crying. It's time for bed.

26 OCT 1979

Morning! We met in the TEC room at 8:30 and sang a song. Then we went over to breakfast. Now we're back in the TEC room. We were each given letters—they're called "palankas." I got three. Lori's palanka for me said she'd put a pebble in her shoe. Everytime she felt it, she'd say a prayer for me.

We went down to a little chapel room afterwards and some people were baptized again. I didn't do it. Rebecca, who is one of my adult leaders, gave a talk about Jesus and her experiences—she got upset—many others did, too. Why? Did they cry because it seemed like the thing to do? Were they really touched by her talk? I was touched, but I couldn't cry. I don't know why, either.

A talk by Sister Diane—about God and Jesus always being around you. Where was He when my mom was having trouble from my brother's death? Where was He when my mom was going through the change? Is He there now that she's doing better?

Lynn is talking about piety. She said she believed in God, but in what else she didn't know. Security? In the Lord? My horoscope tells me I'm always looking for security. Lynn is right—I feel more comfortable today. It was easier for me to laugh, and I almost started to cry. I don't know if I should even question why I cry. I clapped for that talk . . . the clapping wasn't so bad.

130

Lunchtime. We had a break and came back. I wrote a note to Rebecca telling her how much I liked her talk. Now we're singing. I can feel myself getting into the music. I'm also feeling closer to the people at my table, especially the ones on either side of me. Music can really affect you.

Another talk. When I've found out what my gift is, I'll find God. Bingo—it just hit home. Listening to problems. But I take them as my own. Heavy silence. More tears. What am I to do? This atmosphere creates emotional reactions. Should I react and not hold back, or should I wait until I'm sure? I feel foolish showing my emotions. What will people think?

Signs and meanings—removing masks of this weekend. Holding hands with the ones next to us. My hands were cold; someone noticed.

More talk with Father Scott—about eating at the table and being given so much more than just food. I don't see or feel the things that he's feeling. I never used to enjoy meals at home. He and Sister Deborah only mention how everything is supposed to be—do they really do all the things they say? Sister Deborah just described my situation—"If you don't feel the concrete, you'll never see the abstract." I need a break! I wonder what time it is? I think I heard some of the kitchen girls playing basketball outside a while ago.

27 OCT 1979

We got dressed up today and went to Mass. One of the members of my group asked me if I remember the Masses at Camp Buckner. My answer: I never went.

I was okay at Mass until the priest said, "Let us offer each other the sign of peace." Then I lost it. Or maybe I found it. I was crying on this woman's shoulder—I didn't know her; she wasn't even in my group. It took me a while to recover, until I felt I couldn't cry anymore. Cathy got into it, too. She told me to let go with my head, to let my heart rule the rest of the weekend. If I did that, I'd be in tears all the time. Maybe if I let out my emotions when they need to be expressed, they wouldn't become uncontrollable.

We're back from dinner and we're singing. I find myself smiling as I write this. I don't know why, but I know I feel better. I wish we could sing songs for the rest of the evening. I don't even feel like writing anymore. I just want to enjoy the presence of all this closeness—I'm happy.

12 NOV 1979

Veterans' Day. When I got back to my room today, there was a note on my door that said, "Keep Out—by order of the Tac." Someone had driven a saber through Michelle's bed and smashed a bottle of ketchup on top. I can't believe someone would do that. What kind of sick mind would think that was a joke? Michelle is really upset, too. I don't blame her. C.I.D. [Criminal Investigation Division] came in and dusted the whole room for fingerprints. I hope they find out who did it, and I hope whoever did it gets kicked out.

The culprit was never found.

13 JAN 1980

Classes start tomorrow. My last semester here—less than 140 days. Please help me reach the end, Lord. Good night.

22 JAN 1980

A two-cadet room. Robin and me. We chose our branches today and will find out who gets what tomorrow. Selections are given out in order of academic rank—they march us into a big auditorium, and when our names are called we stand up and announce what we want. Projected on the screen in front of us are all the positions still available—and the desirable ones go fast. I asked for Transportation Corps first, then Air Defense Artillery.

24 JAN 1980

My new branch is Air Defense Artillery. I'm not that upset. It will be interesting, I'm sure.
I got fitted for some of my officer's uniforms today. I didn't think I looked like an officer until I put on the uniform. It seemed to change my looks.

26 FEB 1980

Tonight we picked assignments. I'll be assigned to a unit within the 32d Army Air Defense Command, which means I'll be spending the next three years in a Nike Hercules missile battalion in Germany.

7 MAR 1980

I've decided I really want to throw myself into the Army. I'm looking forward to leaving here and starting a new life. I was planning to get out "in five," but now I'm not so sure. Germany will be the deciding factor.

30 MAR 1980

I have started to address my graduation invitations. If only I could be certain I was going to graduate.

School is really getting to me. I failed the "History of Military Art" midterm, so that put me "D" [Deficient]. I'll have to really buckle down. I'll even risk getting sick by studying on the bus to away-games. I'm really going to work at it, but still I have some doubts.

It's probably better to have some doubts.

14 APR 1980

Last Tuesday I met a reporter from Time *magazine. Sean Brown and I were sent over to the Hotel Thayer to speak with her over dinner. She seems to be on top of things around here, but I hope she understands enough to interpret what we said.*

Friday night, Katie Simms gave a surprise wedding shower for Robin Bach. About twelve of us were there at Colonel White's. We carried on like a bunch of civilian girls. If we hadn't been wearing uniforms, no one would have ever known we were cadets.

I still can't believe that Robin is getting married. I told her, "I know you love Kevin, but we've been cooped up here for four years, and now you're entering into a commitment for the rest of your life." Robin just looked at me and said, "If we get married now, we have a better chance of being assigned together."

West Point cadets have to get married within sixty days after graduation to be stationed at the same post for their first assignment. The Army's current policy on the assignment of military couples is known as the "Married Army Couples Program," and stresses that while the Army's "requirements and readiness goals are paramount," those husbands and wives who wish to establish a common household whenever possible ("joint domicile," in Army jargon) must first enroll in this program in order to be automatically considered for joint assignments worldwide. Only married couples are eligible for the MACP—engagements and other live-in arrangements are not considered—which often accounts for the rush to marry on the part of many Academy graduates and other service people. Couples who enroll in the program recognize that they still might be apart for a year here or there because of courses or other movement, but overall they will be together.

In 1985, Secretary of Defense Caspar Weinberger called for greater

efforts to be made in disseminating information about the options provided to military couples by the MACP, and this reflected a definite shift
in attitude. The Army evidently had begun to realize that if they wanted
to keep military couples in the service, one incentive obviously was to
provide a way for them to remain together. When my class was graduating
in 1980, however, more traditional attitudes about dual-career couples still
prevailed.

Lieutenant Colonel Jerome Adams recalls, "When we were studying
the integration question, we asked the male and female cadets about their
lifestyle preferences, in terms of marriage, career, and children. About 92
percent of the men in the class of '80 said they expected to marry *and* have
a career, and about 70 percent of the women said the same. Some of the
senior staff members couldn't understand how it was possible for the
women to do both, which was a bit naive. We subsequently realized that
we hadn't properly prepared those first few integrated classes for the kinds
of marriage versus career conflicts that were inherent in the Army. We did
have a 'Marriage and the Family' course, but we didn't have couples who
had gone through the Academy come back to discuss their postgraduate
experiences, because no such couples existed yet; most couples were left
to work things out for themselves."

Kevin and Robin started to date during yearling year. They knew early
on that they were going to get married, and years later Robin would say,
"We actually would have gotten married about a year and a half before
we did, if we weren't at West Point." But cadets weren't allowed to marry
while they were in school, so Kevin and Robin got married the same day
they graduated.

"We had a real rough time in the beginning," recalls Robin.

"I didn't want to get married then, and I told Kevin that, but I wasn't
strong enough to stand up to the fear of loneliness and say, 'Hey, let me
go and be an individual first.' I mean, my sense of who I was at that point
was nil. I always described myself as an egg. I had a tough-looking outer
shell, yet the inside was mush, which I think the military fosters in both
men and women. After all, there aren't many other professions where you
are constantly being uprooted, sent halfway across the world, and forced
to develop new friendships again and again. You do develop support
networks through your battalion. Still, life is not the same as it is for
civilians. They grow up someplace, go to school someplace, get a job;
they've got friends and family around them. Military people don't have
that. So it's easier to have a spouse. A lot of people get married right out

of the Academy because they don't want to be alone in some Godforsaken outpost. With a spouse, at least, they have somebody they can take with them.

"Unfortunately, the trouble with this scenario was that the cadets were walking from womb to womb—direct from home to West Point to marriage, and so they'd remain embryonic. It often seemed as if it were a very unconscious move on their part. They'd rush into it, and a lot of those marriages didn't last."

15 APR 1980

My grades seem to be stabilizing. After this week and next, I should be okay. I gave my speech in Military Art today—I was MacArthur. I found a corncob pipe, a general's hat and a bathrobe and really layed it on thick. The "P" gave me an A.

Meanwhile, there are rumors flying about Captain Morrison—supposedly she turned in to the commandant some list of women at this school who might be lesbians. What is the matter with these people? Why can't they just leave other people alone?

The men at West Point don't suspect homosexuality among themselves the way they suspect lesbianism among women. Women at the Academy, I found, don't really care as much about homosexuality existing among the cadets. The males, of course, are adamant about it, but they're particularly adamant when it comes to females. Vigilante groups go on hunts and accuse women. Cadets pass stories through the rumor mill, which spread like wildfire, though they're usually hyperbolized renditions of events that have been misconstrued. But these accusations really crush a lot of women. Such rumors would have to be substantiated before they could ruin a woman's career. Just to be associated with such a rumor, though, is not a good thing. It breeds suspicion in people's minds and closes doors that a woman may not want to be closed. Friendships and professional liaisons may be adversely affected. People become less open. Even if people are merely friendly with a homosexual, they are discouraged from continuing the association.

And yet, sexuality was an important part of what went on at the Academy, and of the dynamics of being a woman there. Because, obviously, the perception was that any woman who'd even consider going to West Point had to be very "masculine"—otherwise, why would she want to attend such a masculine place and do such masculine things?

135

It was very scary in the beginning. All the men were watching us to see how we acted socially, and I thought that was pretty weird. After a while, it made me angry; there was so much paranoia.

The fact was, we were just learning about our sexuality. We ranged in age from seventeen to twenty-six years old, and West Point was not a very healthy place to learn about sex. The one course given by the Academy called "Marriage and the Family" was run by an instructor who'd pass around condoms, then a diaphragm, and spermicidal jelly.

"He'd have everybody taste the jelly," Julie Hawkins recalls, "so they'd know that it wasn't something really horrible. He'd taste it first, and then pass it around, and we were all supposed to taste it, too. I was the only woman in my class, and I thought I was going to die."

Paula Stafford also remembers some kind of medical lecture—a class on sexually transmitted diseases where they showed a whole bunch of really disgusting slides. One of the lectures was about a penis getting caught in a window and being bruised. She wasn't exactly sure what the point was, but the allegory was obvious.

Everything went on behind closed doors, in the woods, in cars. Getting an abortion was just about impossible, since we couldn't leave West Point whenever we felt like it. We weren't even free to go to a private doctor or to the local civilian hospital. Sometimes cadets would sneak out anyway, or they'd wait for spring leave. One of my classmates said she knew of a female plebe almost five months pregnant, who finally ran off to a clinic— she hadn't been able to get away before then. In plebe year, especially, you could never leave. So there was a lot of fear, including the fear of going to the gynecologist on post.

Another of our classmates suspected she might be pregnant, and told one of the female phys ed instructors about it. The instructor arranged for her to take a confidential pregnancy test at Keller Army Hospital, but— unknown to the instructor—someone from the hospital must have reported it to the commandant anyway. The woman found a note on her bed summoning her to see the commandant immediately. The very next day she was gone, which was a tremendous shock to her. She ended up having the child. But it was a shock to all of us. Even though we knew the rules, and knew that if we got pregnant and chose to continue it we would obviously be kicked out, we all thought that we at least had control over our options.

(The Academy has subsequently changed its policy on pregnancy. A female cadet who becomes pregnant is now allowed to take a leave of

136

absence and come back, as long as someone else assumes guardianship of the child.)

MAY 1980

It's been a couple of weeks since I've written. Everything is going so fast now. Mailing away all of our belongings, finals, parades . . . God, to even think about leaving. We're so protected here. I wonder what the Regular Army is going to be like? I've got so much running through my head about being an officer. I'm only twenty-one years old. Can I handle it? Everyone says we'll be fine. Besides, they say, our peers are really the hardest ones to lead. After four years at West Point, I'd have to say I agree.

Cadets who graduate from West Point are probably ahead militarily for their first couple of years in the Army, but well behind in social skills, because they've been so far removed from reality for four years.

Discipline and order and marching and cleaning our rooms were supposed to help us become well-rounded individuals, geared to the "whole man" concept. But the Fourth Class System was a game in which fear was always evident. There was always an underlying tension, an undertow of anxiety. And once we got caught in the cycle, it became very hard to break out.

The Academy didn't teach us much about how to deal with subordinates. At West Point, we didn't have to care about our people. We just made sure that they were ready for inspections and formations. There was accountability, but no real concept of caring and ownership. No sense of belonging beyond getting things done. West Pointers are notoriously task-oriented. The Academy taught us how to cooperate as a team, but it didn't teach us to care about the people with whom we worked or to be genuinely concerned about them. In fact, there were times when we'd overlook our friends because of the task at hand. As plebes, we were even afraid of visiting a friend in another company; we didn't want to go through the anxiety of walking into a different company area, because companies tended to be hostile to one another. Esprit de corps was only within our own unit.

Small wonder, then, that our attitude toward the cadets coming up behind us tended to be circumspect. What's more, unless we were involved in Corps Squad athletics or some other club, it was difficult to get to know women from other classes. While I made a concerted effort to help the younger women on the basketball team who I knew were struggling, other

137

female classmates of mine were evidently less willing to take the risk. Lieutenant Colonel Jerome Adams observes, "The women in the class of '80 were asked in exit interviews about what we call "mentoring" relationships. That is, 'You've finished—now, what have you done for female members of the classes of '81 or '82, to help them through the rough spots?' And many reported back a disappointing reluctance to call attention to themselves by bringing up another woman, because a group of women together was always seen as a cabal. So the classes that followed didn't get much of a helping hand. However, the bonding of the women of the class of '80 was extraordinarily strong. They still keep track of all their female classmates in a newsletter—even the ones who didn't finish at West Point. But one mustn't forget that those women badly needed a support network, which, institutionally, wasn't there for them. They had to create it for themselves."

27 MAY 1980

Wow—what a day it was. Our graduation parade was this morning. Firsties marched in Full Dress Gray over white, wearing white crossbelts and sabers, black bell-crowned tarbucket hats with brass insignia and black wool pomps. To distinguish themselves from the rest, cadet officers wore maroon grosgrain sashes and purplish green cock's plumes on their hats.

The graduation banquet tonight was excellent. *The guys in our company bought a bouquet of flowers each for Robin, Kerry, Michelle and me. I almost cried. It's been such a long four years.*

I was going to sneak into Central Guard Room to play "I Am Woman" over the loudspeaker, but I decided not to do it. We all know we've made it through—so do our male classmates—and for now, that's enough.

Well, it's really late. I'm tired, but I am so excited. My life as a cadet comes to an end in a few more hours. I think I'm ready.

Looking back ten years later, my classmates' feelings about the Academy remain mixed. Andrea Hollen says that when she thinks about being literally the first woman to graduate from West Point [because of her class standing], it is almost physically painful to her—because it translates into guilt about the Academy's dual physical standards for men and women. However, she adds, those feelings don't necessarily affect her estimation of her own competence as an officer. She no longer has misgivings about her role in the Army. She has come to grips with equity as a fundamental value—and yet she is still guilt-ridden about being singled out for attention. "The press emphasized the incredible achievement of the women cadets," Andrea says. "As if we had conquered all. But we hadn't."

Robin Bach says, "This is just my personal experience, but I walked out of that place thinking you couldn't force me to go back for any amount of money. With time I have grown a lot more appreciative of West Point, knowing a lot of the things that had happened to me there were not so good, but realizing that a lot of things in life aren't so good, anyway. I began to understand how the training I got at the Academy may have been beneficial."

Paula Stafford recalls, "I was paranoid five years later when I went back to visit. I was scared to death. I felt like a plebe again, as if I were walking around in somebody else's uniform; I was afraid I was going to get caught. I grew up there, so I started remembering how vulnerable I once was. I mean, I was sitting at the Brigade Staff table for dinner. Me—with all these striper dogs [high-ranking cadets], who are really just twenty-one-year-old kids, and here I am a captain in the United States Army. And I thought, Oh my God, I'm at the Brigade Staff table. I couldn't help freaking out about the whole thing. Then came the announcement 'Brigade rise.' And—boom—I was up, until I sheepishly sat back down again, saying, 'Ha ha. Excuse me.' It was so weird. I had to say to myself, 'Paula, get a grip. Remember, you're going home tonight. You don't have to stay.'"

West Point is a closed society, with its own rules. Notably, the Academy gives young people a lot of power over other young people. Eighteen- and nineteen-year-olds have a staggering amount of control over their peers. The kind of power that upperclassmen had over us as plebes, for example, is generally not experienced in an open society. But it happens at West Point. People need to be strong *before* they go there. And they need to know they will probably not be the same when they come out.

A number of my female classmates say they still have trouble crying or expressing emotions. They've become a bit more distant and reticent. They've learned to look within themselves for comfort and support.

The women who are currently attending the Academy say it's not necessarily easier for a woman to be there now. It's different, relative to how one handles stress and to what types of stress one is able to tolerate. Some of the performance standards are significantly higher, but the pressures are similar, though not quite as intense. Being a woman at West Point is still a fishbowl-like experience, but not as much as ours was. And

139

it has to be remembered that many male cadets were genuinely surprised that we actually graduated. Every year they would say, "My God! You're still here!" The women at West Point today are spared that level of attitude.

West Point changes the life of everyone who goes through it. It takes two extremely powerful institutions—college and the military—both of which facilitate maturity, both of which make people face critical questions about the purpose and direction of their lives—and crams them into one experience. Some say that the Academy doesn't perform the function of either one very well. It's not the *real* Army, and it's not a *real* college. It's a hybrid, which makes it unique—and, for better or worse, it has left its mark on me.

GERMANY

★

★

Midnight, 16 January 1981. A second lieutenant shouldn't cry, I kept thinking, as I fought to hold back tears. I was waiting to board a plane at Kennedy Airport, alone, and headed for Germany, traveling blind—moving toward a place I had never seen, to live among people I did not know, in a country whose language I could neither speak nor understand.

I had dressed for the flight in my Class A uniform—a forest green hip-length jacket and knee-skimming broadcloth skirt, black leather pumps, a white blouse, and a tiny black tie that fastened beneath the collar. I wore my second lieutenant's brass on my cap and epaulets, and "Barkalow" on a nameplate pinned to my jacket. I had told myself I was wearing my skirt instead of trousers because this was a special, even formal, occasion: I was leaving home and country for three years. In truth, I had worn it to please my mother.

Practically my entire family had trooped out to the airport that evening to see me off. We sat together for over an hour around a table in the airport coffee shop, drinking tea from styrofoam cups. A sickly, days-old smell of burnt coffee and cigarettes hung in the air. No one said much; we just sipped our tea, and quietly waited.

At ten P.M., an announcement came over the loudspeaker. My flight would be delayed two more hours. I told my family they didn't need to stay any longer; I was on my own now, anyway. Somehow I managed to stoically kiss my grandmother, sister, brother, sister-in-law, niece, and nephew without breaking down. But when I turned to hug my parents, I couldn't stop the tears. My mother, who is usually reserved, began to cry.

After spending four years away from home, I was about to fly across the ocean with nothing but a few old suitcases and a set of travel orders that assured me I'd be met at the Frankfurt airport by an officer from Battalion Headquarters—poor talismans against loneliness, I thought. I marched through the portals of the airport metal detector as if I were crossing a threshold. I had never felt so lonely in my life.

Nor so conspicuous. I hadn't realized that a crying woman in military uniform could be an object of such extreme curiosity for a group of bored civilian passengers on a delayed overseas flight; I could feel their eyes on me as I got on the plane. When the man who took my ticket told me that the in-flight movie was *Private Benjamin*—the 1980 comedy about a pampered blond who joins the Army and finds independence—I braced myself for a long trip.

Once settled in my seat, I decided to rent a headset and watch the film. The caricatures of Judy Benjamin as a soft, spoiled, incompetent female, and of Captain Doreen Lewis as the vindictive bitch who was her commanding officer, were particularly troubling. I can laugh at this movie, I thought, because I know this isn't an accurate portrayal of military women, but what are the people sitting next to me thinking? I regretted that these cartoonish characters were the only images of military women in American popular culture that seemed to exist.

When the film ended, it was nearly three o'clock in the morning. Heads had begun to droop against pillows, blankets were pulled over sleeping bodies, reading lights were snapped off one by one. I was too wound up to sleep. The remaining hours of the seven-hour flight gave me a chance to think about my new life in Germany. Where would I live? Was I going to like my boss? Who would my soldiers be?

At the Frankfurt airport, the promised military escort did not materialize. The Specialist Fourth Class presiding over the airport's U.S. Military Information Booth read my orders and tried to contact my assigned unit: Charlie Battery, 3d Battalion, 71st Air Defense Artillery. We rang Hardheim Military for over an hour, but no one answered.

It would be dark within hours. Sensing my growing apprehension, the Spec-4, whose name was Maddox, made arrangements for me to stay at the military hotel located on the Air Force base at Rhein-Main, and booked my passage on the first bus leaving for battalion headquarters in the morning. He then invited me to dinner. I wondered, perhaps uncharitably, if Maddox extended this courtesy to all incoming officers, or only to those who happened to be females—unmarried, blue-eyed, and blond. I confess that the prospect of spending my first evening in Germany with a total stranger was unappealing, but only half as unappealing as the prospect of spending it alone. Cautiously, I accepted his invitation.

Maddox deposited me at the military hotel to drop off my bags and change into civilian clothes, then returned to his barracks to change as well. This shedding of uniforms at the end of the workday was neither a nod to protocol nor an acquiescence to mere comfort. We knew the presence of American soldiers in Germany was not entirely welcomed by the population; rumors of terrorist attacks frightened soldiers throughout Europe into taking added precautions to conceal their military identities when mixing among the public. It would have been imprudent for either of us to broadcast that we were American soldiers by wandering in uniform through civilian areas at night.

Once safely divested of all visible traces of our profession, Maddox and I boarded a bus for Sachsenhausen, a quiet suburb of Frankfurt. Street-lamps threw long shadows across the cobblestones. The old German houses—with their gables, turrets, arches, and ornaments—looked like fortresses from the outside.

Maddox and I walked through the village until we came upon a tiny, family-owned *Gasthaus* that appeared to have been standing in the same spot for centuries. A beacon of lamplight shining through the front window beckoned us inside. There, a smiling *Kellnerin* led us to a rough-hewn wooden table, where we gorged ourselves on *Schweineschnitzel, Pommes frites,* and *Salat,* washed down with enormous mugs of rich, golden beer.

During dinner, Specialist Maddox told me the story of his life. Born in a small town in Indiana, he'd joined the Army to get away from home and see the world, but now he spent most of his days seeing little more than the Military Information Booth at the airport. Still, he was enthusiastic about being in Germany, had been there about a year, and was eager to show me around.

His steady stream of conversation turned to chatter as I began missing home very badly. In the meantime, Maddox kept ordering rounds of the proprietor's delicious home brew, and in a determined effort to anesthetize myself, I kept drinking.

It grew late. Maddox escorted me back to my hotel. We exchanged phone numbers, and he said I'd see him soon. I didn't want to contradict him, but I knew I'd never lay eyes on him again.

Lying alone in my narrow hotel bed, I realized I was undergoing the Army's process of loosening ties to what was familiar, realigning private allegiances for the sake of a greater good. It was a process that would teach me to let the "Army way" suffuse my life; a process that forged bonds among all soldiers. But even then I knew the Army could never fully

145

replace the world I had left behind. Wherever I went, I would need temporary substitutes for home and family. Professional superiors would serve as surrogate parents, though their value might go unarticulated. Troops would stand in for a brood of children. A simple room in the Bachelor Officers' Quarters would simulate home.

Perhaps the most unsettling adjustment would be to the military's attack on language. A battery of code words and acronyms—indecipherable to outsiders—was already replacing the words of my everyday speech. Fluency in Army rhetoric insulated my conversation from civilians, and was one of the first prerequisites for being recognized as an initiated soldier. It was all part of the transformation—aided by visual cues such as regulation haircuts and little green suits—that miraculously converted almost a million distinct personalities into a single, ideologically unified armed force.

Gradually I would adapt myself to this way of life, grow comfortable with it, even come to prefer it. I would find it easier to busy myself with military ritual and professional relationships than to look closely at what was happening in my personal life. But as a new second lieutenant, the lowest ranking commissioned officer, I hadn't yet perfected the seasoned soldier's ability to detach oneself from private emotions, and replace them with public form.

The wind blew hard against the windowpane. I felt far away from everyone; I wanted desperately to hold onto something I knew. Instead, I wrapped the hotel blanket tighter around me, and settled for sleep.

The next morning, Saturday, I woke up early and rode the bus to Battalion Headquarters in Stuttgart. The dull winter sky reminded me of Gloom Period at West Point, those dismal weeks from late January to mid-February when the river and hills of the Hudson Valley were shrouded in gray, and gray was the color of everything we felt.

When I arrived in Stuttgart, the bus dropped me off right in front of Battalion Headquarters at Ludwigsburg Kaserne. A *Kaserne* is a military camp; the Army has more than a hundred of them all over Germany. This one was fairly small, comprised of a handful of two- and three-story concrete buildings that skirted the edges of a single elliptical road which served as both its sole entrance and exit. The headquarters building for my battalion—the 3/71—was located at the far end of the lot. Since Specialist Maddox had called ahead to let the battalion know I was coming, when the bus drove up, an enlisted soldier came outside to escort me into the building.

146

In the 3/71 battalion, it was the prevailing custom that new lieutenants coming in country would greet the battalion commander upon arrival. The soldier led me down a long, brightly lit hallway, and up a flight of stairs.

At the far end of another long corridor lined with offices, the battalion commander's outer office formed a reception area that opened directly onto the hall. Two desks, one for his secretary, the other for his XO, flanked the office door like a pair of guard dogs.

The battalion commander—Colonel Paul Baumgarten (alias, 'the Dragon')—was not available to meet with me when I arrived. I learned from Colonel Baumgarten's secretary that the colonel was participating in an Inspector General inspection—a complete audit of the supply, personnel, training, and financial records of the battalion. Faithful to protocol, I decided to wait until he made an appearance. I heard him before I saw him, in fact, loudly marching up the steps with two other officers in tow. Clearly looking for someone in particular, the lanky, mean-faced man scanned the second floor hallway from the top of the stairs, then spotted his quarry—an unsuspecting lieutenant—emerging from one of the long row of offices. Without pause, the colonel strode up to the young man and immediately started screaming at him, nose to nose.

"*Goddamnit, Hardy!* You *knew* this inspection was coming. It was no goddamn surprise. You want a surprise? I'll throw you a goddamn birthday party. Get caught with your pants down like this again, and you'll find yourself up to your ass in alligators. *Do I make myself clear?*"

As suddenly as he had arrived, Colonel Baumgarten turned on his heel and stomped off, presumably to continue the evaluation of the battalion. As he passed his office, however, he stopped to check in briefly with his secretary and, for the first time, noticed me.

"So," he began casually, "is this the new lieutenant we've been waiting for?" He posed the question as if I weren't there to answer it.

"Yes, sir," I said, venturing a response. "Lieutenant Barkalow reporting for duty, sir."

"Haven't got time to talk to you now, Lieutenant," he replied gruffly. As an afterthought he added, "Welcome to the battalion." Then he was gone.

I signed in at the personnel section down the hall, and with no further drama, was taken by my lieutenant sponsor to a residence hotel at Robinson Barracks, another American *Kaserne* where I'd be living temporarily. My living quarters were very plain, with barely enough space for two single

147

beds, one desk, one nightstand, and a tiny refrigerator. Major Roberta Parker (my roommate) and I shared a bathroom with two male officers who lived next door. Major Parker lit a cigarette the minute she woke up, and chain-smoked all day. I used to choke on the fumes from her cigarettes, but as a lowly second lieutenant, I could hardly ask her not to smoke. I simply stayed away from the room, and Major Parker, as much as I could. My only consolation, I wrote in a letter to my mother, was that, fortunately, she was a light sleeper, so at least I could disturb her in the middle of the night with my snoring.

Within two days of my arrival, I was assigned to the Operations Section at Battalion Staff Headquarters. Though originally I'd been slotted for Charlie Battery, it was not uncommon for assignments to be changed according to the Army's immediate needs. It seemed that a male second lieutenant named Tony Loquasto had arrived unexpectedly at the battalion a week before I did, and Colonel Baumgarten hadn't yet made up his mind where either of us were going. Fortunately, I had received my clearance for admittance into the Army's Personnel Reliability Program (PRP) during my six-month course of basic training in Air Defense, which meant I had met certain character requirements that convinced the Army I was responsible enough to be assigned to a missile site. Disqualifications could have occurred over a variety of character flaws: alcoholism, drug abuse, or a proven history of psychiatric disorders, not to mention more discretionary failings, such as a poor attitude, contempt for authority, and a lack of motivation. My personal records—medical files and military evaluations—had been examined in detail, and would be reviewed again every six months to make sure I hadn't developed any drug abuse or discipline problems, or any evidence of unreliability that would make it seem as though I were likely to sabotage the weapon system. Were I to fail at any point to meet the PRP requirements, I'd be taken out of the program, and subsequently denied any position of substantial authority.

Twice daily, from January to March of 1981, I made the forty-minute drive (I'd had my car shipped over from the States) between Robinson Barracks and the Battalion Operations Center (BOC)—a twenty-four-hour-a-day combat command center located about fifteen miles from Stuttgart in the otherwise sleepy village of Grossachsenheim.

The BOC was the nerve center for all combat operations within our battalion. None of our battalion's four missile batteries—Alpha, Bravo, Charlie, or Delta—were permitted to fire at a target without the authorization of the commander at the BOC. I spent most of my days there studying Air Defense tactics, in preparation for a series of qualification tests I'd be required to pass within ninety days of being sent to a missile battery.

My nights, meanwhile, were spent on the road, traveling with the Battalion Operational Readiness Evaluation Team (ORE Team) as an additional part of my training as an Air Defense officer. The ORE Team—whose job it was to evaluate a battery's ability to prepare a missile for simulated launch within a designated period of time—was comprised of a commissioned officer, a couple of warrant officers (experts in missile technology), and a senior enlisted ("noncommissioned") officer, more commonly known as an NCO. I tagged along to learn how these very important missile inspections were done.

Whenever individual batteries were "up" in firing status, they would have an average of three ORE Team evaluations per week. There were four types of firing status on a missile site. While complete "downtime" never existed so far as the missiles were concerned, each type of status varied in its intensity. Maintenance Status was the lowest—when soldiers usually performed their equipment checks, and would need at least a day or two to prepare a missile for launch. The next two levels were Twelve-Hour Status, and Three-Hour Status (also known as Back-Up Status), which meant the missile crews would need at least those amounts of time to ready a missile for firing. The final, and most acute, level of status, known as Hot Status, demanded that the crews have a missile ready for launch in less than forty minutes.

The evaluators would normally descend on the batteries at night—either close to midnight, or right before dawn. The missile crews would get a call from the gate guard, letting them know that the ORE Team was on-site. It typically worked out that the crews would have just finished some checks and gone back to the barracks area when *bang*, the team would hit. A time limit was imposed, then all hell would break loose as the soldiers tore back to their battle stations. Once the crews were alerted to our presence, we would split up into two teams, in order to evaluate two sections of the battery at the same time. There were all kinds of verifications to be made on the equipment—the crews would have to check the connections between the missiles and the launcher, ensure that the communications between the missile area and the control room were clear, determine if the missile's electronic flight commands were being received, and dozens of other tasks that would keep the soldiers working till the last second when the command would come to fire.

The evaluators would keep their eyes on the missile crews constantly. They weren't friendly about it, either, even if they knew the soldiers. The slightest mistake by a crew member, or an "out-of-tolerance" computer or radar reading (which meant that a reading fell outside the established parameters) was enough to provoke a reprimand. Sometimes the crews couldn't tell if their tolerances had been correct until after the missile was fired. If there were problems, they would usually surface during crew drills, but occasionally the crews would fire, and everything would seem right, but the tolerance checks would later show that something had gone wrong.

To make things even more difficult, our battalion was a Nike Hercules dual-capable (high-explosive/nuclear) missile battalion—and Nike Herc was an old system that was starting to fall apart. Consequently, in the heat of these evaluations, the unit's mechanics would always be running around changing parts at the last minute. It was wild.

Traveling with the ORE Team to different batteries, and observing operations at the BOC, gave me a bird's-eye view of the entire battalion. It was considered by many to be a good first assignment, and, if I'd wanted to, I could easily have chosen to remain a staff officer and taken a job working shifts at the Battalion Operations Center. But I knew early on that the life of a staff officer was not for me. I wanted to be directly involved with the training and the lives of enlisted soldiers. I wanted to lead a platoon.

In late February, I began asking Colonel Baumgarten to make me a platoon leader at Charlie Battery. He refused, saying he wanted me to stay at the BOC a while longer, where I could continue to get "the big picture." I knew that in the proud, clubby way of tradition-loving men, Colonel Baumgarten liked the idea of having an all-West-Point-run BOC. Two of my classmates—one male and one female—were working there as well. When the colonel began to talk of sending Lieutenant Loquasto to take the position that had been originally promised to me, however, I knew I had to move quickly. Aside from undergoing the rigors of becoming fully qualified to work with the Nike Herc missile system, and surmounting the challenge of fair competition, I knew there was going to be another obstacle to conquer: my gender.

Every day for two weeks I bugged the colonel, making a complete pest of myself, thinking that, if nothing else, he'd send me away just to get rid of me. The problem was, there had never been a female officer at Charlie Battery before, and Colonel Baumgarten was understandably reluctant to make me the guinea pig. It was a remote site, almost exclusively populated by enlisted men and married male officers, and he expressed genuine concern for my safety. He was also worried that there would be little opportunity for me to socialize.

150

At the same time, Colonel Baumgarten understood that the women who were coming out of West Point had spent four years in a fishbowl. He knew that we needed to find out if it had been worth it. Attending West Point was like playing in the minor leagues, I told him. I'd made it through the farm system, but now I had to succeed in the majors. I had to prove myself to others all over again, this time in the real Army.

The colonel did not dismiss me from his office. Instead he looked grim, and was quiet for a long time. Then he gave me his decision. Lieutenant Loquasto was going to make one hell of a staff officer.

I left for Charlie Battery, Hardheim, in early March. It would be my first real job in the Army. I was being sent to replace a platoon leader who, to everyone's relief, had been removed from the site and put to work behind a desk at Battalion Staff Headquarters. Word was that this lieutenant had not been able to withstand the pressures of working on a missile site, and the Dragon had eaten him alive.

Hardheim was located about fifty-five miles northeast of Stuttgart. It was a small German town with narrow cobblestone streets and half-timbered houses rarely more than three stories high. Only two buildings in the area were taller than those at Charlie Battery. They were American-style, modern high rises situated about half a mile from the battery, and I would be living in one of them. My apartment had belonged to the outgoing MP platoon leader at Charlie. It was on the eighth floor, with a good view of the town. I could see the missile site from my kitchen window. My balcony faced south, overlooking a sea of cornfields, and the flocks of sheep that grazed nearby.

Looming distant and high above the roofs of the town was the cement tower where the Military Police kept watch over the site. If one stood in the middle of Hardheim's shopping district, fixed an eye on the tower, and traveled straight up the main road, one would end up at Charlie Battery. Once there, the first thing one would see would be the Administration Area, which included the motor pool (where the battery's vehicles were maintained and repaired), and a long stuccoed building where the unmarried or otherwise unaccompanied enlisted soldiers lived; the female enlisted soldiers had rooms on the first floor. Next to their quarters were the offices of the battery commander and his executive officer, or XO, and to the far right, the Dining Facility. (The Army doesn't like to call them mess halls anymore.)

If not for the steel latticework of the chain link fence and barbed wire that rose six feet above the grassy fields, and a few nondescript structures whose contents were mostly hidden from view, Charlie Battery could have passed for a peaceful German farm.

A gate guard was positioned at the entrance twenty-four hours a day. Depending on the battery's security status, either everyone had to have a valid I.D. card to get in, or only those whom the gate guard didn't recognize.

The site itself was divided into three fenced-in areas: The Administration Area (Admin Area), the Launcher Control Area (LCA), and the Integrated Fire Control (IFC). The Admin Area was where most of the domestic life of the battery was centered. Besides the staff offices, dining facility, and soldiers' living quarters, the Admin Area's main building also housed the battery's supply room, and a small Post Exchange. Unit formations were held, daily, in the parking lot out front.

Approximately one hundred yards to the north was the Launcher Control Area, where the missiles were kept. With the Nike Herc system, the Launcher Area was always directly within the line of sight of the IFC radars, so that standing on the hill of the IFC, one could look down and see the missiles. The Area was surrounded by two fences—a box that was one-hundred yards square, within an even larger rectangle.

In the no man's land between the inner and outer fences stood four more guard towers and two buildings—the Ready Building, and the Maintenance Building. The Ready Building housed my platoon office, and a sleeping bay for the on-duty launcher crew when the battery was at Hot Status. The Maintenance Building was where repairs were performed on the launcher equipment. In that building, too, were the offices of the Launcher Warrants, the battery's true technological experts.

The commander of Charlie Battery was Captain Robert Smith, a West Point graduate, class of '72. I have learned to be wary of male West Point graduates, for I never know what their attitudes toward their female counterparts might be. But when I met Captain Smith, I was naive and optimistic, and looking for a mentor. Unfortunately, having West Point in common made no difference whatsoever in our relationship. Captain Smith was always reasonable and fair, but he was curt and businesslike when he spoke to me, as if a curtain had been dropped between us—a curtain that would vanish in the company of men. I envied the other lieutenants their easy comaraderie.

As Captain Smith's Launcher Platoon Leader, I was responsible for the discipline and training of the enlisted soldiers and warrant officers, for the maintenance and operation of guided missile and launching equipment, and for maintaining the platoon's combat-ready status around the clock. There were over seventy soldiers in my platoon, 95 percent of them male, most of them black. I had two warrant officers, a maintenance sergeant, a platoon sergeant, three squad leaders, and over sixty crewmen. None of these soldiers had ever worked for a woman before.

Here I was, fresh out of school, being thrust into a position of awesome accountability—for people's lives, for millions of dollars' worth of equipment, and for putting into action the complex and dangerous battle strategies that would be handed to me from above. Only, I had no practical experience doing any of these things. And yet, crazily, I was in charge. So I had to rely on the senior soldiers—especially the NCOs and warrant officers—to bring me up, to teach me about the Army.

Mind you, this was not a simple process. Some of my soldiers took exception to being bossed around by a dewy-eyed kid with no real technical or leadership experience. But they also knew it was part of their job to train me.

When I first arrived at Charlie Battery, I looked to my platoon sergeant, Sergeant Quinn, to be my teacher. Quinn was an E-6 (staff sergeant) doing the job of an E-7 (a sergeant first class, one pay grade higher). He had attained the rank of section leader, but the battery was short senior NCOs, so he'd been booted up in position (though not in pay) to platoon sergeant.

Sergeant Quinn didn't speak to me much when we met. Instead, he waited to hear how I was planning to handle his—now our—platoon. Following a tour of the Launcher Area, I asked him to join me in my new office and invited him to sit down.

"Sergeant Quinn," I began, "I know as well as you that I'm ignorant about the operation of this site, and about the duties of a second lieutenant. I expect you to train me. In the end, I know I am responsible for the platoon, and I take that responsibility very seriously. To my mind, a leader has two responsibilities—accomplishing the mission, and taking care of the soldiers."

Quinn politely responded, "Yes, Ma'am," but the look on his face said, "We'll see."

He and the rest of my platoon would judge me according to their standards, not mine. Apparently, a lot of them assumed I was going to be a wimp, cry a lot, and be intimidated by the whole job. I felt, perhaps unfairly, that I was being watched more closely than my male counterparts. It was West Point all over again; only this time I didn't have my female classmates around me for support. I'd have to demonstrate my abilities as a leader before I could ever expect the soldiers to trust me with their problems; most of these men had never turned to a female officer for help. It would take them a while before they'd accept me as a confidante. To be honest, I grew to know what was going on with them before they even came to see me—credit problems, divorce problems, custody battles, joint property claims, tax troubles. Some of my enlisted soldiers were up to their ears in debt when they joined the Army because they couldn't keep a steady job anywhere else.

Soldiers normally have a lot of financial worries because they come into the Army bringing spouses, children, and other dependents with them. Consequently, platoon leaders and company commanders spend enormous amounts of time dealing with personnel problems that are somewhat more complicated than they used to be: not just requests for reassignments or new MOSs (military occupational specialties), but sick children, aging parents, chronically sick or disabled relatives—the list goes on.

Some of my fellow lieutenants seemed to have entered military service with the crazy notion that they'd be spending all their time zipping up and down the Fulda Gap shouting, "Take that hill!" They didn't understand that they'd be spending eight hours a day behind a desk writing justifications for MOS reclassifications, trying to get soldiers registered to vote, or their driver's licenses renewed, helping them handle changes in their insurance policies, writing to loan companies who were hounding them for payments, or to landlords explaining why they hadn't paid the rent, or even letters to their families because some of them couldn't write.

Many of the men at Charlie Battery were high school dropouts. Some of them were illiterate; either they asked other people to read for them when it was necessary, or they simply learned their duties on the job so they wouldn't have to rely on Army manuals (which were written at a sixth grade level) to teach them.

It never used to matter if E-6's couldn't write. Twenty or twenty-five years ago, if people could sign their names, they could stay in the service until retirement. All they had to undertake were some manual procedures with weapons; they had to know how to lead people, how to talk to them, how to develop them. They needed verbal and physical skills, but not much else. Now they've got to know, for instance, how to decipher a computer keyboard. There are rules and restrictions. If soldiers don't fulfill specific learning requirements, they are not allowed to reenlist.

Overall, however, soldiers in Air Defense are well educated. There is more illiteracy in the Infantry, for example. A soldier intent on joining Air

Defense has to achieve a certain level of aptitude test scores. To work directly with the missile system, the scores have to be even higher.

Interestingly, for most of the 1980s, enlisted women recruits tended to be of a slightly higher caliber than men. Women had to rate proportionately higher on physical exams in order to be admitted into military service, while men were accepted with lower scores. The female recruits were generally better educated than the males because they needed at least a high school diploma to enlist. (Recently, according to a source at the Women and the Military Project of the Women's Equity Action League, the high school diploma requirement for enlisted women entering the Marines and the Army has been dropped.)

The Army did offer the soldiers at Charlie Battery an educational program; members of the community came on-site to teach reading or math. Like many things in the military, these classes were optional but "encouraged." Soldiers knew they could not be forced to attend, but they also knew they wouldn't be promoted unless they met Army standards of basic computation and literacy.

These fundamentals, however, were not the only ones that many soldiers needed, and lacked. I had one Spec-4, for instance, who got himself deep into debt by writing bad checks. The battery had received a list of those checks from his creditors, and Captain Smith asked me to investigate. I called the soldier into my office to question him about his finances, and he told me that he thought checks were like money, that he could keep writing them as long as he had them in his checkbook. I thought he must be joking, but he seemed so genuinely bewildered by his predicament that I knew he was telling the truth. So, after straightening out his problem, I gave a class to my platoon on how to properly handle a checking account. I was surprised to learn how little they knew about it; some of them had never written a check in their lives.

But these were just the responsibilities of a platoon leader; a battery or company commander encounters much more. As a commander, you learn about the dark side of humanity. When you stand in front of your soldiers during a formation you know secrets about them that they would never tell anyone else—child abuse, drug abuse, wife-beating, sexual deviance; it all comes across your desk. Everything comes to you eventually.

Deep in the heart of the Launcher Area, at the entrance to the inner fence, sat Post 4, the building which housed the on-duty MPs, whose primary job was to guard the site. The MPs worked a grinding schedule of twenty-four hours on, twenty-four hours off. At least fifteen MPs were on duty at any given time, though their force would sometimes be supplemented with Launcher Crewmen. The rest of us used to joke about them, saying that only one MP had to stay alert on the job—so he could wake up the others when the inspector was coming.

Enclosed within the inner fence were the missiles. Colonel Baumgarten—the Dragon—loved to inspect them. There were three sets of missiles, and each set was inside a structure somewhat whimsically called a barn, even though its flat roof and sheet metal walls made it look more like an oversized garden shed. Some of the battery's missiles, even more whimsically called birds, were kept outside on launcher pads, while others were laid horizontally on platforms inside the barns. (Nuclear missiles were brought forward on NATO's decision to go nuclear.) The missiles were huge—nearly forty feet long and, in prone position, about seven feet high.

The three different missile sections—Alpha, Bravo, and Charlie—were separated from one another by huge mounds of grass and dirt that camouflaged underground panel rooms, six feet square, from which commands could be directed to the launcher pads.

The colonel would drive up from Headquarters for a surprise visit and, as Launcher Platoon Leader, it would be my duty to escort him downrange. Before we were allowed within twenty yards of the barns, one of the barn guards would tell me to halt. He'd then say, "I recognize you as Lieutenant Barkalow. Advance." After taking a few steps I'd be halted again. The barn guard would then ask, "Do you vouch for your party?" When I'd answer "Yes," the guard would tell Colonel Baumgarten to advance. A regulation known as the "two-man rule" ensured that no person would ever enter a missile barn alone. A soldier had to be accompanied by at least one other person, both of them carrying valid I.D. badges, so that if one began to behave in a suspicious manner, the other would be present to do whatever it took to stop him or her. Even if it meant killing them.

Meanwhile, the barn guards, who were responsible for missile security, kept watch according to a strict body of regulations, the most critical being the Five Rules Governing the Use of Deadly Force; that is, the professional soldier's license to kill:

1. A soldier is empowered to kill in self-defense.
2. A soldier is empowered to kill in defense of another battery member.

3. A soldier is empowered to kill to avoid the potential overthrow of a site.
4. A soldier is empowered to kill to prevent the destruction of equipment.

Rules one through four are simple enough. Soldiers are empowered to take action in direct response to a threat. The threat may be real or perceived, but the decision is theirs, as is some measure of responsibility. However, the fifth rule, "A soldier must kill when ordered to do so by a superior officer," is the most potentially problematic for any thinking person, because to carry it out is never an act of reason, but an act of faith, although each soldier does have a responsibility to determine if the order is "legal." Nevertheless, to abandon one's own will, to become an instrument in someone else's hands, is an odd liberation. It leaves one in a state of moral limbo, a condition tolerable only if supported by fear, indifference, or something that is, peculiarly, very much like love.

On this particular afternoon, Colonel Baumgarten decided he wanted to inspect the missile barn in Charlie Section. In another charge of military ritual, I had already quizzed the barn guards on their required knowledge, and was feeling confident when Colonel Baumgarten marched up to one of the guards himself and started shooting the same questions.

"Soldier," the colonel began, "Who's your battery commander?"

"Sir," the man replied, "my battery commander is Captain Robert Smith."

"Soldier," the colonel said again, "give me your general orders."

"Sir, my three general orders are:

"I will guard everything within the limits of my post, and quit my post only when properly relieved.

"I will obey my special orders and perform all my duties in a military manner.

"I will report violations of my special orders, emergencies, and anything not covered in my instructions to the commander of the relief."

The soldier was able to recite his general orders correctly, but when he got to the colonel's last question: "What are the Five Rules Governing the Use of Deadly Force?" he froze.

Colonel Baumgarten tried to get the man going again. His voice was rising. The veins in his neck were becoming as taut as guitar strings. But the poor guard couldn't speak. He couldn't move. He had forgotten.

All the soldier could do was stare, his face a blank. The more the

Dragon yelled, the more panic-stricken the guard became. Seeing he was getting nowhere, Colonel Baumgarten turned to me.

"Lieutenant!" he barked. "You are not to leave this site until this soldier knows his Five Rules and can recite them to me. Is that clear?"

"Yes, sir!" I said.

With that, the colonel strode off down the road to Post 4. In a flash, I was on the phone to the MP on duty there. "This is Lieutenant Barkalow. Do not let Colonel Baumgarten leave this site until I give the order to release him."

Granted, Baumgarten was a lieutenant colonel and I was only a second lieutenant, but I didn't care. My soldier knew his stuff—he'd just become scared. The fact was, Colonel Baumgarten could have left any time he wanted, but I knew he loved it when his lieutenants took charge.

I grabbed the platoon sergeant, the section chief, and a few of the other guys from Charlie section. We sat the soldier down and drilled him until he could recite those five rules backward and forward. It felt as though I were drilling a West Point plebe.

After forty-five minutes, the guard was ready to perform. I walked down to Post 4 and found the colonel sitting, arms folded, in a chair. He looked up when I approached and said, "They won't let me out, Lieutenant, until you say it's okay."

I drew a breath. "That's correct, Sir," I said. "I wanted you to reinspect my barn guard in Charlie first."

Without another word the colonel followed me back to the section. I was nervous as hell, but I tried to hide it. Colonel Baumgarten stood toe to toe with the guard and put the question to him as before. "Do you know the Five Rules Governing the Use of Deadly Force, Soldier, or am I going to have to demonstrate them on you?"

The man cleared his throat. In a steady voice, he recited them flawlessly. The crew nearly burst into applause. Colonel Baumgarten nodded to me, and left. I was especially thankful, because the last time a guard had failed to recite his required knowledge, I saw Baumgarten replace him with the platoon leader. I was not about to let that happen to me.

Between the inner and outer fences surrounding the Launcher Control Area, four guard towers were fixed fifty feet in the air like treehouses perched on gray cement poles. A winding staircase led to the top of each pole, where a four-foot square platform was enclosed in plexiglass, and had a wraparound deck. The deck, which the guards had to circle periodically, was only two feet wide. The MPs, holding loaded M-16 rifles, pulled four-hour shifts in those tiny belfries and had to remain alert at every moment. I knew I never could have survived as a tower rat, but I did have to pull my share of all-night duty, since a Staff Duty Officer had to be on-site at all times. My inspections of the towers took about forty minutes to complete, and involved climbing the stairs to the top of each tower, quizzing the guards on their required knowledge, or just finding out how they were doing. To get from tower to tower, I had to walk across the open grass between them, always staying between the two fences. It was a long, solitary walk, which was scary because tensions were on the rise within the country, and the threat of a terrorist attack was always present. The Red Army Faction (also known as the Baader-Meinhof Gang) was perhaps the most famous terrorist group in Germany at that time. In August 1981, according to a terrorist group profile later published by the U. S. Government Printing Office, the group was responsible for bombing the U.S. Air Force Headquarters in Ramstein—injuring eighteen Americans and two Germans. The following month, they fired two RPG-7 grenades at U.S. Army European Commanding General Frederick Kroesen's car, injuring both him and his wife. Acts like these affected all American soldiers in Germany. It brought home the harsh reality that we were potential targets.

Thick woods bordered the northern part of the missile site at Charlie Battery; large stadium floodlights lit the area, and as I made my lonely walk around the towers, I felt completely exposed. Though I couldn't see into the pitch-dark woods, I knew that anyone who might have been lurking there could definitely see me.

The level of stress on a Nike Hercules site was extraordinarily high. As an officer, I worked in a constant state of controlled hysteria; any error concerning the missiles, even a minor infraction, could have ended my career. Every operation was an ordeal, every inspection a potential crisis. Before I was permitted to participate in missile-firing exercises with the battery at Back-Up or Hot Status, I had ninety days from the moment I arrived on-site to earn my qualification as a Battery Control Officer, or BCO. This involved passing a written test on Air Defense tactics, performing checks on the radars and the missile launcher, and running a hands-on missile crew drill while assuming battle stations. Even after I'd become BCO qualified, however, it still would have taken only one malfunction—human or mechanical—for me to be summarily dismissed from my post. I was never permitted to relax my vigilance, not for a second. No matter how tense I was, I wasn't allowed to show it. An officer had to be alert and in control at all times. Or at least appear to be.

159

While my civilian friends back in the States were struggling with basic issues of identity, I, at the age of twenty-two, was being entrusted with the final button-pressing task of unleashing a missile—possibly one that was nuclear.

Imagine how being placed in this position can affect you. If you're young, it ages you. If you're frivolous, it makes you sober (though sobriety in this case should not be mistaken for maturity). Mostly, it mixes a highly charged fear and a sense of unspeakable power with a release from everything in your life that's mundane and without greater purpose. The intensity of the experience makes you forget about everything else. And yet, if you dwell too much on the gravity of the situation, your life on-site will be dismal. And so, despite our serious feelings about defending American interests, performing the tasks at hand became a form of gamesmanship, a contest of will.

In my battery, crews from different missile sections often competed against each other to see who could have a missile raised in the air and ready to fire first. We staged rodeos between whole batteries, complete with trophies. This was regarded by the chain of command as positive reinforcement.

We knew, obviously, that no one was going to hand us a trophy for firing a missile in wartime, nor would we ever think in those terms. But during peacetime, soldiers need incentives. The soldiers I knew were very proud of their accomplishments. They enjoyed it when they could point to a trophy that said, "Best Platoon within the Battery" or "Best Battery within the Battalion."

When I led my platoon through an exercise, we operated in a state of urgency that gave us a powerful high. I know, because I've succumbed to it. That jolt of adrenalin, the heightened sense of power and focus, is what makes war an addictive experience in some people's lives. In an exercise, of course, one is treated to the thrill without the horror. And it is the horror which, invariably, is first severed from one's mind.

In the classes which followed mine at West Point, I was told that, as an enjoyable way of reinforcing their training, cadets would play a complicated computer game based on the major REFORGER exercise—the annual Return of Forces to Germany, to demonstrate our commitment to the NATO Alliance. This particular game had, as its objective, the defense of the Fulda Gap, the low-lying region where Soviet tank forces would be expected to penetrate if they crossed the Alps into Germany. Cadets would play this game for hours at a stretch. The goal was to prevent the Soviet capture of the Wiesbaden Air Base. If the Soviets succeeded, the game was over, and the Americans would have lost.

If I had come upon the cadets in the middle of their frenzied play and said, "Drop a tactical nuclear warhead on the Russians," they would have responded by saying, "But we don't have tactical nuclear warheads in this game." Well, I'd think, what kind of wargame is that? We have hundreds of nuclear warheads in Germany, and yet there isn't one in that computer game. It's a denial of reality. Most civilians divorce themselves a step from the nuclear reality. Military people divorce themselves another step. We talk about fighting conventional warfare, we talk about fighting guerrilla warfare, even chemical warfare, almost as if the nuke doesn't exist. Mainly what we're trained for is conventional land war in Europe, even though the basic defense in Western Europe is still nuclear.

I know of a young American soldier in a rocket-launching division who is currently babysitting a nuclear weapon. A civilian friend once asked him: "What are you going to do with that thing if the Russian tanks cross the Alps? You're either going to destroy the missile, so that it doesn't fall into enemy hands, or you're going to launch it. Those are your options. There are only two. Has anyone explained this to you? You're sitting on that nuke like Slim Pickens in *Dr. Strangelove*, waiting for it to be dropped."

He considered this for a moment and replied, "Well, I'll do what I'm ordered to do."

His mission is his safety valve. That young officer doesn't concern himself with much beyond the technical aspects of his job, because his superiors are making the decision.

It's true that soldiers in the field are only permitted to "go nuclear" upon the president's direct order. Nevertheless, that officer, or I, or the hundreds of other people in our position would be exercising the president's command. When asked whether we would feel ourselves capable of unleashing the violent forces entrusted to our care, most of us would answer stoically, as the young man did: As long as they are neither illegal nor immoral, we will obey orders.

The difficulty is that the lines between a legal or an illegal order, a moral or an immoral act are too often blurred. Yet we remain incorrigibly romantic about our roles as officers; and in some ways, out of step. We respond to the facts of our profession, and to the fears that accompany them, by clinging to a childlike hope—that we will never be forced to find out exactly what we are capable of.

. . .

The Nike Hercules system, first built in 1958, operated by firing missiles at enemy aircraft from a launcher on the ground. The system could fire only one missile at a time, and the crews had to keep track of each one until its target was destroyed. The Nike Hercules system was eventually replaced with smaller, more advanced medium-to-high altitude, surface-to-air weapon systems such as Hawk and Patriot, which are still in use. Nike Hercules, meanwhile—after being tested and fine-tuned by American technicians for twenty-five years—was phased out by the Americans between 1983 and 1985. It was then sold off.

Because the weapons were located in the so-called rear of the battlefield, Nike Hercules battalions were among the few in the Air Defense Artillery branch that had been opened to women. In the 1980s, as Nike Hercules was being phased out of service, women in Air Defense began to wonder whether they would be permitted to work with the newer Patriot missile system, since it hadn't been determined where it would be located on the battlefield. Ultimately, women were permitted to work with the missile system, but it depended on where and with what type of battalion their units were assigned. If the missile units were co-located with an Infantry battalion, for example, women would not be allowed to work there. The notion, however, that placing women behind the Brigade Rear Area is somehow going to protect them from exposure to combat, is wishful thinking. The Army's current AirLand Battle Doctrine acknowledges and accepts the "fluid and lethal" quality of the hypothetical modern battlefield, and yet location remains a primary criterion for the placement of Army women.

In the spring and early summer, an endless round of German beer and wine fests coincided with our preparations for Charlie Battery's largest and most critical exercise of the year—the Allied Air Force Central Europe Tactical Evaluation, known as the AAFCE TAC EVAL.

This dreaded three-day period began with the arrival of NATO officers on-site for an extended evaluation of the battery's ability to prepare for and survive in a combat environment. The evaluation was made up of two parts; both were extremely tough, and thoroughly exhausting. First, we'd build up to a state of preparedness for combat—we'd send soldiers to man foxholes and bunkers around the site, initiate a thorough check of the missile system, and ensure that our communication lines were up and running. Then we'd have a simulation of combat itself. The build-up took about twelve hours, starting at 8:00 P.M., and continuing through the night. Under close surveillance, a huge mock battle would rage at Charlie Battery for the next two and a half days. This was called our "sustainment in war."

Virtually everyone at the battery stayed on-site for the duration of the exercise. For three days we lived on C-rations in the field, and dressed in suits designed to protect us against nuclear, biological, and chemical warfare attacks. Our Load Bearing Equipment belts, which we strapped around our waists, carried two ammo pouches, a first aid pouch, a canteen, and a rain poncho. To complete the costume, when required, we wore protective masks pulled over our heads.

Whether it was eleventh-hour maintenance on one of the radars or missiles, or some other type of fine tuning, the work was a nonstop, potentially volatile combination of stress and sheer exhaustion that had been known to send some soldiers completely over the edge.

After midnight of the second day, nobody had slept for nearly forty-eight hours. I was hopping mad, because I had ripped my boot falling over a tent peg in the dark. Sergeant Quinn and I took a walk from my office down to Post 4 on my way to inspect the missile area. When we arrived, Specialist Wilson, a Spec-4 from the launcher crew, was inside the building arguing heatedly with one of the crew members. Wilson was furious because he had just finished pulling guard duty in the towers, and was now being ordered to man a guard post in the bunker. Taking shifts back-to-back was strenuous, especially since the soldier had already worked an eight-hour day. But then, so had everyone else. It was his turn to guard the bunker. He simply had to do it, we told him. We were understaffed, and he wasn't going home. Evidently, this was not what he wanted to hear.

Specialist Wilson marched out of the building. Sergeant Quinn and I knew he was still upset, but we assumed the discussion was closed. The next thing we knew, he was screaming his head off at the entrance to the inner fence, dangerously close to the missiles.

The sergeant and I rushed outside.

"I'm not going to pull guard duty!" he was yelling. "I'm tired! I want to go home!"

I wondered briefly if he were drunk, but his speech sounded more spent than slurred. Sergeant Quinn moved forward slowly, promising the man he'd have time to rest later, firmly insisting, however, that he was needed at his post.

Wilson was becoming desperate. Yelling was getting him nowhere. It suddenly must have dawned on him that he held a much greater power of persuasion in his hands. Without any warning, he raised his loaded weapon, and aimed it directly at Sergeant Quinn.

Sergeant Quinn stopped. His body tensed. He was not armed. Neither was I.

The bright lights from the towers set the two men in stark relief against the woods. I hung back in the shadows, too terrified to move, fearful of what the man would do if there were even the slightest interference from me. This wasn't supposed to happen, I thought. Our troops weren't supposed to be the ones we had to watch out for.

The three of us stood frozen, poised between safety and calamity for the next half hour. Sergeant Quinn continued to speak to the soldier, calmly and steadily. His voice became a soothing drone, intoning over and over that everything was going to be all right.

When it finally became apparent to Wilson that no one was going to make him pull guard, he lowered his weapon. An MP appeared and stepped forward with Sergeant Quinn to disarm the frightened soldier. Wilson handed over his rifle, without incident, and allowed the MP to lead him away. He was never given another weapon again. Instead, we made him a cook. That's what usually happened to those who were disqualified from pulling guard duty. They didn't leave the unit, they just helped out elsewhere.

Three weeks later, I was working in the Admin Area when I ran into Sergeant Quinn again. He was coming down from the Launcher Area, charging like a bull. I asked him where he was headed in such a hurry.

"Ma'am," he said, shaking his head, "I'm sorry. But I've had it. I am going to get out of here. I'm going to walk through those gates, and never come back."

But Sergeant Quinn didn't leave, not then, nor later that day, nor for as long as I remained at Charlie Battery.

The first time I disciplined a soldier, I felt like a priest—sitting in my confessional, doling out penance, or offering absolution. It made me uncomfortable, but hell, in the Army, you get used to anything if you do it often enough. One of the basic principles of military justice is to develop discipline—the state of mind in which soldiers are willing to obey orders, no matter how unpleasant.

At this stage of my career, I was not empowered to deal with major offenses. A platoon leader handles a fairly limited range of disciplinary actions, such as penalizing a soldier for being late to formation or missing it altogether. The guilty soldier would come to my office after his or her transgression had been brought to my attention by the section leader or platoon sergeant. The NCO would relate the details of the incident and recommend a suitable punishment. Since the NCO was closest to the soldiers, I usually followed his recommendation.

For a first offense, I gave the soldiers only an ass-chewing, but if it happened again they would find themselves pulling extra duty, such as cutting grass, painting walls, or stripping barracks floors on their own time at night. At most, I could recommend Article 15 proceedings to the battery commander, who would summon the soldier to be formally charged. The soldier then had forty-eight hours to decide whether he or she was going to accept the Article 15, or demand a trial by court martial. Usually, soldiers preferred to accept the Article 15. These nonjudicial punishments for minor offenses—going AWOL, for instance, or showing disrespect to a senior officer—reminded people that they were still in the Army and not just working for some mammoth corporation. When soldiers talk about the awesome power of command, they're describing the Uniform Code of Military Justice (UCMJ). The UCMJ makes the commander both judge and jury. Fixed sums of money can be withheld from soldiers' paychecks. Rank can be taken away. The penalty depends on the commander's discretion, and the seriousness of the offense.

Though a soldier can try to appeal the punishment further up the chain of command, it takes a strong case to overrule a commander's decision. In truth, as a commander you have tremendous power over people, including the power of life and death. Which is why command is considered the "holy of holies," and why the officer must have some understanding of what the hell he or she is doing.

It can be a very heady experience. Imagine having a couple of hundred people under your command, and when you say "Jump!" goddamnit, they jump. You can fall in love with the trappings of authority, or you can slash your wrists from despairing that you will ever live up to what's expected of you; the struggle is to strike a balance somewhere in between.

Colonel Baumgarten was right. I did not have much of a social life at Charlie, or a great deal of time to develop one. Male soldiers at the battery either had their wives to go home to, or could find some release in the bars and brothels that have always been a part of the military landscape. Even in Germany, single men might be invited to homes within the community where there were unmarried daughters or sisters-in-law. There is quite a bit of matchmaking that goes on in the Army. Eligible bachelors, especially young lieutenants coming right out of the Academy, are still considered a real catch.

Socially, women officers had a much tougher time. Our outlets were fewer. Of course, we were surrounded by men, but most of them were unavailable—because they were either married or lower-ranking, or perhaps somewhere within our chain of command. Unlike our male counterparts, women officers in Germany couldn't pick up dates in bars. Soldiers have certain expectations of their superiors; watching a woman officer get drunk and turn slovenly would have been the quickest way to kill her authority. The world we lived in as American soldiers overseas was very small, so my troops would invariably see me if I went out on the town. Some of them were understandably very curious about their officers' personal lives. But I felt the same way about my soldiers knowing me as an actor does about an audience; it's better they don't know too much about you, so they can have faith in what they see.

Even though as a female officer I'd become accustomed to being in the minority, my tour of duty in Germany was an isolating experience. The few other females in my platoon were lower enlisted; there were no female noncommissioned officers. I couldn't pal around with the enlisted women any more than I could socialize with the married male officers. And they were all married, except one warrant officer, Richard Paulson.

At that time, in the Army's social hierarchy, warrant officers were neither fish nor fowl. They weren't commissioned officers (though it's possible now they can receive a commission), and they weren't enlisted. Richard's rank did not make him the ideal companion for a single female commissioned officer, but a friendship between us should at least have been permissible. The situation was further complicated because Richard worked directly for me. Because of Army regulations against fraternizing within one's direct chain of command, open friendship became a highly risky proposition, and romance a near impossibility.

Still, at a remote site like Charlie Battery, friendships among soldiers were born of necessity—from living together, pulling duty together, and keeping each other awake through the long nights of work. Being an American soldier in a foreign country was difficult. Drinking grew into a way of forgetting one's loneliness and blending in with everyone else. After inspections, a few of the officers would meet at a local *Gasthaus* and drink. Many times we'd end up closing the place. When I was stationed in Germany, drunk driving wasn't considered as severe a problem within the Army as it is today. Back then, I would have received perhaps nothing more than a verbal reprimand if I were caught. Now if I got picked up for drunk driving, my career would be ruined.

Nonetheless, the Army continues to have its share of alcoholics, particularly among the older NCOs. In fact, one of the male soldiers at Charlie Battery had a drinking problem. He had been picked up three times for Driving While Intoxicated, and yet it wasn't until the third time that his driver's license was revoked. His platoon leader tried to get him kicked out of the Army, but he had been in the service for many years, and in those days, the Army was reluctant to dismiss a veteran soldier. Not anymore, however. The demands of modern military technology preclude a tolerance for human foibles. The Army will now dismiss soldiers, even those who are just about to retire, if they defy the Army's code of behavior.

Aside from my recurring bouts with loneliness, I found that being unmarried in the military had its unique set of problems. For one thing, living quarters for single soldiers are generally less desirable than married quarters, which is one of the reasons I have always chosen to live off post. Also, many job policies are prejudicial against single people. If you are married with children and have just arrived at a new installation, you are normally given two weeks to find housing and schools, and to become acclimated. But if you're single, it is assumed that you will report to the unit within twenty-four hours of landing and be ready to start working right away. There is a climate in which a single person is expected not to have a social life, or, rather, it is expected not to be important.

Though marriage is not always possible, or even desirable, the social pressure on military women to marry can be tremendous. Whether we're married is usually the first question asked of women officers at any military installation. This is not solely for practical reasons—determining our entitlements, for example, or helping us decide where to live. There is a moral tone to the question, a sizing up of character.

If for whatever reason, we do not marry, we are certainly not encouraged to seek friendship and support among other female soldiers. Gatherings of women are perceived negatively in most military circles. (The tradition of holding "Coffees"—social gatherings for civilian spouses, usually wives—stands as the rare exception.)

And so, despite all the flap that goes on in the military about how desperately men need to bond with one another, male soldiers seem categorically unable to perceive, or to forgive, a similar need in women. In fact, they often appear to possess an irrational fear of women's groups, believing that, in their midst, men will be plotted against or, perhaps worst of all, rendered somehow unnecessary. If women soldiers do try to develop a professional support network among themselves, they are faced with the dilemma that something as simple as two women officers having lunch together more than once might spark rumors of lesbianism—a potentially lethal charge, since even rumored homosexuality can damage an officer's career.

Participating in sports remains one of the few acceptable ways for military women to connect. In Germany, sports were my refuge. I played basketball in winter, and in spring, I would drive for an hour and a half three nights a week from Hardheim to Stuttgart for softball practice. Most of the women on my team were in the Army, the rest were Army spouses. They all lived close to town, but I had to face a long trip back to the battery after midnight. Sometimes I would sleep on the couch at a friend's place, then leave around 3:30 A.M. in order to arrive back at Charlie by dawn. As inconvenient as this routine was, I could not have survived three years in Germany without it. When I played basketball, I could remove my military uniform and escape my responsibilities as an officer for a little while. (I'd always have to let my battery commander know if I were leaving Hardheim, however. Freedom was never complete.) Basketball was my element; it was a sport I had grown up in, and returning to it made me feel at home. Being a member of a women's team also gave me the rare chance to relax and spend time with friends. At the battery, I had to maintain a certain amount of distance from everyone—I was a single female officer, which meant I had to be on my guard. But when I played basketball, I was just one of twelve women on my team—I didn't have to be anyone's authority figure.

In the summer of 1981 our unit began preparing for the Annual Service Practice (ASP), a live fire exercise that would take place at the end of September. The Army usually chose Crete as the location for the exercise, because whenever it was held in the States, some soldiers, facing the bleak prospect of being shipped back to Germany for another year or so, would find their daring and go AWOL as soon as they set foot on American soil.

There was a lot of pressure from above to produce outstanding results on the ASP, so we practiced rigorously throughout the summer. We worked feverishly every day, sweating through our crew drills no matter what the weather. Each day the schedule was the same. We'd wake up, form up, bring our equipment to the missile site and start our routine checks—monthlies, weeklies and dailies—designed to monitor missile security and combat-readiness. Commanders from the battalion and the

168

brigade would come out often to inspect us. Even our practices were graded.

One small bonus was that many of our usual tasks took a backseat to this evaluation. Everyone in the battalion knew to go easy on a unit that was preparing for Crete. It made life a bit simpler, but we still had to deal with the ORE team, which was always hovering, fierce as hornets, and making us extremely nervous.

The normal progression of a lieutenant in an Air Defense battery was from Launcher Platoon Leader to IFC [Integrated Fire Control] platoon leader to XO, and then, customarily once he or she was promoted to the rank of captain, to battery commander. By the time we had begun preparing for our ASP that summer, I was ready to take the next step. I didn't know if I'd be promoted all the way to battery commander before I left Germany, but I knew I'd learned quite a bit in the Launcher Area. Now I wanted a job in the IFC.

In the Launcher Control Area, I was in charge of the maintenance of the missiles. In the IFC, however, I'd learn, among other things, how the radars interfaced with the missiles, and how the BCO found and identified targets. The Command Post, where the battery commander sat, was also in the IFC—and was the focal point for any decision making. Being an IFC platoon leader would give me a much broader understanding of the complex inner workings of the entire Nike Hercules system. I was ready for some new challenges, and I wanted to see what life was like in a different battery. It was not uncommon, after all, for lieutenants to move from battery to battery within a battalion. In fact, it happened all the time.

In late August, I heard of an IFC platoon leader position becoming available at Delta Battery, a sister battery within the battalion. I already knew Delta's commander from my BCO classes, and thought he'd be a great guy to work for. His name was Captain Dave Porter, and, like Captain Smith, he was a graduate of West Point as well.

Captain Porter was younger than Captain Smith by about six years. Because he was nearer my age, I thought that perhaps I'd have better luck with him as a commander. He seemed easier to get along with, and his personal credo, "Work hard and play hard"—sounded just fine to me.

The next day, I got in my car and drove to Headquarters to meet with Colonel Baumgarten. I told him I'd heard about the position at Delta, and asked him if I could be transferred. He knew I'd been getting antsy at Charlie Battery, and was perfectly willing to send me somewhere else, but he didn't know if Delta should be the place until he figured out what else was going on within the battalion. Within a week or so, I received a phone call from the colonel. He agreed to transfer me to Delta as soon as my unit returned from the ASP exercise in Crete.

On a beautiful Saturday afternoon in late September, forty soldiers from my unit flew to Crete on C-141's—those huge, noisy, windowless planes we used to jump out of in Airborne School. As soon as we arrived on the island, we settled into our military billets, which were located about eight miles from where the missile launch was scheduled to take place. The ASP evaluation would begin the moment we left the garrison area and drove through the gates of the training area on Monday morning. If weather permitted, and all systems were go, we would end the exercise early Wednesday afternoon with the firing of a Nike Hercules missile carrying a conventional warhead into the Aegean Sea.

We spent a wild Saturday night drinking *ouzo* in a local bar in Iráklion. Starting on Sunday, however, we observed an 8:00 P.M. curfew every night. From then on, no one would be allowed to leave the site until we fired out on Wednesday afternoon.

Over the next few days, we worked from morning till night performing hundreds of minute checks on the missile, the launcher, the radars, and the IFC computer. On the day of the launch, everything was running smoothly. The sky was a solid and luminous blue. The launch would proceed as planned.

Because of our close proximity to the launch pad, and in order to avoid possibly being hit with flying debris from the explosion, none of us sitting inside the Launcher Control Trailer was allowed to watch the missile take off. My job during the exercise was to relay commands over a headset from inside the trailer to the IFC—the section of the Nike Hercules site that regulated the missiles' flight patterns. My soldiers told me they had heard that the last female lieutenant in Crete had gotten scared during the missile launch and had screamed into her headset. They were taking bets that I would scream, too.

When the missile finally lifted, the noise wasn't all that frightening, but knowing the men were expecting it, I let out a small squeak—just so they wouldn't be disappointed. Everyone laughed on the line.

Scoring 98 out of 100 percent on our evaluation gave us another reason for elation, especially since Captain Smith had promised that if we scored high, he would shave off all his hair. Well, we kept our part of the bargain, and so did he. The guys in the battery wanted me to shave my head, too,

but I said no. Esprit de corps was fine, but I had to draw the line somewhere.

Delta Battery was situated near Pforzheim, a city at the edge of the Black
Forest, about sixty-five miles southwest of Charlie Battery and twenty-five
miles northwest of Stuttgart. Pforzheim had been a German industrial
town before World War II, but was nearly demolished by British bombs
in 1945. Since then, the city was rebuilt, and in 1989 Pforzheim signed
a sister-city pact with Guernica in Spain. The bombing of Guernica on 26
April 1937 not only marked the first tragic aerial bombing of civilians, but
it also destroyed the notion of a containable battlefield, deeming previous
assumptions about limited warfare obsolete, and setting a terrifying precedent for all wars to come.

After the little town of Hardheim, I felt fortunate to be living within
walking distance of a city of approximately 100,000 people. American
soldiers in Europe often live near tiny villages with a population of two
hundred or so. Pforzheim was large enough for us to blend in comfortably;
we were less conspicuous, and therefore less vulnerable, in our uniforms.

Delta Battery was divided into three areas. The Admin Area—consisting of the soldiers' barracks, the dining facility, the motor pool, and the
staff offices—was in Bückenberg. The IFC was five miles south, in a small
town called Wurmburg, and the Launcher Control Area was between the
two towns.

The Delta IFC was a makeshift site—with only one concrete structure
called the Ready Building, which contained six rooms, among them a
sleeping bay with ten bunk beds, a kitchen with a refrigerator, cabinets,
a sink, and an old beat-up stove, and an office for me that was rather
monastic, with just a desk and a small single bed. The bed was for the Duty
Officer remaining within the IFC all night. There was also a game room
in the building, where the soldiers worked out with some free weights they
had brought from home. We kept a pool table in there for a little while,
until the felt cover was ripped in the course of Army wear and tear. Soldiers
can be hard on their toys.

There was only one bathroom in the building, with two sinks, one small
mirror, a toilet, a urinal, and a disgustingly dirty shower. As hard as we
tried, we could never get that shower clean. The engineers from Karlsruhe
(where we received our logistic support) wouldn't help us with any building
renovations, either, because the Nike Hercules system was a dying breed.
In two and a half years, the missile site would be closed.

171

The sixth room was the battery's communications center. Our unit didn't have the luxury of regular telephones, but we did have a switchboard that could put us in contact with any country in the world. Getting it to work was another matter. It was no surprise that the Army's phone system in Germany was called "Hitler's Revenge." To make an outgoing call, we had to go through the "Switch"—a weary-voiced operator who faithfully manned the phones twenty-four hours a day, seven days a week. To reach the battery from the outside, callers had to first contact the Stuttgart operator, and then ask for Wurmburg Military. There was one civilian phone in the Admin Area, but it was reserved for emergencies. Any personal calls had to be made from home.

Our work area consisted of five vans—some were old, discarded refrigerator truck vans, others were trailers that the Army had newly purchased specifically for the Nike Hercules system. They looked like the backs of moving vans—about six feet high, six feet wide, and twenty feet long. One van held the radar controls; another housed the computer that created the artificial targets we used in our training; the third contained all the unit's tools and repair equipment; and the fourth transmitted the classified message traffic. The fifth, the Battery Control Van, was my domain.

Each van rested on metal stilts about three feet off the ground. A central building made of wood and concrete with similarly raised wood floors, and five six-by-six foot openings around it, adjoined four of the five trailers, which were in a kind of backward E formation (E), and sealed to the building with tar paper and shingles to protect their interiors from the elements. To gain access to any of the trailers, one first had to pass through the central building. Off to the right side of the central building and adjoined to the fifth trailer, stood a Command Post made from two Expando vans bolted together. The five vans, the central building, and the Command Post formed the nucleus of the IFC area—a secret, self-contained world that seemed impregnable.

Sometimes at night I'd steal away from the vans and climb to the top of the dark hill just to watch the lights of the Launcher Area—a large, glittering rectangle—shining in the distance like a constellation brought to earth.

As Delta Battery's IFC platoon leader, I was once again in charge of the welfare and training of anywhere between fifty and seventy soldiers (depending upon fluctuations in the battery's personnel assignments), and the maintenance of equipment. I was the Emergency Message Action System (EMAS) officer, a Battery Control Officer (BCO), the Classified Documents Custodian, and the Communications Security (COMSEC) Custodian. These last two were highly sensitive positions, since they involved classified information that had to be carefully safeguarded. A number of times I had seen officers reprimanded or suddenly relieved of duty for security violations.

I was also the Redeye Officer. The Redeye was a tubelike weapon fired from the shoulder—a very low-level type of Air Defense. Redeye teams were usually found within Infantry battalions, but there were a few in Air Defense Artillery. It was the Redeye Officer's job to deploy teams on missions that required shooting down enemy helicopters and other incoming aircraft. Because Redeyes were intended for use near the front lines, the position of Redeye Officer was coded as having a high risk of exposure to combat, and women were barred from holding it. However, the position happened to be an integral part of the IFC Platoon Leader's job at Delta Battery, and I thought it was ridiculous to have to turn it over to someone else just because I was a woman.

This was when I first learned about expediency; how things in the Army are not always done according to strict regulations. My conclusion was confirmed a few years later when, based on interviews I conducted with American Army commanders in Europe for a 1985 U.S. Army Logistics Center Study entitled "The Use of Women in the Forward Support Battalion," I discovered that, out of sheer necessity, women had been temporarily filling combat support positions, such as tank and truck mechanics, which were technically closed to them. Of course, this depended on the attitude of the leadership within the particular unit. When there was a maintenance job to do within a combat unit, for instance, a job that was too large or complicated for the unit's own maintenance section to handle, a support team from the Forward Support Battalion would be sent in. And if that support team happened to include women (leftover from the period prior to when the Army changed its configuration in 1984–1985), then those women, who were gradually being transferred out of the Forward Support Battalion, would be allowed, meanwhile, to remain a part of the team. Soldiers in the field knew that if their unit were called into a conflict, there would be no time to bring in male replacements, and these women would continue to perform their tasks.

I remained the Redeye Officer at Delta for as long as I was the IFC platoon leader.

When I left Charlie Battery, I was coming off a high of having done well in Crete, and was looking forward to the environment at Delta Battery as being more compatible with my style of working. Captain Porter, the battery commander, seemed to have a hands-off approach to leadership, and to be open to new ideas. At first, I was very excited to be working for him. He was a West Point graduate, class of '78, and a former football player—good-looking, tall. Despite his West Point training, though, Captain Porter never ran much PT. He smoked a lot, and he had a favorite expression. Invariably, during the course of a conversation, Porter would sit at his desk, squint his eyes, take a long drag from his cigarette, look you square in the face, and say, *"I don't give a shit."* People said Porter ran his battery like a football team. He was also the type of man, I discovered, who would slather a coat of white paint over a rotting door jamb to make the problem look pretty, rather than fix it. Perhaps this was a byproduct of his West Point training, a system that did not encourage delving into anything too deeply. Just get the job done and move on.

The effect of this sort of training can make people seem very efficient, but it can also create tunnel vision, and—deadly for an officer—cause people to lose their human touch. The private changes the tire, the mission is completed, and you forget to thank the private. When you become too task-oriented, you can begin to think of life as a series of assignments to be accomplished, and then forgotten before you go on to the next. I know this, because I have sometimes suffered from West Point-itis myself. Nevertheless, I was surprised to find Captain Porter so different from what I had expected. He seemed to be such a hard worker who got along well with people, and cared for his soldiers; in other words, he seemed to be a good leader. But, gradually, I began to realize that perhaps he wasn't quite as dedicated to the welfare of his soldiers as I had thought.

It didn't take me long to settle in on the Hill, which was what we called the IFC. My days would begin at 5:30 A.M., with a formation in the Admin Area. There I would receive my daily work instructions from Captain Porter, or from First Lieutenant Frank Parrott, his XO.

Porter had two pals. One was Parrott, the other was Second Lieutenant John Corey, the MP platoon leader. Privately, I called them "the Three Stooges."

Parrott and Porter were like Pete and Re-Pete. They were a dangerous combination. Parrott was constantly worried about covering his own ass and Porter's, but no one else's. He was about five-ten, had dirty blond hair, and a terrible slouch; his hips always seemed to walk ahead of his body. Frank never did anything he didn't want to do—and Porter never pushed him. If you ever pissed Frank off, you could be sure he'd find a way to make you pay for it. His wife was in the Army, too. She worked on a *Kaserne*, managing an Officer's Club, and was promoted to captain before Frank. I thought that was great.

John had been in the Army as an enlisted soldier before earning his commission as an officer. He was also about five-ten, blond, wore a moustache, and a had a nice muscular body. John genuinely cared about his soldiers, but his style was a little too casual for my taste. He was what you might call a guy who liked to "stop and smell the roses"—he'd take his own sweet time about everything. In addition, John thought he was God's gift to women. He'd be nice to your face, but then talk trash about you behind your back. There wasn't much love lost between us.

When I had received my orders from either Porter or Parrott, I would pass them along to my section chief, who in turn would transmit them to the platoon. After spending my first day getting used to the battery, and discovering that most of my soldiers were down in Crete going through the same type of ASP exercise that I had just finished, I was assigned to all-night IFC duty, which was where I met Sergeant Christopher Jones.

Chris was one of the most respected soldiers in the battalion. A handsome, black sergeant from Virginia, Chris had a soft southern accent, a moustache that barely skirted the regulation length, and a bodybuilder's physique. He was a weightlifter, and had a wonderful sense of humor, although he and his crewmen did have a terrible habit of calling the soldiers in the Launcher Control Area "Rail Apes." Chris said it was because the IFC people figured that monkeys could do their job. All they had to do was push the missiles out of the barns and make sure the simulator was on so the Nike Hercs wouldn't, literally, fly off their rails. They also guarded the missiles and took care of maintenance, but the guys in the IFC didn't think much of that. They would laugh about how the launcher soldiers' knuckles dragged through the dirt on their way to the Admin Area.

Chris said that the first time we met he didn't know how to speak to me—like a gentleman or a soldier. I thought he was a clown—always playing for laughs—but as I got to know him, I saw another side to his character that was sensitive and warm. Chris had an air of independence about him that I admired. In this respect, he reminded me of Mike Truxel.

Chris and I loved working together in the IFC. We made life on that remote site in Germany a little more bearable for one another. People from the battery would often see us together—in the Battery Control Van, with

Chris sitting in a chair immediately to my left, advising me during crew drills, which would last for hours, or standing around in freezing cold weather, burning classified documents and laughing to keep warm.

One time we put the documents into the burn barrel—a fifty-five gallon drum punctured with holes—then poured gasoline into it, leaving a thin trail of gas for a fuse. When we lit the gas, the whole barrel blew up. People came running from every direction. Chris and I grabbed each other and screamed, laughing until tears ran down our faces.

The other soldiers thought that either something was going on between us, or else we were both just plain crazy. But Chris used to say that a person needed to be a little crazy to stay sane on-site. Sometimes Chris and I would spend all night together locked inside the windowless COM-SEC van. He was worried that this didn't look too kosher, but I told him I didn't care. As far as I was concerned, people would simply have to get used to it. After all, no one would have blinked an eye if there had been two men together in the van.

Chris was one of the most experienced Nike Herc NCOs I'd ever met. Of course, a lot of the experience he received was on-the-job training. More often than not, that's what happened in Air Defense. Enlisted soldiers were given only about eight weeks of formal advanced training, as the joke goes, "to show them the exits in the van." Chris said success or failure as a "scope dope" (a soldier who monitored the radar screens) came down to having intense self-discipline coupled with intuition. It was a talent. Often, the officer sitting in the IFC van was nothing more than a rookie lieutenant, while the NCOs were the ones with real experience. Like Chris, they tended to be E-5's, E-6's, or E-7's, having served eight or nine years in the Army. The Battery Control Assistant (BCA) manned a radar scope to the left of the Battery Control Officer (BCO), and the Acquisition Operator kept watch on a similar scope to the right. The only person legally allowed to push the button, however, was the BCO, who also had to understand and infallibly respond to a host of tactical alerts—all with split-second timing.

The fourth person on the crew would wait for the target to be locked into place by the computer. Once it was tracked, a confirmatory message would be sent back to the van. The computer emitted a frequency like morse code. A "friendly" aircraft had the same frequency and could emit a response. If the aircraft did not emit a friendly response, it was identified as negative, and considered a foe.

176

If one was sitting inside the van when this happened during a tactical exercise, one would hear something like this:

BCA: *Target. Inbound. Negative SIF, IFF.*
BCO: *Designate!*

This meant that the incoming aircraft had been identified as hostile and the crews would then prepare to fire. The BCA and BCO would speak over the microphone to the Radar Control Van, and when their radars located the target, the BCO would get a message from the radar van to "Track!"

It would then be up to the BCO to decide whether to engage, or to drop the track. If the decision were to engage, the crew in the BCO van would check one more time to see whether the aircraft was friendly. If not, the BCO would give the warning, *"About to engage."*

Then the BCO would push the button and say: *"Fire."*

When we were up to speed, we could complete this entire process in less than twenty seconds.

Whether we went nuclear was determined by NATO. We often simulated going nuclear in our exercises. Our leadership believed in preparing us for the worst case scenario, presumably so we would be able to handle anything. It gave us a rather all-or-nothing view of warfare, somewhat skewed toward the catastrophic, but it was never dull.

Though the president gave us our nuclear clearance, it was the Air Force that established most of our rules. They seemed terribly nervous about the Army having all of these missiles. They called us "Duck Hunters," and balked at what they believed to be the Air Defenders' earthbound philosophy: "Shoot everything down and sort it out on the ground." Or, put even more crudely, "If it flies, it dies."

The Air Force set up a complicated morass of barriers, flight patterns, and zones. If an incoming aircraft didn't follow their carefully prescribed patterns, they would counsel us, then, and only then, should we treat it as a foe, and blow it out of the sky.

I had two section chiefs—Sergeant Fielding and Sergeant Wood. It would be hard to find two more opposite men.

Sergeant Fielding was nicknamed "the Mouse." The missile crews walked all over him, which made him inefficient at his job.

The other section chief was Sergeant Wood, who had no trouble whatsoever at getting the soldiers to obey him. He was black, about six-four, and weighed almost three hundred pounds. Sergeant Wood was very knowledgeable about the Nike Hercules system, so he was a great asset to me. But his way of maintaining control was strictly by intimidation. Sometimes I found his tactics a little hard to take.

One day, Sergeant Wood stomped into my office and said, "You know, Lieutenant Barkalow, if a firefight ever breaks out here, I'm going to shoot all the women."

As though this were not an attempt to frighten me, I calmly asked, "Sergeant Wood, why would you do that?"

"So they won't be in my way," he said.

"Sergeant," I told him, "you're a bag of hot air. If you're ever caught in a firefight, the only thing on your mind will be saving your own ass."

On another occasion, he confronted me and insisted I was out to get him. I knew he was testing me again, trying to find out what I was made of. It was his way of showing me his power. When I ignored his absurd accusation, he accused me of being prejudiced against black soldiers.

That made me so angry, I stood up and said indignantly, "Sergeant Wood, if I were prejudiced against black soldiers, you certainly would have realized it before now. There's nothing more to discuss. Now, get the hell out of my office!" He turned and left, and I never again had another confrontation with him.

Despite the occasional challenge to my authority, the male soldiers at Delta seemed to have no problem accepting me as their platoon leader. I must say, however, that many of them didn't seem to know what to make of me. A few of my troops even gave me the nickname "Jane Wayne." When soldiers from the IFC would have to supplement security in the Launcher Area, and I would head over there carrying a PRC-77 radio (known affectionately as a Prick-77), the guys simply couldn't stop themselves from making fun of Jane Wayne running around the Launcher Area with a Prick on her back.

The Launcher Platoon Leader was Lieutenant Larry Perkins. Larry and I had to communicate daily because of the integrated checks between the Launcher Control Area and the IFC, but it soon became apparent that he'd been working at Delta Battery for nearly four months without being BCO qualified. I finally asked Larry whether he was ever the least bit curious about the reason why every other officer in the battery was pulling BCO duty except him.

No, he said, he hadn't thought about it.

When Colonel Baumgarten heard that Larry was not yet BCO qualified, he locked him on-site at the BOC for a month until he passed his exams.

Typically, two warrant officers would alternate being on call for Nike Herc repairs twenty-four hours a day. Warrant Officer Bill Moss, however, was the only warrant officer at the IFC, so he did have an unusually heavy workload. He was always on call, which made him cranky.

Bill and I got along all right until I learned that warrant officers had a reputation for jerry-rigging equipment—in other words, giving a quick fix without bothering to check the manuals. Parts for the Nike Hercules system could be exceedingly hard to come by. We often made do with whatever we had on hand. Bill's repairs were temporary, he said, until the inspection was over; he'd go back and fix the equipment properly when he had more time. But, somehow, the time never seemed to come. Many of Bill's repairs rarely lasted beyond a single evaluation; sometimes, not even that long.

When a critical part of the system was down, and stayed down for at least four hours, the warrants were supposed to inform Battalion Maintenance. Every month a report was filed of each battery's "downtime." The less downtime officially recorded, the better off you were. Consequently, if a warrant thought the weapon system could be fixed in less than four hours, he might not call it in. If it took longer than that, he still might try to fix it without letting anybody know, and before anyone showed up at the battery for another inspection.

The problem was, when Bill quick fixed one part of the system, it invariably had an effect on an equally critical part somewhere else. Naturally, this wouldn't be discovered until we were in the middle of a battalion ORE, which would cause us to fail the evaluation, and put heat on the battalion commander, which would put heat on the battery commander, which, in turn, would put heat on me.

As IFC platoon leader, I was held directly accountable for Bill's actions. No matter how trivial or extreme the offense, as conventional military wisdom goes, a commanding officer is responsible for everything a unit does or fails to do. At my level, this meant that I was responsible for every action committed, or omitted, by the soldiers in my platoon. It was a peculiar way to live in the world, as if I were being trailed by a platoon of inextricable, wayward, yet autonomous shadows.

On the other hand, being a female officer seemed to have little appreciable difference on the success or failure of the women in my platoon within the battery. During the course of my tour at Delta, I had three women assigned to me, but I lost them one by one.

The first was Joan Keegan, my communications sergeant. She left the battery on a normal rotation not long after I arrived. Joan was a fine soldier and I was sorry to lose her. Her successors, unfortunately, were not as good. Mary Edwards, the second of my female soldiers, was an E-5, married to an E-6. The two of them worked together in the IFC—hardly a bower of marital bliss. The woman was overweight, and was constantly struggling to stay on a diet. This didn't endear her to many people at Delta, although it happened to be a period in Air Defense when PT wasn't a high priority. A number of the male mechanics, the old NCOs, for example, had enormous beer bellies. They claimed to need them as a place to set their cups of coffee in the morning. In the early eighties, there wasn't the same kind of rigorous physical fitness testing that goes on today, so overweight men were more or less tolerated. The same clemency, however, was not extended to females. A potbellied woman just didn't do much for the image of women in the Army.

Mary's husband, meanwhile, had his own problems. He had the unfortunate habit of bad-mouthing the officers in front of their troops, which eventually cost him his career after eleven years in the service.

The couple was going through a divorce, and it was hell for all of us. We lived out of each other's pockets in that platoon. It was too damn small for people not to overhear their continual bickering. Telling the couple not to bring their worries to work would have been ridiculous, but their relationship was becoming a total headache for me.

One day, I'd had enough. I called them both into my office for counseling. I did not profess to be a marriage counselor, but it was within my power to send them to one, or, if necessary, to get them the proper legal advice. Although they agreed to try and straighten out the situation, nothing seemed to work. The bickering persisted and I realized that I would have to do something about it on my own.

I remembered that Mary had expressed interest in training soldiers, so I shipped her off to the Admin Area, where the battery's training section was—without her husband.

The third woman at Delta Battery was simply a mess. She was an MP sergeant who believed she had gotten a raw deal while she was working downrange, and was extremely bitter about it.

The woman had been assigned to the Admin Area, but she argued so much with everybody there, she lasted only a month. By the time she was sent to me, her attitude had gone completely sour. She couldn't seem to see past her anger, and had developed a real knack for pissing people off. When people would say to her, "Hi, Sarge!" she would answer, "Don't call me 'Sarge.' A sarge is a fish, and I'm not a fish!" She wanted to be called *Sergeant.* Although I tried on numerous occasions to talk to this woman about her attitude, she remained steadfast in her belligerence.

"Look," I said, "I know you've had a bad go-around, but I don't care whose fault it is—you're starting fresh here."

Unfortunately, the woman was convinced that everyone at the battery was out to get her, and so she would try to get them first. She didn't get very far in the IFC, however, and with nothing but a year of largely negative evaluation reports, she didn't stand much of a chance of being promoted. Eventually she left the Army and I knew what people would think: they'd generalize about whether women should be in the military from one bad example. But there was really nothing I could do. In the Army, you can't just quit if you don't like your job. You have to stick with it for a while, and be flexible, and somehow hope you survive.

28 November 1981. I received my promotion to first lieutenant, along with ninety-six percent of the other second lieutenants who entered the Regular Army in the spring of 1980. The promotion was fairly automatic—the ceremony took place eighteen months from the day my classmates and I had graduated, as well as all the other commissioned lieutenants from whatever schools they'd attended.

Our entire unit was lined up in formation for the occasion—the Headquarters Platoon, the IFC Platoon, the MP Platoon, and the Launcher Platoon. Each of the four platoon sergeants stood in front of their respective platoons, and First Sergeant Jeffries called the battery to attention. Captain Porter assumed command, and called: "Post!" then executed an About Face, while the platoon leaders (officers) and platoon sergeants (NCOs) exchanged places—the officers walking to the front of the formation, and the NCOs stepping to the back. Colonel Baumgarten, who'd been watching from the steps of the Admin Area building, took his cue when Captain Porter turned to face him. The two men exchanged salutes, and Porter approached the colonel and stood at his side. The Dragon called out, "Lieutenant Barkalow, front and center!" I left my position in front of my platoon and marched up to Colonel Baumgarten, stopping five feet in front of him. I saluted and said, "Sir, Lieutenant Barkalow reports as ordered." Colonel Baumgarten turned to the battalion adjutant. "Post the orders!" he commanded. The adjutant then read, with minimal expression, the form letter that would change my status and raise my pay grade. "The president of the United States has reposed special trust and confidence in the patriotism, valor, fidelity, and abilities of Carol A. Barkalow. In view of these qualities and her demonstrated potential for increased responsibility, she is therefore promoted in the U.S. Army to first lieutenant." As the battalion adjutant spoke these words, Colonel Baumgarten pinned the subdued black first lieutenant's bar on my collar, and gave me a short, motivational pep talk about all the good things I could look forward to at this stage of my career. Then he did something totally out of character— he leaned over and kissed me on the cheek. Sensing my surprise and embarrassment, the colonel quickly said, "I kiss all the female lieutenants I promote."

I didn't want to make a big deal out of it, but I wished he hadn't done it. A few of the guys in my platoon teased me about it later. I just shrugged them off. They knew I hadn't asked for any special treatment.

Because the IFC was five miles away from the Admin Area, I felt as if I were in charge of my own little command. I tried to run it that way, too, which sometimes turned out to be a mistake. You have to strike a delicate balance between ambition and obedience early on in your military career. And while you don't want to squelch your enthusiasm, you have to be the one to figure out which of your ideas are acceptable, and which are not.

In the spring of 1982, I decided to institute a No-hat Policy in the IFC. This meant that the soldiers, who were obliged by regulations to wear their hats outdoors at all times, wouldn't have to wear them as long as they remained inside the gates of the IFC. My reason for this new policy was to protect the soldiers from getting into trouble when they were spotted outside "without a cover," since most of them left their hats inside the vans while they were working. The IFC wasn't a very big area, after all, with the furthest distance between the Ready Building and the vans being only about ten yards.

I told Captain Porter my idea, and since he seemed to take it in stride, responding neither positively nor negatively, I activated the policy. The soldiers were pleased. It seemed fine for a couple of weeks, until the brigade commander, Colonel "Wild Bill" Freeman, decided to pay one of his surprise visits to Delta Battery.

Colonel Freeman was one of the older colonels in Germany at the time. He looked like a philosopher, I thought—tall, thin, and wrinkled, with a large nose. He spoke like a philosopher, too—slowly and deliberately, as if he'd been pondering what he was going to say all day long. He'd utter a few words, then pause. A few more, and there'd be another pause. Then a look of deep concentration would settle on his face.

I always thought that Colonel Freeman got a kick out of me because he liked outgoing officers who were candid about what they felt. I also thought I reminded him of his daughter—an image that often gets projected onto young women soldiers by senior officers.

Colonel Freeman first drove to the Admin Area to pick up Captain Porter and Lieutenant Parrott, who would escort him around the site. I got a call from Porter's office, letting me know they were on their way.

I stood at attention, hatless, beside the gate of the IFC when the three officers drove up. I walked over to the car to open the door for our brigade commander. I saluted respectfully, eyes front. But I couldn't help noticing a confused expression on the colonel's face as he emerged from the backseat.

"Lieutenant Barkalow, where is your hat?"

Proudly and without hesitation I replied, "Sir, I have deemed this IFC a no-hat area."

Colonel Freeman didn't say another word. Porter and Parrott had kept their hats on during this exchange, but when the colonel remained calm at my declaration, they removed them. I was feeling pleased with myself, satisfied that the colonel wasn't questioning my new policy. But I couldn't have been more mistaken.

Later the same afternoon, I received a call from the Dragon.

"Barkalow," he said, "Listen to me, and listen good. You will get those goddamn hats back on your heads and you will keep them there!"

"Sir! Yes, Sir!"

I was being scolded like a plebe again, jumping to attention even as I was talking on the phone. That was the end of my No-hat Policy. The soldiers went back to wearing their hats, and leaving them in the vans.

It was shortly after this incident that I began having real problems with Captain Porter. Since the Nike Hercules system was being phased out of the Army, it had become very difficult to get replacements when the soldiers rotated to other assignments. We were given some relief from batteries that were closing farther north, but it wasn't enough.

We had reached a critical point for manning the site by April. I had three IFC crews, with only ten people in each; normally I would have had fifteen. Because an IFC crew required at least ten people to function, and the system demanded daily checks, there was barely any leeway for soldiers to be sick or unavailable. I kept losing people to attrition, and wasn't getting replacements. With people dropping out, it was becoming harder to maintain three full crews. The crews would rotate duties—one would perform daily checks, while the other would do chores around the battery. The third would then take off and get some badly needed rest.

When I no longer had enough people to maintain three full crews, I decided to consolidate to two crews, fourteen people in each, who would work on alternate days if the battery were at hot status, and take turns doing chores and dailies, if we were at regular status. Obviously, this put a lot of pressure on the troops, and demanded even more of their time, but I felt that it had to be done.

The following morning, I assembled my platoon sergeant and section chiefs, and told them we'd be rearranging the platoon into two crews instead of three. They complained a little, because it meant they'd each be working longer hours. One of the section leaders (the most junior) would lose his section altogether. But personnel was short, which we were powerless to change, so we rearranged the crews that afternoon.

Later that same day, Captain Porter phoned me at my station on the Hill. "Lieutenant Barkalow," he said, "I need four people from your platoon to combine with the MPs. They need people to sit in the towers."

He told me that the MPs needed these soldiers for at least thirty days. I reminded him that they already had some of my people, and, at this point, my guys were having to pull their own guard duty in the IFC. But this news seemed to be of no consequence. That's when I knew that, one way or another, it was time to take a stand. Certainly it's important for a lieutenant to obey the commander, but it is also important to take care of the soldiers. My decision would depend on what I felt was my immediate priority—loyalty to the unit commander, or loyalty to the platoon. In this case, I chose the platoon.

"Sir," I said, "I don't think I'll be able to give you those people. I'm already down to two crews as it is, and I wouldn't have enough soldiers to man them. Don't you think there's another solution somewhere?"

"No," he said curtly.

"Well, Sir," I said, "I'm sorry, but I can't supplement the MPs without seriously degrading my ability to accomplish my mission in the IFC."

There was silence on the other end of the phone, so I hung up and went back to observing dailies. I didn't quite hang up *on* the captain, not exactly. There just wasn't anything more to say.

The reasons for my decision were twofold. My primary allegiance was to my platoon, and so I chose to intercede on their behalf since the captain didn't seem to appreciate fully what had become a difficult situation for them. Moreover, I felt that perhaps Captain Porter was placing his pal

John Corey's needs over those of my soldiers, which was something I didn't want to support. I was tired of Porter playing favorites.

Eventually, I learned that John had apparently allowed too many of his own people to take leave at one time. He needed to make up for his error by filling in with whomever he could find. It was an internal problem within the MP platoon, not a legitimate reason for me to give up my people at all, or so I thought.

Every decision has its consequences, however, and this one was no exception. The working relationship between Captain Porter and me was permanently scarred. What had been an attitude of cool tolerance turned into open hostility, more or less. Not only had I brought down the wrath of Porter, but that of Parrott and Corey, as well. So be it, I thought.

About a month later, another incident occurred in which my authority was put to the test. Since Sergeant Fielding had been doing a less-than-splendid job in the IFC, I gave him a job overseeing the cleaning of the barracks, while I took care of the IFC myself, doing his job in addition to my own. Porter, meanwhile, had met with Sergeant Fielding privately and worked out a reassignment. Rather than following my order to work in the Admin Area, Fielding had asked Porter for the Housing Engineer's job—a notoriously cushy position that was usually given as a reward to overworked soldiers who had done well and needed a break. Without consulting me, Porter made Fielding the Housing Engineer. The old Army truism—"Screw up and move up"—seemed to be at work again.

I felt powerless. Not only had my authority as Fielding's platoon leader been disregarded, I was at a loss to explain to my good soldiers why a poor performer had been rewarded with an easy job. I told myself I'd just hold on until July, when Porter would be leaving this command.

At the same time, I began looking for a way out of Delta Battery. At first I thought there must be something wrong with me—here I was in my second battery, and I wanted to leave it. I knew it wasn't the soldiers; the problem was with the command section. Finally, in May, I heard that Colonel Thomas Giordano, a brigade commander in 32d AADCOM, was being promoted to the rank of brigadier general. Colonel Giordano was interviewing for an aide.

Each battalion had submitted someone for the job; my name had been forwarded from headquarters along with four others. Giordano was a West Point graduate, and so I felt certain he would want a West Pointer as his aide. Sure enough, three of the five candidates who were being considered were Academy graduates, and two of those three were women—Angela Parker and I.

185

I went for an interview at 1300 hours at Colonel Giordano's office in Darmstadt, about an hour-and-a-half drive north of Delta. I wore my Class A uniform, and even put on a little makeup. I wanted that job.

Colonel Giordano was a distinguished-looking man. He was tall, with dark wavy hair graying at the temples, and a pleasant smile. We shook hands when we met; his grip was strong, and his gaze was steady and direct. He seemed very personable, and I liked him at once.

The colonel invited me to sit down in his office, and together we discussed the responsibilities of the aide's position. As his aide, he told me, I would make all of his travel arrangements and accompany him on those trips approximately three days a week. Colonel Giordano said he didn't believe in working on weekends unless something important came up—a philosophy I certainly appreciated. He asked me when I'd be available to start. "Whenever you need me," I told him. As far as I was concerned, there was nothing tying me to Pforzheim.

When I left the colonel's office, I felt good about the interview. I had wanted to be a general's aide for a long time. Some called it a glorified secretary's job, but it had its benefits—mostly the prestige of being selected for the post, and the chance to travel and be exposed to top-level staffs.

It took Colonel Giordano nearly three weeks to make his decision. I learned of his choice through Frank Parrott, who had a friend stationed at Darmstadt. As I had predicted, the position went to one of the three West Pointers, but it was given neither to me nor Angela. The job was given to our male classmate.

I was crushed. Colonel Baumgarten had called to break the news to me officially, and to relay a message from Colonel Giordano. Evidently he had said that I should spend as much time as possible as a platoon leader, because that was the best way to develop a successful career as an officer. While that may have been true, it seemed like a weak explanation. But there was nothing I could do. The decision had been made.

A few months later, Colonel Baumgarten admitted to me that I hadn't been chosen because I was a woman. A tainted reputation can cause real harm to a military career, I realized, and this would have been the picture: Good-looking, fast-burner, one-star general with single, blond, female aide—traveling together all over Germany for days at a time, dining together—sometimes late at night—sleeping in the same *Gasthaus*es, working closely for long hours. Questionable appearances might have led to rumors, which in turn might have affected my career as well as ruined Giordano's chances for further rank. He had enough to worry about in his position as general without having to look over his shoulder every time we went away together. I was still disappointed, but when the reason was explained to me, at least I felt I understood it.

The worst part of it, though, was that I was stuck at Delta Battery, with Captain Porter.

Earlier that year, I had been required to rate the performance of one of the men, who in my view had done a mediocre job, and to whom I couldn't honestly give a maximum rating. Since my experience at writing evaluations was limited, I had consulted Captain Porter on how to do this. I felt I had to lower the man's rating just enough to get his attention, but not enough to ruin him. At the time, Captain Porter had informed me that there was an item in the "Professionalism" category that, if rated below "1," which was the max, would effectively cripple one's career. It was a rating of "2" next to the statement: Displays Sound Judgment.

Because I didn't want to go that far, I gave him a "2" rating for the categories "Clear and Concise in Oral Communication" and "Is Adaptable to Changing Situations." Despite my intended generosity, the man I evaluated was furious over the less-than-max rating. He went to Colonel Baumgarten to complain about it. The Dragon called me in to see him. I told him I was adamant about keeping the rating, because I'd already given the man numerous chances to improve his performance. I felt it was my responsibility to show him his weaknesses. The rating stood.

When it finally came time for Captain Porter to leave Delta Battery, it was my turn to be rated. I was certainly not expecting a max rating from him, but I was surprised to see where Porter had hurled his poison darts. He had given me two "2" ratings: one for "Is Adaptable to Changing Situations"; the other for "Displays Sound Judgment"—precisely the category he had told me could destroy someone's career if the rating were not perfect. Fortunately, that has not been the case.

Captain Porter did not discuss my evaluation with me before he left the battery in July 1982. When it came time for his change of command ceremony, I took leave and flew to the States to have a short visit with my family. I didn't care to bid him farewell.

Captain Porter's replacement was Captain Nick Logan. Frank Parrott, Porter's XO, rotated out of the battery at the same time, and I was next in line for his job. Under Captain Logan, I became the XO, as well as the Voting Officer, the Tax Officer, the Nuclear, Biological, and Chemical Warfare Officer, the Dining Facility Officer, Office in Charge of the Unit

187

Lounge, and the Officer in Charge of NATO Secret Documents. Even though I had no formal training in accounting, I also was required to balance the unit lounge's books.

The relationship between a company commander and an XO is a peculiar one. While it's the commander's job to train and discipline the junior officer, the XO, in turn, can greatly affect the commander's career. In the commander's absence, the XO walks in his shoes.

A male commander and a female XO have to tread very carefully, however. Due to the chain of command, there is always a veil between them, a thin but substantial barrier out of necessity. The question is, how much of that veil do you dare to remove? How does a male commander treat a female subordinate whom he is willing to trust with his life? How does he *not* form a deep attachment to her?

Two men in a similar situation might acknowledge and express their fondness for one another by playing golf or shooting hoops together, but men and women tend to talk. Sometimes, Captain Logan told me, I was the only person to whom he would admit his screwups; but it took time for that relationship to develop. If I had been a man, we might have been even closer, because we could have spent more time together as friends.

And yet, given my previous experiences with commanders, it was a revelation to me that my new commander and I could become what I considered to be an extraordinary team.

Nick Logan's command philosophy was entirely different from any I had ever encountered. He was not a believer in leadership by force. "It might work for the short range," he said, "but not the long term. If you were in a burning house and people weren't moving, you'd pick them up and throw them out of the building. In an intense, spontaneous environment like combat, drastic measures are often necessary. But not in day-to-day life within the unit."

Captain Logan believed in the value of the carrot and the stick—he felt that you had to know when to kick people in the ass, and when to pat them on the back. Of course, the ideal situation was not to have to motivate people at all, he said, but to have them motivate themselves. What really meant the most to soldiers was the feeling that they mattered, that their contribution was valuable.

"Most people in the Army are not terribly talented," Captain Logan said. "We're just average people who, together, can achieve amazing things. Back home, one of my guys might be running a gas station, but in the Army, he's 'the Motor Sergeant.' He passes inspection and accomplishes something, and I think he gets a certain amount of satisfaction from that, and from knowing he can perform tasks which his civilian friends can't, or wouldn't even attempt."

More than either of my commanders, Captain Logan was a great supporter of PT. He'd say, "Why do PT? Well, when kids sit around saying, 'My Dad is meaner than your Dad,' they don't really want a mean Dad. In the Army, it's just being able to say 'Our unit is tougher than your unit—you ran four miles, we ran six.' It gives the soldiers something to brag about, and ties them together, particularly in units like the ones we have in Germany, where athletic facilities are limited. It's as if each of us were living in a six-by-eight-foot cell doing two hundred push-ups a day. Prisoners don't like push-ups, but they've got to do *something.*"

"Mainly," Captain Logan would say, "you do PT to get the soldiers so tired, they won't go out at night and tear up the town."

As one of my first and most enjoyable missions, Captain Logan assigned me to lead a surprise attack on the Battalion Operations Center during their preparations for the AAFCE TAC EVAL.

To determine an Air Defense unit's ability to defend itself, a second unit within the battalion is given the task of acting as aggressor by launching a raid on the site. Delta was chosen for the tasking this time, and I was made Officer in Charge of the Aggressor Unit. I took nine other soldiers with me, and together we plotted our takeover of the BOC. This was tactical level involvement—the kind of hands-on soldiering I'd been waiting for since I arrived in Germany.

The attack would not be a complete surprise, since the unit knew that another unit was going to come and aggress them at some point during their TAC EVAL. Everyone knew the best time to do this was at night, so our opportunities to take them unawares were narrowed even further.

Sergeant Jones and I drove a jeep out one afternoon to reconnoiter the area. The BOC site was fenced in and well protected. Along the northern border of the site was an open road, to the south were fields of grass— neither would make a good avenue of approach for our assault. Beyond the fields, however, was a stand of trees—woods deep enough to hide in. Of course, the soldiers at the BOC were aware of them, too. It was time to be inventive.

Although our adversaries already expected us to strike under cover of darkness, I decided it was still our best shot. We would wait for the final night of their deployment.

When the moment arrived, we split our small band of marauders into five teams of two soldiers each. Armed with blank M-16 ammo and a case of star clusters (explosive signal flares) we began our mission. Loaded into three jeeps, we left Delta Battery at midnight, ready to overtake a site manned by more than 150 soldiers. We daubed our faces with camouflage sticks and wore dark clothing to protect us against detection. I had forgotten how low the temperature could drop in Germany, even in the summertime, and had neglected to wear much underneath, so I nearly froze my ass off.

It took us forty-five minutes to reach our assembly point in the woods, about a mile and a half from our target. Before leaving Delta, I had drawn a simple diagram of the area and briefed the assault team. Since the BOC would presume we were going to attack within the next few hours, I said we should wait them out. At 1:00 A.M. we would begin to disperse from the assembly area and surround the site. We would launch our assault right before daybreak.

Four pairs of soldiers concealed themselves near the entrance to the woods. Sergeant Jones and I worked our way across the open field, crawling on our hands and knees for one hundred yards until we reached the road. At times we had to drop to our bellies and low-crawl through the high grass. The moon that night was bright enough to betray us.

The plan was, at the stroke of four, the pair of soldiers farthest from the fenceline would unleash a burst of fire. Then each team would open fire in sequence—at a rate of one minute apart. This was intended to create a diversion that would allow Chris and me to cut through the fence with a pair of bolt cutters, infiltrate the site, reach the command post, and capture it.

I had made one major tactical error, however, which I later realized could have been fatal to my troops in a real combat situation. At the last minute, I had decided to leave the star clusters back in the jeeps because I didn't want my soldiers blowing off their fingers in the dark.

At 0330 hours, from inside the fence, dozens of star clusters suddenly shot up overhead, illuminating the black sky. The BOC must have sent out a search party to look for us, we realized, and when they came upon our jeeps, they helped themselves to our star clusters. They were lighting them in hopes of routing us from our position.

But Chris and I pressed on to breach their defenses. In the confusion that followed, all ten of us took possession of the site. We made it back to Delta Battery just as the sun was rising and PT was ending. We were tired and ragged and looked like hell, but we had accomplished our mission.

Each member of the team received a certificate of achievement, commending us for our professionalism and discipline while infiltrating and destroying the enemy. My sense of accomplishment was tempered by the thought of how hellish it must be for soldiers in the field who live in fear of enemy ambush day after day. Despite the fact that I was in the Army, living the regimented life, I had never come close to knowing the true horrors of war. I accepted this as the reason we were always being called upon to prepare ourselves for that eventuality.

One morning in October while we were finishing a run, an evaluation team arrived unexpectedly in the IFC. The unit was returning to the Admin Area when my clerk, Sergeant Mulligan, stood on the steps and said, "Guess what, Ma'am? The AAFCE TAC EVAL team is on the Hill."

This was the first time the team had shown up at Delta Battery. Captain Logan was on leave, and I was acting commander.

We had practiced for this moment many times; I knew I had to get things going right away. Everyone from the unit was called back from their pass or leave, including Captain Logan, whom I immediately telephoned at his home five miles away. First Sergeant Jeffries and I then alerted the soldiers to begin making their checks on the equipment, in order to bring the unit up in status.

The evaluation was a three-day test designed to see how well the unit could perform its mission. We were plunged into a simulated battle—worst case scenario—and given a barrage of targets to which we had to respond instantly and correctly. The NATO evaluators were from Norway, West Germany, the Netherlands, and Belgium, the Belgian being one of the toughest evaluators NATO had to offer. And these guys took this stuff *seriously,* particularly since we were using their countries as our battle-fields.

Within the hour, Captain Logan had returned to Delta. His job during the exercise was to take control of the battery by manning the command post. Larry Perkins (who had taken my place as Delta's IFC platoon leader) and I rotated between the Battery Control Van and the secure communications area, taking turns firing missiles and decoding messages.

To run a crew drill in the IFC, two vans were the most important—the Radar Control Van, and the Battery Control Van. In the Radar Control Van sat the following six operators: the Range Operator, the Elevation Operator, the Target Ranging Radar Operator, a Section Chief, a maintenance person, and the Azimuth Operator, who would orient our direction. These six people maintained constant contact with the Battery Control Van, which also carried six people: the Battery Control Officer (BCO), who sat between the Battery Control Assistant (BCA) and the Acquisition

191

Operator; they were flanked by the Computer Operator, an Early Warning Operations Plotter (EWOP), and a maintenance person. All of these positions—except for the BCO and sometimes the EWOP—were held by enlisted personnel.

Near the end of the exercise, the BOC sent word that they were giving us authorization to use nuclear, as well as high explosive, weapons. Everything was rolling along smoothly when the Belgian evaluator, who had been observing operations, suddenly rushed out of the Battery Control Van, calling for Captain Logan. During this highly critical stage of the battle, when the Acquisition and BCA scopes were bristling with targets, the evaluator had watched in horror as Lieutenant Perkins had fired a nuke at a friendly aircraft.

If you are the BCO, once you've been given the release to fire a nuke, you have the option of issuing a command to launch either a conventional, high-explosive missile, or a nuke (prior to receiving nuclear release, you would have only been permitted to launch the former.) The high-explosive missile is designed for a "one-kill target;" if, on the other hand, your intention is to shoot down a number of aircraft at once, you would use the nuke to perform what is called an "area burst." Once the command to fire has been made, the BCO repeats it to make doubly sure of the intent. When Larry pushed the button that activated the nuclear weapon, his command was relayed by secure radio network to the Launcher Control Station, which informed the Launcher Crew of the IFC's decision.

Even in a dual-capable system, a BCO cannot simply fire off a nuke accidentally, although there is still room for human error. Once the authorization is given, the missiles are brought forward, and the necessary cable hookups are made, it is then entirely possible for an officer to fire a nuke at the wrong time, or at the wrong target, the way Larry did.

The Belgian evaluator returned with Captain Logan in tow. Both of them were steaming mad. The irate Belgian looked as though he were about to pick up Larry and throw him bodily out of the van. Through clenched teeth, he said, "Captain, get this guy out of here." Logan relieved Larry of BCO duties at once, and sent him to decode messages in the EMAS Van. Then, Captain Logan came looking for me.

For the next five hours, I acted as BCO in the Battery Control Van. Four of those hours were spent in full MOPP (Mission Oriented Protective Posture) gear—a heavy chemical protection suit consisting of pants, a jacket, gloves, boots, and a hooded mask. The van was already warm with so many people crammed inside it, but when we put on our MOPP gear, the temperature skyrocketed. I was sweating heavily. Wearing the mask also made it harder to communicate with the Radar Control Van and the crew in the Launcher Area. First I had to determine whether the targets on the scopes were friend or foe, and, if foe, whether to fire off a high explosive round or a nuke. The evaluator hovered over my shoulder for five straight hours. I almost made a few small errors but caught them before he did. My buddy, Chris Jones, was there beside me, helping me all the way.

I was under tremendous pressure to redeem the unit after Larry's mistake, but I survived it. In fact, when the exercise was over, our battery was rated Number One among all the batteries in the battalion. What meant the most to me, however, was the evaluator's comment to Captain Logan that even though he'd never seen a woman serve as a BCO before, he was impressed. Chalk one up for the American female soldier.

Three months later, in January 1983, we lost Larry Perkins for good. At the time, only three officers at Delta Battery were BCO qualified— Logan, Perkins, and I. One of our duties was to inventory the communications security equipment in the IFC. Every day the Duty Officer and an enlisted soldier would list and then burn used or unnecessary classified code books. After the code books were burned, those responsible were required to sign a statement verifying that the records had been destroyed.

On this occasion, one of the enlisted soldiers who'd been taking inventory of the code books discovered that Perkins had neglected to destroy some top-secret information. When the incident was investigated, it came to light that he and the enlisted soldier who'd been on duty with him at the time had falsified the information on the destruction certificate (claiming they had witnessed the burning of the documents when they hadn't), and then signed it. Logan was forced once again to relieve Perkins of duty, this time for good.

It just so happened that immediately after we lost Larry, Delta Battery was given the order to go to hot status. Pulling that off was difficult enough with three BCO qualified officers on site. Now we had only two—Captain Logan and me. For the next three weeks, the two of us worked back to back, taking turns pulling all-night duty every other night. Since our unit was also under fire from above because of Larry's security violation, we had to be extra careful. We knew we were being watched.

This did not prevent other traumas from occurring, however. One of our sergeants was suspected of selling cocaine, and we'd gotten word that there were other guys in the unit who were smoking dope. I gathered my

193

platoon together and told them, "Listen, I cannot control your actions off site, but when you're in my barracks, or in my platoon, if I catch you with the stuff, that's it. You've had it."

Some of the soldiers got caught. The battery commander, all his lieutenants, and an MP would bring a dog through the barracks sniffing for drugs, and when they were found, I had the unpleasant task of reading the culprits their rights. These soldiers were handled with an Article 15—they'd be busted a rank or two, half their salary would be taken away for two months, and they'd be restricted to their barracks after work for at least two weeks. Then they'd be placed in a mandatory rehabilitation program.

Captain Logan was tough but caring with these soldiers. He would assist with their drug rehabilitation and meet with their counselors, something which I never saw either of my previous commanders do. When I asked him about it, the captain would quote the philosophy of General Omar Bradley, "The greatest leader in the world could never win a campaign unless he understood the men he had to lead."

Overseas units are unique within the Army; they are like an extended family. It's different in the States, where soldiers have more of their own lives off post. But in an isolated place like Delta, so much of the soldiers' lives rotate around the unit that it practically becomes another culture. With Captain Logan as battery commander, Delta became very paternalistic. He was our Father Superior; it wasn't unusual for him to receive phone calls in the middle of the night, asking him to bail out a soldier. More than any other officer I had known, Captain Logan was always available. The only time he reserved for himself was an hour of running each day; he said it was the only way he could avoid the phone, and no one could find him.

I also found the captain's attitude toward women soldiers refreshing. He had served with a female officer in Alpha battery, who had been the first female platoon leader in the battalion. He said there had been some problems with enlisted women when they initially came on-site, but most of the trouble was logistical. The tactical sites had been built for a society of men. They didn't have "His" and "Hers" bathrooms, and the living arrangements were a problem; it was hard to ensure adequate privacy for enlisted women.

Further, Captain Logan observed, enlisted women didn't do as well at Alpha Battery until they had female officers and NCOs out there to act as role models. He said that sending women officers to those remote units was the smartest thing the Army could have done. The old Army tendency would have been to make them clerks at headquarters, or drivers for the colonels. He said that he didn't recall "the question of women" being an issue at Alpha. If they carried their workload on-site, nobody objected to their presence.

According to Captain Logan, the only time the idea emerged that women were a possible hindrance was when they got pregnant. He once called the female section of Alpha barracks "the Maternity Ward" because eight of the twelve women in his battery were pregnant at one time. The issue was not whether they were unwilling to work, it was just that the Army would no longer permit them to operate the radars or push the missiles. They had to be transferred to the Dining Facility, or to offices to perform clerical work. Moreover, the MPs were already pulling long hours, and if a soldier were pregnant, the other troops would have extra duty because she'd be unavailable. That, he said, was when some resentment and hostility set in. When the female officers and NCOs arrived on site, however, the trend reversed itself. Captain Logan recalled having more trouble with the civilian wives than the female soldiers—wives who were nineteen or twenty, homesick and lonely, with husbands who worked long hours on-site. Apparently, infidelities were common.

Captain Logan's wife, Meg, on the other hand, belonged to the set of more progressive Army wives, many of whom had their own jobs or careers, and respected other professional women. They were not, for example, as threatened by the fact that women were working with their husbands. The other set consisted of wives who didn't work, and who had more traditional opinions and jealousies. Some of them would ask Meg, "How can you let Lieutenant Barkalow work all day with your husband? Aren't you worried? Aren't you jealous?" I knew such gossip might be going on, so I had made a conscious effort to befriend her. I wanted Meg to see for herself that I was not a threat to her marriage in any way, and we eventually became very close. But Meg was unusual.

One night I was at a battery party in a schoolhouse near our *Kaserne*. I was telling a joke to an enlisted man and busting his chops a little. Sort of teasing him. Then, just as I was about to tell him the punch line, I put my hand on his shoulder. All of a sudden, from across the room, his wife tore through the crowd, grabbed my hand, threw it off his shoulder, and said, "Excuse me, but my husband doesn't do that!"

I was stunned. I felt so awkward and embarrassed that I left.

Obviously, it was hard for me to relate to these women. We didn't have much in common, and so social gatherings were especially difficult. The wives would talk about their kids, or they might talk about their jobs, but

I felt much more comfortable among the men. I don't think the wives saw me as an ordinary woman. I was a strange creature. I was an officer, and in some cases, their husbands' boss. I could tell they were more at ease with civilian women.

And yet, being accepted among the men professionally, not to mention socially, wasn't the easiest thing, either. Omar Bradley's sentiment may have been fine for a commander like Captain Logan. But how could a woman get close enough to "understand" her soldiers without meeting a wall of resistance? The concept of a female in a position of real authority was, surprisingly enough, still unusual in 1983—and not only to American soldiers and their wives.

During my tenure as XO, I learned that one of my enlisted men had gotten a German girl pregnant. The soldier wanted to marry her, but that was impossible at the time, because the Army was shipping him back to the States. Then, one Saturday afternoon in October, while Captain Logan was away from the battery, I was in my office doing some paperwork, essentially functioning as acting commander, when the CQ [Charge of Quarters] came to the door and said, "Hey, Ma'am, we've got three Germans out here."

"Three Germans" could have meant anything from three antinuke protestors to three bomb-toting terrorists to three spies trying to gain access to the missile site by posing as foreign diplomats.

"Don't just tell me they're here," I said. "Find out who they are."

My three German terrorists turned out to be the pregnant girl and her parents. They had come to find out the American soldier's intentions from his commanding officer. I didn't speak much German, but some of my soldiers did, so one of them acted as interpreter.

I went to the main gate to meet them, since none of them were allowed inside the area. The girl's father took one look at this twenty-five-year-old *Fräulein* coming toward him and immediately turned to ask the interpreter, "Where is your *commander?*"

The soldier pointed to me and said, "This *is* our commander."

The man and his wife stared at me, and then stared at each other. Together they said, "What?"

They couldn't believe it, and had to spend a few moments recovering before they could actually speak. Meanwhile, I told the interpreter to explain to them that I understood the situation between their daughter and my soldier, and that I believed my soldier was a trustworthy individual; he had already informed me of the circumstances and assured me that his intentions were honorable.

At last, the girl's father seemed satisfied I was telling the truth. The girl left with her parents, and my soldier flew to the States. A month later, he returned on leave to pick up his bride and bring her to America.

By the time my tour of duty at Delta ended in December 1983, there were few things keeping me in Germany, but Chris Jones was one of them. Saying good-bye to him would be hard. I was anxious to return home to the States, but I knew it meant leaving behind my confidant and friend. The day before I left Delta Battery, Chris and I drove to Wagner's gym in downtown Pforzheim to lift weights together one last time. I wanted us to say our farewells in private, without being subjected to the prying eyes of the battery. I feared I'd become visibly upset, and I didn't want my other soldiers to see me. After four years at West Point, and nearly three years in Germany, I still wasn't very good at good-byes.

When, finally, we had to part, Chris and I could only stand dumbly in the gym's parking lot and look at each other. I wanted to say *something,* but I knew the waterworks would start the moment I opened my mouth. Chris must have been feeling uncomfortable, too, because I saw his eyes were misty. Suddenly, we each bent forward to embrace and bumped our foreheads, which made us both laugh. Then I hugged him, hard, and got into my car and drove away.

My last evening in Germany was spent drinking wine and reminiscing with Captain Logan and his wife. Leaving Captain Logan felt like flying the nest once again, only this time I was eager to arrive at my destination. I had decided back in May to request a branch transfer from Air Defense Artillery to the Transportation Corps. As I saw it then, unless the Army's Combat Exclusion Policy were changed, my opportunities for career advancement in ADA—a combat arms branch—were limited and would continue to narrow. Permission was granted for me to transfer upon my return to the States. Captain Logan had advised me to seek out a company command as soon as I had finished my Transportation Officers' Advanced Course. Seeing how troops responded to good leadership, feeling the satisfaction that came from accomplishing a unit's mission, and carrying out the responsibility for the lives of soldiers were the rewards of being a commander, Captain Logan assured me, experiences that no good officer should miss. So, on my "dream sheet" (a list of personal preferences for assignments) I asked to be assigned either to Fort Eustis, Virginia (home of the Transportation Corps), Fort Lee, Virginia, or Fort Meade, Maryland.

Once the Army decided I was headed for Fort Lee, I immediately

197

asked my assignments officer for a listing of available Transportation Corps positions on post. She informed me that there was a truck company at Fort Lee—the 57th Transportation Company—where a captain would be rotating out of his command in about six months. I was determined to make that company mine.

COMMAND

★

Fort Lee, Virginia, off Route 36, set halfway between the slow-paced southern towns of Petersburg and Hopewell, was first established as Camp Lee on 24 April 1917, a mere eighteen days after America declared war on Germany. Responding to the sudden need for mobilization, the Petersburg Chamber of Commerce leased the Army a generous 450 acres for the camp area and an additional 15,000 acres for maneuvers, from land bordering the eastern edge of town. During both world wars Camp Lee served as a basic-training and branch-training post for Quartermaster personnel, but it did not become firmly entrenched as a permanent part of the Virginia landscape until the Cold War era when its status changed from Camp Lee to Fort Lee in April 1950.

Fort Lee abuts the famous Petersburg Battlefield to its west (now a tourist park), where General Ulysses S. Grant's indomitable siege, beginning in mid-June 1864, sparked one of the longest and most critical battles of the Civil War. Here, General Robert E. Lee's Confederate Army of Northern Virginia made its final heroic stand against Grant's Union forces; the struggle ended nine and a half months later with Lee's woeful surrender on 9 April 1865 at Appomattox Courthouse nearly one hundred miles to the west.

I can only imagine Grant and Lee's astonishment had they lived to witness the accession of a woman to the rank of company commander at a post so close to the site of their historic showdown. I found out after my arrival, however, that I'd have to wait longer than expected before I'd be able to receive my first command. The company on which I'd set my sights—the 57th Transportation Light-Medium Truck Company (or "57th Trans")—had been given to a senior captain already working on post. In two years, when his assignment was over, the reins of command would be handed to me.

The Fort Lee I encountered in September 1984 was relatively open, relaxed, and friendly compared with my Germany experience. No ominous guard towers housing armed MPs existed here; no barbed wire gates controlling access to the post. Unlike the missile batteries, Fort Lee was well integrated into the surrounding civilian community. The post employed a high proportion of local civilians within its offices and facilities, its centers for child care, recreation, and community counseling (marital and financial), as well as in the PX. The grounds also included a gymnasium, four chapels, a theater, and a golf course. A self-contained world within a world, Fort Lee provided its inhabitants with every necessity, maintaining the illusion of so-called normal life. Daytime traffic, whether military or civilian, was not restricted; the post gates were guarded only at night.

Fort Lee was a TRADOC (Training and Doctrine) post with two FORSCOM units (Forces Command, or deployable units); the 85th MEDEVAC Hospital (medical evacuation—a deployable hospital that could be picked up and moved to wherever it was needed); and the 240th Quartermaster Battalion, of which the 57th Trans was a part. It was also the home of the U.S. Army Logistics Center, a centralized planning cell for the movement and maintenance of Army forces. As it turned out, the "Log Center," a two-story white-cement-and-glass box with a central courtyard, was where I'd be pencil-jockeying on a logistics assessment task group while awaiting my company command.

Since the daily mission of Fort Lee was not as urgent as either Charlie or Delta Battery, the atmosphere was far less stressful. In Germany, for instance, I had routinely handled classified documents; this rarely happened at Fort Lee. And without having to operate a sophisticated weapons system like the Nike Hercules, the technical demands were not as great. Soon I began to feel as though I were working a regular job—fifteen- and sixteen-hour workdays had been relegated to the past; no longer did I have to spend the night in my office or sleep in my boots in anticipation of an all-night exercise. I lived in a little townhouse a mile and a half from post, occasionally drove into the "big city" of Richmond for the only entertainment available for miles, and showed up for work every morning at the sinful hour of seven. The change of pace was a relief, but it was an adjustment as well. I'd become so accustomed to working under extreme pressure that I found myself missing the excitement. I started looking for ways to fill the empty hours. One of these, I later learned, nearly cost me my command.

Ever since my days of lifting weights with Sergeant Jones in Germany, I had entertained the notion of becoming an amateur bodybuilder. The owner of the gymnasium in Pforzheim had encouraged me, saying that if I lost weight and developed my muscles I might be good enough to compete. To me, bodybuilding seemed a logical extension of the lessons I'd been taught at West Point. Achieving and displaying bodily perfection seemed an appropriate endeavor for a professional whose primary purpose was to inspire subordinates to feats of heroism and sacrifice with mythical images of physical prowess.

My sedate schedule as an "action officer" at the Log Center finally gave me the chance to work out on a regular basis. For the next year and a half, I spent most of my time reading technical documents in the office and pumping iron in the post gymnasium. Eventually, after long deliberation, in January 1986 I decided to enter my name as a contestant in the Ninth Annual Roanoke Valley Open Bodybuilding Championships. The competition would take place in May at a high school in Roanoke.

Then, for the first time since I'd entered military life, I imposed a strict discipline on myself, rather than merely responding to the demands of an external authority. For the four months leading up to the event, I ran at least six miles every morning and lifted weights for two hours at lunchtime and another hour or so when I came home at night. Charlotte Dimirack, my forty-six-year-old trainer and a former champion herself, choreographed my routines and advised me on exercise and diet. As an inveterate junk-food lover, I found that subsisting for months on the bodybuilder's simple fare of fish, chicken, low-salt cereals, and fruit was the hardest regimen to maintain. I had to lose fifteen pounds before the contest and, in the final days before the competition, needed to reduce my water intake dramatically. I practically had to be dehydrated for the "cuts" in my muscles to appear in sharpest relief. To acquire even greater muscle definition, and to avoid being washed out by the harsh glare of fluorescent lights, I had to roast my fair skin under the ultraviolet lamps of a local tanning salon every day for a month.

Learning the performance poses was a grueling and complicated process that demanded more focus than I was accustomed to giving. A ninety-second routine required absolute concentration in order to keep all of my muscles tensed, while simultaneously isolating each group and showing my well-oiled limbs and torso to the judges.

Most critical to my success, however, was my attainment of the body-builder's ability to strike and hold excruciating contortions, yet continue to smile and breathe naturally, as if standing serenely at rest. Fortunately, as an officer, I was already well practiced in this art.

The event itself would be delivered in two parts: the contest and the Show. The serious competition began at 10:30 on Saturday morning, 3 May, and all the winners were chosen by early afternoon. Joanne Dugan, a civilian friend of mine, drove me to the high school on the day of the competition. I could have driven myself, but the ride was two and a half hours long and I preferred to conserve my strength. Other friends had offered to come along, too, but I couldn't bear the thought of an entourage. I was nervous enough.

For at least six days before the contest, I cut down on my liquid intake. My allowance of three glasses of water on Monday evaporated to one by Friday. On Saturday, I thirstily sucked out half a grapefruit for breakfast, but nothing more. By the time Joanne and I arrived at the auditorium, I was feeling rather lightheaded. Then, for the next two hours, I (along with fifty-three other contestants) was put through my posing paces like a prize racehorse. Before doing so, however, we each pumped some preparatory iron for about twenty minutes with the long, heavily weighted barbells and smaller handheld dumbbells that were conveniently stashed backstage. And, during the moments we waited in the wings for our names and numbers to be called, we pumped a little more, all the while gazing fixedly at our rivals.

The contestants were called onstage by category. The contest opened with the Men's Novice competition and was followed by the Women's Open (consisting of Short and Tall groups), the Men's Open (comprised of the same two subgroups), and finally, the Senior Men's competition, for male competitors over fifty. (The sport has yet to become widespread among women; bodybuilding contests are still predominantly male.)

When it was time for the Women's Open, all the female contestants within each category were summoned onstage at once to take their places before a row of seated judges. Each of us stood approximately four feet apart, waiting for the Master of Ceremonies to bark out the posing calls.

"Ladies, let's see a chest shot!"

"Give us a triceps shot!"

"Let's see those hamstrings!"

We'd turn to the side, back, and front, completing a 360-degree

204

rotation. I knew I was doing well when the judges asked me to move my place in line.

"Number 39, please stand next to Number 42!"

It meant they were going to judge me against that woman and wanted to compare our bodies at a closer range.

The entire competition, including the category judging and the performance of individual routines set to music, lasted about three hours. All of the contestants performed admirably, but the morning's main excitement occurred when we heard a huge *thud* onstage and looked up to see that one of the men had fallen over; in a particularly heightened moment of performance, he'd forgotten to breathe.

While the morning's atmosphere mostly had been tense and subdued, the evening show was positively raucous. At precisely 7:30, two scantily clad professional male posers leapt onto the posing platform, which stood a foot above the auditorium stage, and began to display their shining bodies under the hot lights. As these two professionals pulsed and bulged to the pounding of prerecorded drums, all fifty-four contestants were asked to line the aisles of the auditorium and pose along with them. This had the desired effect of working the audience into an absolute frenzy of whistles, footstompings, and cheers.

The evening show followed the same order of procedure as the morning show. Each contestant was given the chance to mount the stage and perform the ninety-second highlights of his or her personalized routine, and once again I found myself pumping iron in the wings, silently waiting my turn.

Backstage, meanwhile, chaos ruled. Like a Greek frieze come to life, a tableau of statuesque men and women stood together boasting and joking, trying to psych each other out by showing off their "cuts." I think I disarmed at least one cocky male by asking if he wouldn't mind oiling me up.

As the female contestants took the stage one by one, I evaluated them carefully. I knew my legs were weaker than they should have been, but my upper body was larger and more developed than any of the other women contestants. Suddenly, my name and number were called. As I stepped onto the platform and into the grueling lights, I realized that I was still on public display but that the gutwrenching part was over. I could now relax and have some fun. I had geared my routine to accentuate my back, shoulders, triceps, and calves (my most developed features), so I emphasized those positions—transitioning as gracefully as I could between each static pose and gliding through a fluid dance of tension and release. When my ninety seconds in the limelight had ended, I stepped down lightly from the platform and ran backstage to apprehensively await the judges' word.

When the winners were finally announced, I had taken second place in the Women's Tall Class category, beating some of the more-experienced competitors. The photographers immediately began snapping pictures while I dutifully posed with my trophy, but my mind frankly wasn't on the fanfare. It was on the nearest Italian restaurant, where Joanne and I were headed, and where, after months of junk-food deprivation, I could blissfully indulge in a large sausage-mushroom pizza with extra cheese and a magnum of cold beer.

Two weeks after the contest, a Fort Lee public affairs officer ran an article about my victory in *Traveller,* the post newspaper, with full-length photographs of me in my bikini posing suit. Unknown to me at the time, a copy of this picture was circulated around the battalion by some rather indignant soldiers. The picture reportedly found its way to the battalion command sergeant major's desk, where he deliberately propped it up to taunt any member of the 57th Trans who would wander into his office. "See," Sergeant Major Dick Bridges would proclaim disdainfully while pointing to my ingenuously smiling image, *"this* is your new company commander."

Some months after I became commander, one of my NCOs finally had the nerve to confess the havoc that nearly set back my career, perhaps permanently. The soldier and I were walking through the motor pool one day, discussing how I liked being a company commander, when suddenly he said, "You know, Captain Barkalow, there was some trouble a while back when your picture appeared in *Traveller.*"

Apparently, this NCO had been working as a driver for our brigade commander, Colonel John Houston, and had overheard a conversation following the article's publication—purportedly prompted by a number of NCOs within the battalion—between the brigade commander and the general of the post regarding my imminent future as commander of the 57th Trans. Evidently, there were some who felt that my indelicate press appearance had disqualified me for the job.

Years later, now-retired Colonel Houston explained what had transpired. "I was bringing in a new company commander," he said, "and I'm sorry, but I didn't need any problems. I was up to my ass in alligators, and I didn't need none of 'em in my swamp. I wanted someone who could help me drain the swamp.

"Then, all of a sudden, here comes the post newspaper. And I'll be goddamned if Carol Barkalow didn't do just what I told her not to do. When I interviewed her for company command in the summer of 1985, I told her, 'Don't do nothing *dumb.*' To me, that picture was dumb. She became the masturbatory fantasy of every goddamned male noncommissioned officer in the company. The problem wasn't that she had developed her body or won at a competitive sport. I applaud her success to this day; I thought it was fabulous. She did exactly what a commander should do. But we had some real old-line noncommissioned officers in that battalion, and, goddamnit, her half-naked picture didn't have to appear in a newspaper whose only readers were the soldiers she was going to command!

"Now, I knew it really wasn't deliberate on Carol's part, because she didn't run the newspaper. I wasn't after her. I was after that goddamn public affairs officer. How dare the dumb son of a bitch run that story two goddamn months before she took command. I never said a single word about the incident to Carol Barkalow. Never did! But I went after that public affairs guy—you talk about chewing someone's ass, he lost fifteen pounds within minutes in my office. I did a raindance on him."

Fortunately, I realized, the previous battalion commander had given me his solemn promise in writing that I would be the next commander of the 57th Trans. Had that promise been seriously challenged, my only recourse would have been to pit letter against photograph and wage a militarily uncharacteristic war against image with the power of the written word. Armed only with that fragile slip of paper, I knew I would have raised whatever bloody hell was necessary to make sure my place within the company was secure.

From the safe perch of hindsight, however, it was a battle I was just as happy not to have fought. Still, I was angry, even in retrospect. I felt like the creature in Mary Shelley's *Frankenstein.* These men had inculcated their values in me, had created me, and now they were calling me a monster. If I were a man, I felt certain the battalion would have been proud that the 57th Trans was getting such a fit commander. My idea was confirmed because one of the male NCOs on post had taken third place in the men's division in the very same competition. It was the second time he'd competed as a bodybuilder, and his unit had even given him time off to train. His troops obviously respected him for the discipline it had taken to achieve his goal. But because I was female, the automatic assumption about the effect of the photograph was that my soldiers would *not* respect me; they would regard me as a "sex symbol," instead of a leader.

This was, ironically, the very circumstance I'd spent a good part of my professional life trying to avoid. I had imagined, perhaps naively, that by presenting myself as a physically strong and disciplined woman—frankly, unabashedly—without hiding behind the easy authority of a uniform or the barrier of captain's bars, I would earn the confidence of my male soldiers and set a positive example for the females. Clearly, some of the men had not come to accept this in women quite yet, though they just as clearly resented it if we were not physically fit.

My West Point classmate Captain Denise Gavin recalls reading, as a cadet in 1979, former Secretary of the Navy James Webb's ten-page diatribe against the congressional decision to admit women into the nation's service academies, published in a magazine called *The Washingtonian*. The article's title was simply "Women Can't Fight."

At the time, Captain Gavin says, she was struggling with some of the Academy's physical demands, so her reaction to Mr. Webb's argument that women were both physically and emotionally unsuited to receive combat leadership training was to feel guilty. "God," she remembers thinking, "I thought I was truly a worthless human being, utterly unfit to lead American soldiers because I could only do ten pull-ups."

"Now," says Captain Gavin, "having been a company commander in the Signal Corps, I have witnessed other qualities—like courage, stamina, and teamwork—which have counted a lot toward my assessment of officers and enlisted soldiers. Far more than how many pull-ups they can do.

"And yet," she acknowledges, "PT programs *are* important. I always took the physical training tests with my troops, and I agree that one's bearing as a soldier depends upon one's physical conditioning. I also know that putting up rigs and wearing chemical suits can be physically exhausting. But I've seen women who have somehow made it as soldiers on pride and adrenaline alone, and musclebound men who bungle things miserably. Competent garrison soldiers can easily fall apart in the field, and when they do, it's usually due to a lack of perception and teamwork.

"All this finally led me to understand that what really matters in the military is competence, compassion, and the ability to make the Officer-NCO relationship work. This realization cast a whole different light on my West Point experience, where I had gone through moments of dark despair. For someone like me, it had been a daily struggle to 'get with it' physically. I kept banging my head against the wall, trying to be a man. It was a relief to discover that it wasn't necessary."

.   .   .

208

As Captain Gavin realized, inherent in the work of any female soldier is the call to invent, or reinvent, herself. It isn't enough to be lifted out of context, slapped into a uniform, taught a new language, and dispatched whimsically around the globe. Accompanying these generic changes is a much slower, frequently painful, and highly individualized process of self-definition. In the military, it is a challenge merely to function as best as one can within the system without losing one's sense of self. Meeting that challenge as a male within a male-oriented institution is tough enough; as a female, it can sometimes prove devastating. Women who cling to traditional ideas and images of female identity may find very few places to gain a foothold.

And yet, it is that very footlooseness that, for some, can provide the most satisfaction. Like the bob-haired, uncorseted, trouser-clad women of the 1920s who mimicked male attitudes and dress—not because they wanted to be men, but because they wanted to be free—a woman in the military is granted a surprising freedom of movement. One is allowed—no, encouraged—to be physical. A uniform may be a rigid requirement, but in military circles it denotes respect. And perhaps more important, the female body usually is not imprisoned in pantyhose, high heels, and skirts that render one incapable of any activity more vigorous than a measured walk. One's nails don't have to be long and lacquered like bird's talons; one's hairstyle is not the center of one's existence; one's face does not need to be painted before being exposed to public view. For me, one of the greatest and most paradoxical attractions of choosing a life in the military, after accepting the yoke of missions and regulations and standards and uniforms, was living in a way that would not tie me to a fixed place, or to people, or to the obligations of domestic drudgery. If I kept body and soul together, that would be enough. The stream of my energy was channeled into work that gave me purpose and direction. Although I paid dearly for this independence with long periods of loneliness, as a professional officer with some measure of authority, I found it a relief to assume a role among men that enabled me to deal plainly and straightforwardly—a role that did not require me to project myself as a coquette, temptress, or helpless damsel in distress. Within certain professional parameters—applied equally to all soldiers—my body and image would be under my control and no one else's. Or so I believed.

I was introduced to the key people in the 57th Trans for the first time in June 1986. The outgoing company commander had called a meeting of the platoon leaders, platoon sergeants, the first sergeant, and the supply NCO, to make arrangements for the Change of Command Inventory. I had to account for all the property in the unit before I assumed command, which meant I literally had to count every truck, bed, sheet, dish, tent, stove, wrench, rifle, generator, and camouflage net in the company and ensure that every item listed on the hand receipts was truly present. This tedium would take approximately three weeks to complete.

A quorum gathered in what eventually would be my new office. In my company, the officers were white and the NCOs predominantly black. My first sergeant, otherwise known in military parlance as "Top," was among the first to greet me. He was an elegant man—tall, slim, and soft-spoken— with a fatherly good humor that made him extremely popular among his soldiers. Top was a Vietnam vet—one of three in the company—and, by his own account, had volunteered in 1967 to avoid the roulette wheel of the draft. "I was classified 1-A when I got out of high school," he recalled, "and I knew I was going to be drafted. I knew a lot of guys over in Nam were getting killed, so I thought if I joined up and got trained in the mechanical field, then I could basically go where I wanted. When I finished school, there were seventy-two guys in my class. Out of all of them, only two were sent to Vietnam—me and another guy. So my whole idea didn't work.

"I hadn't planned on staying in the Army after the war," he admitted, "but when my three years were up, I was down in Texas and had gotten engaged and didn't know if I wanted to go back to school. So I reenlisted. And here it is, nearly twenty years later, and I haven't left."

Staff Sergeant Kevin Randall, the supply NCO, and I spent most of our initial meeting simply leafing through the hand receipts. The supply room was right down the hall from my office, so it was easy for me to sit and chat with him, which is how we came to be friends. Privately, I referred to him as "The Quiet Man"; Sergeant Randall was a gentle, deeply religious soldier who I felt needed to be more involved with troops. So rather than having him merely in control of the Supply Room, I appointed him Headquarters Platoon Sergeant. Until then, he had worked only with property; now he'd be responsible for human beings.

When the meeting ended, Sergeant First Class Michael Sweeney, the NCO in charge of First Platoon, escorted me to my car. My first impression of Sweeney, a sharp-looking, bespectacled sergeant, was that he was quickwitted, squared away militarily, and respected by his soldiers. One of Sergeant Sweeney's favorite expressions was, "That dog will hunt"— meaning he had an order and would comply. To be sure, if Sergeant

Sweeney were a dog, he'd be a bloodhound—hardworking and tenacious. Unfortunately, he did possess one prejudice: He did not want females in his platoon.

"I'd been in the Army seventeen years, and Captain Barkalow was my first female commander. My *first*. It was tough," Sergeant Sweeny still laments. "And when she arrived, what I wanted to know was, Did she have herself a set of balls? I mean, all the guys were glad to see a blond, blue-eyed young lady, but would she make a strong commander? That was my major concern. If I had a problem, and I brought it to her, would she be able to help me?

"I remember the very first thing she said to me. 'I'm not a politician; my command starts at the ground level.' And I thought, Yeah, sure. Because even though most of the company commanders I'd seen had the power to go against the battalion commander on behalf of the company, they'd all been afraid to do it. Once a colonel reams off on a captain's butt, the commander gets paranoid and becomes like a panic button stuck on hold. But Captain Barkalow didn't care. She didn't care. She'd go against any man. She never let her feminine structure get involved in her business as commander. But that's just Captain Barkalow. Captain Barkalow'd cuss out the Pope if she had to. Straight up.

"Still, it took me a pretty good while to catch on to the whole idea of female responsibility. See, you take a beautiful young lady who comes in as a 64 Charlie [driver]. She was probably bullshitted by her recruiter, who said, 'When you join the Army as a 64 Charlie, you can drive the colonel around in a nice sedan, and you'll never be around tactical work, you'll never have to go to the field.' But then she gets assigned to a unit like this one, and suddenly she's got to drive two-and-a-half-ton trucks, and she's not ready to do that. For one thing, she's not conditioned properly. Her basic training got her squared away on her military knowledge, and her AIT [Advanced Individual Training] course prepared her for a specific job. But her permanent duty assignment was a future shock.

"Now, I told Captain Barkalow that I didn't like having females in my platoon, but she put two of 'em in there anyway, and I had to deal with it. Well, if that's what she wants to do, I thought, fine. But I said, 'They get no favoritism. I ain't giving them no damn breaks, now. They'll get cussed out just like everyone else. And if they can't take it, then *they* have a problem. I don't.' Because I asked some of them how they ended up driving trucks in the first place, and they told me, 'It was all the Army had to offer.'

"It all goes back to that damn recruiter. You know, meeting a quota, getting in x number of people. They don't care what MOS [Military Occupational Specialty] they put 'em in. They tell 'em, 'You'll wear a Class B uniform, you'll never get dirty, and you'll never see a motor pool.' That's all they know. And they go freaky-deaky once they get here. They've got to contend with *me,* and I don't cut them no slack.

"So, I say, when the recruiters put people in the military, they should tell them the truth about being in the Army and about the job they'll be doing. You know, if it's pole climbing, goddamnit, tell them, 'You're going to be climbing this pole, and you're going to have shit on your feet. It ain't no easy job, and it ain't no piece of cake.' But I come from the old Army. And I'll tell you what, I've got a lot of disciplined soldiers. Those who can't take it go AWOL."

The Change of Command ceremony was scheduled to take place on a grassy field just east of the company area. Since a third of my company had been deployed to Yakima, Washington, in support of a fuel- and water-pipeline exercise, only eighty soldiers stood in formation for the ceremony. Six deuce-and-a-half's (two-and-a-half-ton trucks) were parked behind the unit formation to create the illusion of a crowd. One of my lieutenants was away on leave, and Top was at home nursing a migraine. At least my family was able to come.

The uniform for the troops was BDUs (battle dress uniforms) with soft caps and stripped pistol belts—green web belts without the .45s, ammo pouches, and other accessories of battle that would usually adorn them. My BDUs were heavily starched, and my black leather combat boots were spit-shined.

The morning of 1 August had begun for me before daybreak, but I wasn't nervous until the stroke of nine, when the battalion commander and I commenced our slow march together into formation. As Lieutenant Colonel Edward Schuller and I approached the area, my heart started to beat fiercely. My body began to shake while I stood so rigidly at attention, and I was certain that even the meager crowd of soldiers assembled on the field could see it.

With choreographic precision, the battalion commander, the outgoing company commander, the acting first sergeant, and I maneuvered ourselves into a four-pointed diamond, then turned to face each other expectantly. In a sequence of quick, decisive thrusts, the guidon pole was passed from the acting first sergeant to the company commander to the battalion commander and, finally, to me. It crossed my hands with an authoritative slap, and the orders appointing me commander of the 57th Transportation

Light-Medium Truck Company were read. At the close of this simple ritual, I was in command.

This was what I had been waiting for, it seemed, since the day I entered West Point. Assuming command of my own company would be the true validation of my military career.

My first official day on the job—Monday, 4 August—and the first order of business was to count heads. As it turned out only a third of my unit, and no lieutenants, were present. Some of my soldiers were on leave, others were down at Fort Pickett, Virginia, providing drivers, military escorts, and clerical workers in support of a Logistics Exercise, and still others—an entire platoon, in fact—had been deployed to provide transportation to the battalion's Quartermaster units who were participating in Operation Yakima 1986, testing a 37-mile pipeline that would carry fuel and water to remote sites during times of war.

The aboveground pipeline was designed to carry liquid from a tanker docked in the water to a designated transfer point, where it would then become the job of a POL [Petroleum, Oil, Lubricants] Company to truck it into another area so various combat units could be refueled. Third Platoon was charged to transport construction materials in order for the pipeline to be tested. The exercise had begun in June and wouldn't conclude until October. But I did have contact with my absent soldiers by phone almost every day and made two trips out west to see them, though I could stay only four days each time. Naturally it was difficult for me to get to know any of them under those circumstances, and I felt bad for them. The living conditions in Yakima were awful.

The site was on the Yakima Firing Range, a desert terrain not far from the Columbia River, about 120 miles southeast of Seattle. Rain was scarce, vegetation was sparse, and the only living things that managed to survive the region's frequent, violent dust storms were a few scrubby cactuses and the rows of hardy apple trees that bordered the main road by the river. When the storms were at their height, people couldn't see much farther in front of their faces than their own outstretched hands, and if you'd been riding around in an open jeep all day, by evening your body was guaranteed to be completely caked with dust. Major Frank Nichols, the commander in charge of the exercise, had even tried to keep down the dust by trucking in tons of gravel to cover the site's dirt floor. This helped somewhat, but unfortunately it resembled living inside a giant litter box.

To make matters more complicated, not a single structure had been erected, so everything took place in tents. Our encampment—aptly

213

known as "Tent City"—was located just to the east of the Saddle Mountains, a low range of bare, rocky protuberances that looked more like plain hills to me. North of Tent City was a makeshift motorpool, where all our operator and direct support maintenance was performed. The Tactical Operations Center (TOC), only one hundred yards to the south, was where the officer and NCO staff received daily briefings and progress reports on the status of the pipeline. Whenever military or civilian dignitaries came to the area (as they often did, since this was the largest petroleum operation the Army had undertaken since World War II), they were briefed at the TOC before having a guided tour of the grounds by helicopter.

But even our guests could see that my soldiers were having a hell of a time—driving heavy pipe-laden deuce-and-a-half's and five-tons over Yakima's ribbonlike dirt roads in the hot, dusty afternoons, then sleeping on cots in canvas tents during the windy, bone-chilling desert nights.

Once, while I was on-site and we all were asleep, our maintenance tent—the largest in camp—was uprooted by the wild northwest wind and blown directly into the river. When, after four months, my soldiers finally returned to Fort Lee, they brought back everything with them but the maintenance tent. I was never issued another one. The soldiers joked that it was my only casualty.

The 57th Transportation Company had been in existence for fifty years by the time I arrived on the scene. Constituted on 1 May 1936, the company had been inactivated and reactivated numerous times and tasked to drive every type of vehicle from trucks to cars to helicopters and back to trucks again. The 57th Trans had participated in many campaigns during World War II, including Algeria, Tunisia, Anzio, the Rhineland, southern France, as well as the Tet '69 Counteroffensive during the Vietnam War. For its service in Vietnam, the company had received the Meritorious Unit Commendation and the Vietnamese Cross of Gallantry with Palm. These awards had been hung ceremoniously in my office, on the wall behind my desk.

The rest of the room was less pretentious. Cinderblock walls painted blue and white surrounded a large wooden desk and swivel chair, two brown leather armchairs (for guests), a small refrigerator (brought from home), a wall locker that held a spare uniform and my "war gear"—tent, poncho, canteen, web belt, and sleeping bag—everything I needed in the event of sudden deployment. There was also a bulletin board, a calendar, and, in one corner, a flagpole stand that held both the American flag and

214

the maroon-and-gold company guidon suspended in crossed union. Mud-brown wall-to-wall carpeting covered the linoleum floor.

For the first couple of weeks, I drifted like a phantom around the company, quietly observing. I'd leave the confines of my office and spend an entire morning and afternoon raptly watching my mechanics working in the motor pool, the immense garage that stood about a quarter of a mile away. Each company within the battalion had its own separate area within the pool and its own maintenance building containing jacks and tools for repairs. Most of the vehicles—five-quarter-ton (ton-and-a-quarter) pickup trucks, CUCVs (Commercial Utility Cargo Vehicles—a type of covered, two-door, four-wheel-drive, cargo-carrying, all-terrain vehicle that is fast replacing the traditional jeep as the Army's vehicle of choice), deuce-and-a-half's, and five-ton trucks—were lined up outside in seemingly endless rows of wheels and chassis. It was an orgy of machinery, painted olive, tan, and brown, to match the soldiers in camouflage.

Though I possessed no overriding passion for fixing motors, as com-mander of a Transportation company I did want to know how things were done. If one of my soldiers was working underneath one of the vehicles, sometimes I'd crawl below the chassis with him, to watch and learn. That way I'd be capable of doing more than performing only a few standard preventive checks on a vehicle's oil, breaks, and fluid levels.

Ultimately, though, my presence in the motor pool was superfluous; it was the soldiers' domain, not the commander's. After keening around for a while, I decided that the best approach would be to take things day by day. I never knew precisely what would happen when I showed up for work in the morning. Invariably, someone would walk into my office with a new set of problems to solve. This, I realized, was the commander's lot. Al-though I knew I'd have to take my unit through an ARTEP in May 1987, and that we'd also get hit with an EDRE or two, I never had a clear-cut itinerary.

An ARTEP (Army Readiness Training and Evaluation Program) was a sustainment exercise that tested how effectively a unit had been trained to function during times of war, similar to the AAFCE TAC EVAL in Europe. The EDRE (Emergency Deployment Readiness Exercise), on the other hand, tested the speed with which a unit could build up for deploy-ment. In the case of a unit like the 82d Airborne, if it were called to deploy, the soldiers might have to get on a plane that very same night and *go*. Because my mission was trucking—not fighting—the 57th Trans would be given at least 72 hours to react to a declaration of war. It would take my soldiers that much time to gather their personal belongings, load their equipment, make sure their records were straight, and see to it that they'd had their shots (depending on where in the world they were going).

Before one could ever hope to deploy, however, the equipment needed to be arranged in some kind of order. As the self-proclaimed "Susie Home-maker" of the 57th Trans, I insisted that our company be tidy. One of my first projects was to clean up our chaotic company warehouse. I had each platoon build its own storage closet with plywood sheets and two-by-fours, providing a place for every piece of equipment—except the ammunition and the weapons. The live ammunition was kept at the Ammunition Storage Point across the post. Throughout the battalion, weapons were kept under lock and key behind heavy steel doors in each company's Arms Room. These included the soldiers' M-16s and M-60s and the command-ers' .45s.

Commanders were among the few people in each company who could demand access to those rooms, although we didn't possess the keys. The keys were left in the care of the Armorers—trusted soldiers appointed by the commander within each company—who would turn them in for safe-keeping to a protected vault at night.

We rarely ever saw these weapons. Nobody but the MPs was armed, and my soldiers never went anywhere carrying live ammo, unless they were going to the firing range for their annual qualification test. This gave the post a peaceful atmosphere, but made it that much harder to instill a sense of urgency and inspire the soldiers to do their daily jobs. In Germany I had a very serious mission, and the threat of attack had been real. I didn't need to be reminded of my importance. Fort Lee was so quiet, however, I had to invent a lot of trumped-up ways to raise the soldiers' enthusiasm.

In effect, this meant that I had to create as many "real" missions as possible to maintain the interest in the upkeep of equipment and vehicles. This was a bizarre task, really—like trying to persuade an orchestra to sit inside the pit of a darkened theater and keep their instruments in perfect tune for a concert that everyone hopes will never happen.

In order to do this convincingly, I had to show them that at least somebody cared about what the hell they were doing, namely their com-pany commander. For example, we had an E & B Team—Environment and Beautification Team—whose job it was to drive around in a pickup truck and collect the trash scattered on the post grounds. It was a mindless, mundane job, and I knew my soldiers hated to do it. Some of them would joke about it, making fun of the Army's television commercials as they speared each piece of litter. "Hi!" they'd say to one another, "My name is Spec-4 so-and-so, and I'm bein' all I can be!"

So, I'd go out with my driver and talk to the guys who were stuck with this detail. I'd say things like, "Hey, you're keeping the post looking real good, and that reflects well on all of us." I'd encourage them to believe in the worth of their accomplishments, no matter how small. But it was hard to stimulate patriotic zeal for picking up cigarette butts. When that reality set in, all the images and slogans began to fray at the edges and wear thin. I came to realize that the view from the top remains frighteningly disparate from the one at the bottom.

As Colonel Houston declares, "We have a constant dilemma—how do we keep our fighting edge for forty or fifty years? This is one of those rare times in our history that we've ever had the luxury of trying to figure that out. But I don't believe that anything has changed fundamentally about the nature of military leadership. Somebody still has to 'close with and destroy the enemy,' and do so by example. I happen to believe seriously that we are training for war, something that might occur at any time I'm here as commander. I've been preparing for it since the day I graduated from college. Preparation is my litmus test. War is my master's thesis.

"The true tragedy for the American public, of course, is that we kill a lot of innocent Americans, young men and women, while we're looking for our competent leadership. You see, competence in peacetime doesn't necessarily equate with competence in wartime. After all, we haven't fought a major war in a long time. Ironically, the more successful we are as an institution, in terms of providing a credible deterrent, the less likely we are to be ready to fight if we have to."

Major Joan Parker, a former West Point phys ed instructor, concurs. "If we get called into battle," she says, "there won't be a switch that flips to turn us all into competent soldiers. I don't mean to sound like a warmonger, but we have to be prepared to make decisions that involve life and death. That's the difference between the Army and a civilian corporation. If a civilian corporation says to one of its employees, 'Will you risk life and limb for us?' the employee can say, 'No, I quit. You've stepped beyond the bounds of what I'm obligated to do for this company.' But *we've* raised up our hands and said, 'So help me, God, I will.' When the alarm goes off for us to deploy to a hot zone, we can't all of a sudden turn around and say, 'Well, you know, we were just kidding.' But hardly anyone I know in the military wants to talk about that. It's a very unpopular subject. Peacetime armies get very lackadaisical. The fact is, professional warriors need to test themselves, just as athletes need to compete.

"On the other hand, soldiers are typically the last ones who want to go to war because *we're* the pawns on the battlefield. So the Army has tried

217

to come up with maneuvers and exercises that can at least give us an opportunity to put our theories and practice into play."

Yet, Colonel Houston observes that even simulated worst-case scenario exercises aren't always enough to sustain the flagging martial spirit. "Interestingly," he says, "the Germans are finding that their army has some of the same problems as ours—they have a series of leadership schools now called Inner Fuhrering, or Inner Drive, which are concerned with similar issues—namely, how to keep officership motivated. How do we keep them driving?

"When I was a department director at the Command and General Staff College," he recalls, "we had a situation that caused us to feel we needed to start teaching ethics again. Talk about covering your butt and lying so you're a hero, saying you're prepared to go to war when, in fact, you're not. In October of 1973 we found, lo and behold, that we had to alert our troops to go to the Israeli flap. And we ended up not going, in part because we flat ass couldn't get there—for a lot of reasons, not the least of which was that our actual readiness did not match our *stated* condition of readiness.

"I mean, how can I, as a commander, admit to being C-4 [the lowest condition of readiness]? Hell, I wouldn't make my next promotion. But lying about readiness is no way to be a goddamn hero. Because all of a sudden, there goes your honor. There goes your Code!"

If I had to describe Colonel Houston to anyone, I'd say he was like a teapot about to boil over—constantly. Plenty of people in the battalion were scared of him, and he'd say, "By God, you'd better be scared of me. I'll take your job, you son of a bitch!" But I loved working for him; he reminded me of the Dragon.

Colonel Houston was another Napoleonic personality—in the spirit of Mike Truxel—who favored robust military novels (written by robust military men) and popular histories of Caesar and Alexander the Great, all of which he attempted to persuade me to read, to no avail. His bright bursts of laughter and peppery exclamations and his predilection for weekend spiritual retreats made him a bit of a character, but as a brigade commander, his interest in the welfare and training of soldiers was always taken seriously. His predecessor, Colonel Owen Schrader, had been largely concerned with "post beautification," which guaranteed that our grass was always manicured, but frankly did little to boost the soldiers' morale or challenge their complacency. When Colonel Houston arrived on post, however, he immediately put solid tactical training back into the soldiers' curriculum. "Rolling a thirty-eight-car train out of Fort Lee may not sound like much to some people," he once told me, "but it would be the longest train to leave Fort Lee since the Second World War. And we need to know how to run it."

When he was in a particularly good mood, Colonel Houston would settle into one of the leather armchairs in my office and talk to me amiably about the role of a commanding officer. "A commander," he would say, "is like an old GP physician, who has all kinds of specialists telling him what he ought to do, and, hell, he doesn't know what the devil these people are talking about, so he has to rely on his gut. And if he's been properly trained, and his instincts are correct, he may make the right decision. If he doesn't, someone may die.

"But remember, when you're not being a commander, you're an officer on the staff of your superior, and that's when you get to study. As a staff officer, you're able to observe *your* commander screw up one thing after another and learn from his mistakes.

"If you're smart, though, first you'll learn to be an operations officer, then an intelligence officer, then an administrator, then a logistician, and *then* an executive officer. Commanders used to be able to perform all these tasks, but no longer. The theoretical waging of war has become so complicated that now we are generalists in charge of specialists, and to be successful we have to master the art of interpretation. In some cases, if a commander hasn't been doing all his homework, he can be at their mercy. He has to study each discipline. Otherwise, how the hell will he know if they're telling the truth? And yet, ultimately, he makes the decisions. The Army may be getting to a point where command is a specialty, too. But nobody is owning up to it. In my opinion, the Army needs a management training track just for command, because if you fail, you're history.

"A commander usually gets two report cards, one at the end of the first year and one at the end of the command tour. So there will normally be two OERs (Officer Evaluation Reports) reflecting your tenure as a company commander. If you are very, very fortunate and during that time there are no rapes, no riots, no soldiers killed in dumb training accidents you should have known better about and prevented, and you survive unscathed, you will probably get passing marks. You may even get glittering remarks, because you may really be that good. Or appear to be that good.

"On the other hand, let's say the house of cards falls down on your head and there's a murder in the barracks. Or, let's say there's an unfortunate situation in which one of your NCOs is killed. It's your fault, and you have to take care of it because everything that happens or fails to happen is your responsibility. Sometimes that seems grotesquely unfair, but it's a fact. What's more, you're responsible for the actions of at least 140 people, many of whom have dependents, so they're all connected to two or three or four other people. Some may live with them, some may not; some are balanced, some are unbalanced, but they're all your wards. They're all under your charge.

"And, lest we forget, there could be war. And you might not be ready to go. You could screw up deployment. You might not be able to get your shit together in time because you didn't know how to plan it. There are a hundred thousand ways you can get hung out to dry. So don't think that all commanders are happy to be in that position. There are a number of officers who, in their heart of hearts, really would rather *not* command. It's too risky. Well, *I* say, if the risk-takers of our society, who are *paid* to put their asses on the line, for Chrissake, won't stand up and take them, then what the hell is wrong with the Code of Honor? It's grotesque! *God*, the number of captains I've had to go through to find someone who actually wanted to command!"

There would be days when I understood exactly the reluctance of those fellow officers to inherit the responsibilities of a company commander. A commander literally has to be available to his or her soldiers seven days a week, twenty-four hours a day. They can be called on duty at any time. And, as Colonel Houston was fond of pointing out, they are held personally responsible for the welfare and behavior of 140 independent people—both on-duty and off—quite an awesome burden for anyone to shoulder, let alone a junior captain in all her twenty-eight-year-old wisdom.

It was a typical Saturday night on post. People were coming and going; a few were in the company dayroom watching television. The CQ was making his rounds of security checks, a boring job. Not much happened, although the weekends tended to be the worst. Soldiers would come in drunk from a night's revels and get rowdy, and it would be the CQ's job to quiet them down. This particular Saturday night was no different, except that sometime during the night, two drunken soldiers had stolen a headstone from a graveyard in Petersburg, dragged it into the barracks, and left it in front of an NCO's door. I came in for PT at 0600, Monday morning, to find this headstone sitting in the middle of my Orderly Room floor. The CQ told me he'd found it during the night while making his rounds but hadn't known what to do, so he'd stuck it in the Orderly Room.

I was livid. I ordered the soldier to call the police immediately and have them pick up the stone, and to start questioning some of the others so we could find out who had taken it. It was a small gray tombstone, about a foot and a half tall and a foot wide. When I examined it more closely and saw the name and the dates of birth and death that were carved into the smooth granite, I felt sick. The headstone had been taken from the grave of a six-year-old girl.

The first sergeant ran an investigation, and we finally learned which two soldiers were guilty. One of them had already been on restriction for bad behavior, so I gave him a full Article 15. The other soldier, a first-time offender, received only a letter of reprimand and some extra duty.

When the local police showed up, I hoped that the cemetery would file charges against the two men and that they would have to be taken into custody. I wanted them to understand the seriousness of their actions. A few nights in jail would give them some time to ponder it. But the cemetery didn't want to press charges; they just wanted the headstone back.

Eventually, I started grilling Top, my first sergeant, about my soldiers. "What are their complaints?" I wanted to know. "What am I overlooking?" I asked him about their personal histories, their family backgrounds, their aspirations.

So, he told me about the talented jazz saxophonist who'd kept a coffin in his barracks room (until the previous commander made him get rid of it) and who now drove around the post in a long, black hearse. He told me about the motorcycling truckdriver who had dreams of becoming a highway patrolman and about the computer operator who refused to take showers around other men. He told me about soldiers who wanted to go to college and about soldiers who wouldn't clean their rooms. He told me about soldiers who'd been selected for choice assignments driving dignitaries around Washington and about single-parent soldiers struggling to find babysitters for their kids.

Newly armed with all this information, I inquired, "If any of them could be commander for a day, what do you think they'd do differently?" I was attempting to show him that I wasn't a stickler for having things done my own way or not at all. If the soldiers had ideas, I wanted to hear them. I don't know if the male commanders within the battalion believed as strongly as I did in the value of eliciting opinions from subordinates, but I wouldn't presume to call my partiality toward this approach an exclusively female impulse. However, Captain Janice Parker, a graduate from West Point's class of '86, reflecting on her experiences as a high-ranking female cadet, observes, "I think women, as leaders, do tend to be more collaborative. They involve their subordinates in the decision-making process more often than men do, which seems to allow them more authoritative latitude without being seen as castrating bitches—something they need to be very, very careful to avoid.

"When I was at the Academy, I would call a group of cadets together, throw out an issue, and then talk to them about where I wanted to go with it. I'd let them hash it out so the decision would have the feel of a consensus. It was extremely important for everyone to adopt the plan as his or her own. I didn't want them to go back to their companies and say, 'The commander said we have to do this.' I wanted them to go back and say, 'This is *our* idea, so let's do it!' If I could get them to feel like participants, then the company would respond to decisions collectively and adopt them, internalize them, support them, and be loyal to them, as if the decisions were their own.

"Officers—and women especially—have to be smarter than everyone else, and more intuitive, because a decision that depends on deliberate, dynamic group interaction might come down to this kind of rhetorical manipulation for success. Obviously, you can never allow your subordinates to become equals, per se, but you can allow them to feel involved. The final word will always come down to the leader, but you will succeed or fail as a group."

The soldiers of Third Platoon returned to Fort Lee from Yakima on the fifteenth of October; it was gratifying, finally, to have my entire company together. Before they arrived, however, the big rumor going around Yakima had been that the new female company commander was making everybody do aerobics back home.

In fact, we did PT three times a week in our unit—every Monday, Wednesday, and Friday morning at 0600 hours. A typical workout consisted of calisthenics for fifteen minutes on the grass in front of the company area building and then a run of anywhere from two to five miles. When that routine became a bore, I asked a friend of mine who worked at a Richmond nightclub to mix a tape of good dance music for me, and I started teaching Army aerobics in the post Fitness Center.

The female soldiers were pleased. Of course, none of the male soldiers wanted any part of this when they first heard about it; they were convinced that aerobics was a "sissy" exercise. But they quickly changed their minds after the first five minutes of the first day. I went easy on them in the beginning, realizing that most of them had never done anything like this.

We worked out for only thirty minutes, but I heard a lot of moaning and groaning. I had been practicing aerobics myself, so I was fine, but those guys were hurting. For three days afterward, all of them were sore. Top was walking around *real* slow. Even so, I could see a little bit of excitement in their faces, though they tried not to show it. In any case, I never heard any of them call aerobics "sissy" again.

From that day on, we did aerobics every Wednesday morning. Often, soldiers from other units within the battalion would ask if they could join us. We once had a crowd of nearly 120 sweaty soldiers dancing at the same time.

I had a lot of fun teaching them. If one of my guys started messing around, I'd bring him up front to perform the routine with me, a tactic that usually embarrassed him enough to ward off future cutting up. It wasn't a particularly pressured PT, but everyone got a great workout. We eventually worked our way up to a solid fifty-minute routine, which I considered a personal triumph.

Mondays and Fridays, though, were still the days I reserved for the rigorous two- to five-mile runs. I would purposely turn around and run backward in front of the formation to see how many people were holding up and how many had fallen out. I have to admit that I looked specifically to see how many women had fallen out. I was very sensitive to that. Motivating people during runs, especially females, could be difficult, and I knew that some of my male NCOs were afraid to discipline the women for fear of being charged with sexual harassment. There seemed to be a rather pervasive perception among male soldiers that if you dared to cross a woman, she'd ruin you. Men were reluctant to take that chance, so they tended to go a bit easier on their female soldiers. Consequently, some of the women slacked off. But I say a soldier is a soldier, male or female, which also means that if soldiers of either sex think they can "get over," one way or another, they will. Regrettably, I had one of these ne'er-do-wells in my unit.

Before I came to the 57th, Spec-4 Louise Harper would run no more than a hundred yards before falling out. Yet no one had ever taken her to task for this. The first time she tried it with me, however, I started in on her. She complained that she couldn't breathe, couldn't stop coughing. I calmly suggested that she stop smoking.

No response.

Of course, I didn't want to do anything stupid in case the woman really did have a problem, so I sent her to the Kenner Army Community Hospital on post for a complete physical. The doctor gave her a clean bill of health, so the next time she pulled that asthma crap on me, I told her to get her ass moving. Slowly but surely, she stayed in the formations longer and longer. I think she even surprised herself.

Then, one Monday morning during a two-mile run, Spec-4 Harper quit right near the end. Well, I ran to the back of the formation and started shouting at her. She became very upset and collapsed to the ground, sobbing, which pissed me off. I was tired of her lame excuses for why she was in such terrible shape. I also wanted to prove to the other women in the company that they could be physically fit, if they tried. As Harper lay there snivelling on the ground, I yelled, "Get up and finish this run!" I really must have frightened her, because she leapt up and took off like a jackrabbit. She even caught up to the others long before they had stopped running.

I think I demonstrated to my NCOs that they didn't have to be afraid of scolding a woman for not performing up to her potential. Usually, I felt I had to be more firm than soft in these cases. At times I wasn't sure how hard I should be. I never wanted my soldiers to call me weak, so maybe I went to the other extreme to prevent that from ever happening.

"I've trained both males and females," Sergeant Ricki Ellis of the battalion's 555th MP company once told me, "and I'd rather train males any day of the week. Females can be ridiculous. And they *fight*. 'She called me a bitch!' 'She called me a slut!' 'Well, *slap!*' 'Well, *smack!*' Oh, gosh, it's terrible. I mean, guys go into the bathroom and beat each other up. When you see them again and ask, 'What the hell happened to you?' they say, 'Oh, I slipped and fell.' Or, 'A door hit me in the face.' And that's the end of it. The men take better care of things among themselves. They know how to take care of business—beat each other up and then it's over and done with. But the females don't know what to do, so they drag their shit out forever.

"And females can be *funky*. When they were in the field, I had to order my NCOs to clear out the tents so the females could go inside and wash their funky selves, because when I asked them if they were clean, they said, 'We changed our socks.' 'Bullshit,' I said. 'You haven't washed in days.' 'Oh, yes, we did.' 'Really, where?' 'In the latrine.' 'I'm sorry, but you can't wash yourselves in a portajohn.'

"But, really, the males aren't that much better. I went to MP school with a guy who kept throwing his clothes away and buying new ones because he didn't know how to use the damn washing machine. I couldn't believe it.

"Still, I'd rather work with men. I know that may be disloyal to say, but then people do claim I'm much harder on females than I am on males. I don't know if that's true or not. I just want women to do well in their jobs because I know what I've suffered on account of their bad reputations, and I don't want to go through that anymore. And I don't want to watch other good females suffer because of that horseshit. It makes me really mad."

As the months passed and our honeymoon ended, the company finally settled down to the serious business of learning to function in a new configuration. As the autumn days grew shorter, the workweeks seemed to lengthen. And when Friday afternoon arrived, I found I badly needed a place to reflect. Sometimes I would close the door to my office, sink into one of the cushioned chairs in front of my desk, and just think—or have talks with myself, which people would occasionally overhear and wonder what the hell I was doing.

But if I really needed to talk to someone, I would wander over to the Supply Room and sit with Sergeant Randall. Sergeant Randall made me feel like a teacher—or an analyst. Now that he was in charge of forty soldiers, he'd ask me for advice on how to deal with their personalities, and, particularly, for advice on how to counsel them when they got into trouble. I didn't have all the answers, naturally, but I'd ask provocative questions and give him just enough bait to hook him into thinking like a commander and come up with solutions of his own. He was an extremely sensitive and thoughtful man, which was why I liked him so much. I'd be whirling around the company like a dervish, and Sergeant Randall would be one of the few people who could make me slow down long enough to stop and think. His decision-making process was more deliberate, which encouraged me to seek more than one solution and to recognize that situations weren't always black-and-white. West Point had pounded into my head that it was critical for an officer to make quick decisions, for one rarely had the luxury of time on the battlefield. And though this training had proved invaluable, the flaws inherent in relying exclusively on this approach were obvious. The fact was, I was a whiz at coming to snap conclusions. Now I had to study the ramifications. After all, a commander has the power to change people's lives, permanently.

I conducted two urinalysis tests while in command—the first unit sweep was in November 1986; the second, the following July. A unit sweep was a full-scale production, mainly because of the legal implications. There were meticulous ways of handling the urine-filled bottles; from start to

225

finish, everything had to be perfect. Only the commander and first sergeant knew when the sweep was going to take place; in fact, we were the ones to decide when it would occur.

First, I'd have to brief my battalion commander—with a lawyer present—on my plan of action. I'd even have to submit a diagram of the desks that would hold all the bottles, so the exact placement of each bottle could be clearly identified. An observer and a recorder would document the proceedings. We also had to ensure that the clean bottles were being watched at all times, so no one could gain access to them.

The observers would take each of the soldiers into the bathroom, one by one, and watch them urinate. Men watched men, women watched women. This process was strange enough, but the assembly-line character of the drill—the sudden alarm to wake and rise in the middle of the night, the rush to the bathrooms, the waiting rows of empty plastic bottles, and the long lines of impatient soldiers, legs crossed in agony, snaking their way out into the brightly lit hallways—gave the exercise an almost surreal quality. The whole unit was tested, including the commander. Of course, I did have the advantage of knowing when the test would occur, but, unlike the rest of the soldiers, the commander's word was presumed to be good. (Had the battalion commander decided to initiate a test without informing me, I would have been in the same boat as everyone else.)

We'd rust everyone out of bed to begin testing at about 3 A.M., and it wouldn't end until lunchtime. Custody of the bottles was entrusted to a chain of individuals. After being sealed at the unit, the bottles had to be signed for each time they changed hands, affixing responsibility to every member of the chain. The samples were then sent to a laboratory at Fort Meade, Maryland, where it took approximately five weeks to test an entire unit's urine for traces of marijuana and cocaine.

I would be informed of the results only if they came back positive. The battalion commander reserved the right to punish drug offenders, but I could recommend the punishment I thought the soldier deserved, based on his or her overall performance. Adding the results of both testing situations, only five of my soldiers came up positive. I felt fortunate—other units within the battalion had between fifteen and twenty positives. Normally, the punishment would be a bust of one or two ranks, partial forfeiture of pay, and extra duty for forty-five days. Sometimes, if an enlisted soldier had financial problems, the battalion commander might go a bit easy on the fine. But if an officer or NCO were *ever* caught using drugs, even once, the colonel made it clear that his or her career would be over.

"The big scam with my guys," recalled my West Point classmate

Captain Julie Hawkins, "was frozen urine. They'd actually use black market urine *during* the tests. I had one guy who everybody suspected was doing drugs, so I wanted him watched carefully. Of course *I* couldn't go into the bathroom with him, so Sergeant Morris, my platoon sergeant, went, but he was forty-nine years old and a little naive about these things. I had to give him specific instructions. 'When he goes into the bathroom,' I said, 'have him take off his shirt—both shirts, his outer shirt *and* his T-shirt—and have him drop his pants. Then I want you to walk around him and make sure he doesn't try anything funny.' It sounds extreme, I know, but as it turned out, the guy had bought a bag of someone else's urine and taped it underneath his arm, with a tube running down his body and taped again onto his penis. This is big business. A positive result could mean the end of a career.

"I also had a girl who was a heroin user. She'd already been in and out of rehab programs, but when we ran a test right after she came out of one, she couldn't go, couldn't go, couldn't go . . . so, of course, I had her in that bathroom until two in the morning. I thought she was going to split a gut. I mean, it was obvious what was going on. If they try to tell you they can't pee, just keep giving them Cokes."

One wants to be able to trust the people one works with, particularly in a military environment. As Colonel Houston puts it, "I believe it all stems from the relationship in combat, which people tend to forget. If I call you on the tactical radio and tell you the enemy's coordinates, I don't want you sitting back in the Fire Directional Center saying, 'Oh, that's John, that son of a bitch, I never thought he was worth a damn anyway. Screw him' and not fire that mission, or deliberately fire it the wrong way so you end up killing the son of a bitch. It's called getting rid of your contemporaries. Appalling. Appalling! But those things do go on."

As in the case of mandatory drug testing, trust among soldiers is gained by force, if not by merit. In the military, even friendships become occasions for inspection—especially among women. When I befriended Sergeant First Class Ricki Ellis, the battalion's senior enlisted female from the 555th MP company, or the "Triple Nickel," with whom we shared our building, eyebrows shot up immediately. Despite the air of disapproval that surrounded our relationship, however, Sergeant Ellis and I became fast friends. We established our own "old-girl" network; it was rather small, but it worked. If I ever had a question about my enlisted soldiers, I knew she would help me out. If she needed to borrow supplies and I could get them for her, I would. More importantly, we were sounding boards for each other. Even though I was an officer and she was an NCO and we had come from completely different backgrounds and training, each of us understood exactly what the other was going through.

Sergeant Ellis recalls, "Captain Barkalow took command in August 1986, and I came into my unit in November. Before I had even met her, I had heard people talk about her, and the conversation would always swing back to that old cliché, 'He's assertive, she's a bitch'—that word-game thing. So she had a reputation for being a bitch and for being arrogant and obnoxious, as well. Still, she had a good company, and people thought she was good at what she did. She had her ways, just like I had mine, but when guys had their ways—hey, that was just part of being a guy. When *we* yelled at our people, we'd lose them. We knew what our soldiers were thinking: 'Oh, she's yelling at me. It must be that time of the month.' "

Of course, neither Sergeant Ellis nor I dared to overstep the line that separated us as professionals. At work it was never "Carol" and "Ricki." I was either "Ma'am" or "Captain Barkalow," and she was "Sergeant Ellis" at all times. Perhaps it was my West Point training, but I held to a strict maintenance of hierarchy. I knew that other companies had relaxed those boundaries, and officers would call their enlisted soldiers by their first names, or lieutenants would call each other by their first names in front of the enlisted soldiers. And though I didn't find anything wrong with this, personally, I never felt comfortable doing it. I considered it unprofessional. Nevertheless, my mere association with Sergeant Ellis was enough to cause her numerous reprimands.

"The first time Captain Barkalow and I went somewhere together," Sergeant Ellis remembers, "my superiors knew about it before I even got back, and I was called on the carpet. They told me, 'You know you can't hang around with her. She's a captain, and people will talk. You have to watch your actions.' I told them, 'Look, I can hang around with whoever I want.' But we were very careful, anyway. We'd go to lunch in different cars and meet—and I got hassled for it a couple of times. Then I got mad. I said to my commander, 'You can't tell me who my friends are.'

"So, Captain Barkalow and I started eating in the dining facility together, and my two bosses—the company commander and the first sergeant (the guy who writes my EER [Enlisted Evaluation Report])— would just glare at me. Finally, I walked over to my commander and said, 'Sir, I've got to have someone to talk to. I can't go around hiding it, either. It's not fair to me.' After that, they mellowed. My first sergeant even went out of his way to speak to her, too. I don't know if it was because of me or because he'd finally pulled his head out of his fourth point of contact and realized, Hey, it's not really such a bad thing after all.' "

Ironically, the only sexual harassment case I had during my nineteen-month tenure with the company happened as a result of fraternization, or so I thought. About five months into my command, some of the NCOs and lower enlisted soldiers had fallen into the habit of playing cards in the company dayroom during lunch and after duty hours.

One bitterly cold January morning, following an after-work card game, Spec-4 Lily Joyce complained to my first sergeant that Sergeant Roy Livingston had offered to drive her home the previous night and, en route, had leaned across the front seat of his car to kiss her. Joyce claimed that Sergeant Livingston subsequently propositioned her, and when she refused his advances, he insisted that she get out of his car and walk.

I had known from past experience that some male officers and NCOs take advantage of their power by making sexual overtures to female soldiers, typically lower ranking enlisted women, who, in many cases, feel either too frightened or powerless to fight back. My West Point classmate Liz Jenkins had encountered this when we were cadets—one summer she'd been forced to lodge a complaint when a drill sergeant had made it clear that he wouldn't let her have any time off unless she slept with him.

I was aware that Sergeant Livingston had earned himself a reputation as a ladies' man. This middle-aged married man liked to fancy himself as being popular with young women. Sometimes I'd hear him talking cute to the civilian women who worked in the dining facility. Unfortunately, Spec-4 Joyce's reputation was no more sterling than his, but I found both her distress and her detailed account of the incident too compelling to ignore.

Predictably, Sergeant Livingston denied any charges of untoward behavior. He claimed that he had kicked her out of his car when he realized he didn't have enough gas to take them both home. He'd tried to charge her five dollars for fuel, he said, but Joyce didn't have any money with her, so he told her to get out and walk.

Upon investigation I learned that both Livingston and Joyce had been flirting with each other rather crudely throughout the whole card game. It seemed possible, then, that some kind of sexual altercation would have taken place between them, anyway. Meanwhile, I was dealing with two people whose word I frankly doubted in both cases. What could I do?

A sexual harassment charge can be a lethal weapon; if substantiated, it can easily destroy an officer's or NCO's career. On the other hand, a much more common occurrence is the appalling lack of response and investigation into legitimate complaints. It is usually easier for a commander to look the other way and ignore the problem rather than address it. And, more often than not, a woman's so-called reputation—and not necessarily the facts of the case—determines the level of attention her plea is likely to receive.

Part of this problem doubtless comes from an all-too-common impulse to "blame the victim," particularly where questions of women and sexual conduct are concerned. But perhaps an equally large share comes from the military's failure to establish a clear-cut, standardized definition of sexual harassment and a uniform procedure of assessment. Despite the Army's efforts to overcome the problem, by circulating pamphlets, offering educational classes on sexual harassment, issuing three policy statements by the Secretary of Defense over the past decade, and creating various outlets for lodging complaints—through the individual's chain of command, the Equal Opportunity staff, the office of the Inspector General, the chaplain, the Army's Legal Counsel, the filing of a complaint under Article 138 (complaint of wrongs) of the UCMJ, and the writing of letters to Congress—the paths of approach can be intimidating to many young women, especially when they perceive that their claims will be disbelieved or ignored, or when they fear the threat of backlash for being whistleblowers. As difficult as it may seem, however, it's important for women to recognize that they are perfectly within their rights to speak up when they feel they've been mistreated, and that, in some cases, a more serious problem may be averted if their fellow soldiers are set straight from the start.

Sexual harassment among soldiers can, of course, be prompted by mean, or even vicious, motives, but it can also arise inadvertently or out of sheer ignorance. Male soldiers often find themselves making comments that the women consider offensive, while the men don't even think of them as rude. Since educational policies on the subject are inconsistent among the services, overall guidelines are nebulous, confused, and even silly. For example, in the military one is required to say "sexual *har*assment" and not "sexual har*ass* ment" because the latter sounds like one is saying "her *ass.*" Imagine the effort it took to come up with that.

Another instance, less laughable, but illustrative of the reigning confusion, is cited by Captain Bill Thomas, West Point, class of '79. "I once took members of an Infantry battalion up to West Point to help train cadets on the machine-gun range," he explains. "I was with seven hundred guys who, by and large, hadn't had any dealings with women in the Army whatsoever. We were out where the women were shooting, and when a female cadet failed to qualify on the M-60, one of my sergeant instructors said, 'Don't worry about it. You'll probably never see a machine-gun, anyway.' Well, that female cadet complained to her chain of command, and the West Point administration supported her claim that his remark was a form of sexual harassment. As the sergeant's commanding officer, I had to investigate and then determine what I was going to do to the guy. So I counseled him and told him why he shouldn't have said what he did. Meanwhile, I was thinking to myself, Hey, what exactly is sexual harassment? Because if *this* is it, I don't get it.

"I called the head of the Leadership Development Center, a psychologist, and said, 'Hey, Sir, here's what's happening. I need some help with educating my guys on what the heck all this stuff means.' So he came out and talked to us—just the officers and senior NCOs, initially—and now my definition is this: If it *offends*, then it's sexual harassment.

"Originally, we thought it was something *sexual* in nature, something pornographic, which is what we had told the soldiers before we brought them to West Point. But once they got there, we found out it was any remark that was *sexist* in nature. Bottom line, it was anything you wouldn't say to a guy, because then it would mean you were separating the males from the females . . . phew, it was tough."

Sergeant Sweeny acknowledges, "That's why I, as an NCO with two females under my supervision, am careful about how I talk to them. Mostly, though, I don't care what people think, because I've got a job to do, and when I'm on the job, I don't treat the sexes any differently. When I want to counsel a female in my platoon, I call her into my office and shut the door, the way I would with any man.

"But the one thing I would do with a guy that I wouldn't do with a female is put him in my car and give him a ride home. Because of the way the system is designed, I would never do that with a woman. In fact, I remember Captain Barkalow once asking me for a ride when her car broke down, and I said, 'Hell no. You're gonna walk.' And I was serious. She did walk. She wasn't getting in my shit. And I apologized to her the next day.

"Now, if I'd had a witness with me, I might have picked her up. But alone? No, no, no. Hell no. Shit no. I would never let myself get caught in that position. *Never.*"

In the end, I decided to reprimand both of the soldiers in question, and pointedly the older, and presumably wiser, NCO. After conferring with my first sergeant, I wrote Sergeant Livingston a letter of reprimand, and when I presented it to him, I explained why.

"Sergeant Livingston," I began, "I'm not saying I know conclusively what happened. It's her word against yours. But I still hold *you* primarily responsible because of the position in which you put yourself. As an NCO, you should have known better. I also have to admit that I have difficulty believing you kicked her out of your car on a freezing cold night because you didn't have enough gas to take her home. Do you usually let your tank get so low?"

He didn't have an answer for me. But when he read my letter of reprimand, he wanted to make waves. He threatened to go over my head and call the battalion commander. I'd already learned in Germany how to deal with soldiers who tried to intimidate me, so I swivelled around in my chair, picked up my phone, held the receiver out to him, and said, "Let me dial the number for you."

He backed down immediately. "No, Ma'am," he said. "You don't have to do that."

I never heard another word about it.

Still, I felt that the growing familiarity between the NCOs and lower enlisted soldiers was being fostered by these card games and contributing to a breakdown in company morale. Fraternization was laying the groundwork for potential problems, particularly where senior males and lower enlisted females were concerned. In an attempt to prevent something like this from happening again, I delivered an order that no card playing would be permitted in the barracks, or on duty, between NCOs and enlisted soldiers in my company with the rank of E-4 and below. I stated clearly that violators would be subject to UCMJ action (Uniform Code of Military Justice) if they disobeyed my direct order.

The policy had been problem-free for a month or so—I hadn't even been *looking* for violators—when one lunchtime in March I took a stroll down the hall to talk to Sergeant Randall. I opened the door to the Supply Room and found, to my amazement, not only Sergeant Randall but Sergeant Livingston and a male Spec-4 deep in concentration; all were holding fans of cards in front of their guilty faces.

I was angry—and hurt. The only thing I could say to them was, "You guys just put me in an awful trick." Then I headed back down the hall to my office in utter disbelief. I simply couldn't accept that Sergeant Randall—*Sergeant Randall*—would blatantly and deliberately disobey me. For the first time in my career, I felt personally, as well as professionally, betrayed. When I went home that night I thought, I shouldn't be feeling like this. I should just treat him the way I would any NCO. But he wasn't just another NCO, he was my friend. And yet, as much as it disturbed me to do so, I knew I had to punish him. But before I did, I let my feelings simmer for a day or two because I refused to make any decisions based on emotion—I had to think things through. In the meantime, I couldn't even look at Sergeant Randall. For the next few days, I simply stayed away from the Supply Room.

Eventually, after talking to Top about what I should do, I decided to give Sergeants Randall and Livingston something known as a "Summarized Article 15," which meant that a record of punishment would remain in the soldiers' personal files, but only within the unit; it wouldn't be transferred to their official Army files. With a Summarized Article 15, the maximum penalty I could give them was fourteen days of confinement to barracks (after duty hours, of course), fourteen days of extra duty, and a strong letter of reprimand, in which I threatened to ruin their careers if they got into any more trouble while I was commander.

Sergeant Randall had never been reprimanded before. While I read the letter to him, his eyes were downcast. When I asked him why he had gone against my order, he said he had completely forgotten about my policy, but he was sorry and was prepared to accept the punishment he deserved.

After that, it was difficult for me to walk into the Supply Room for any reason except company business, so I kept my distance for a while. When I sat down with Sergeant Randall months later and told him how I'd been affected by the whole thing, he said he'd experienced some of the same feelings. The night it happened, he said, he couldn't eat dinner and couldn't even talk to his wife. He just wanted to be alone, so he went straight to bed. He felt so ashamed about letting me down that he started having difficulties disciplining the soldiers in his own platoon. Since he'd been at fault himself, he didn't feel he had the right to discipline anyone else.

Well, of course, *that* wouldn't do. Sergeant Randall had come a long way since his days of being merely a property master. I knew that if his shame over this minor transgression persisted, I would lose him altogether. I realized it was also my job to lift his spirits, so I asked him to step into my office for a moment. I invited him to sit down, and then I said, "Sergeant Randall, I don't like the way things have been going between us, and I know the only way we can solve it is to talk about it."

"Yes, Ma'am," he said.

"I understand you feel bad," I said as I reached under a pile of papers on my desk and pulled out a flat wooden object that was the size of a small paperback, "but have you ever seen this little plaque I keep on my desk?" Without waiting for an answer, I held it out to him and said, "A friend of mine from West Point gave this to me. May I read it to you?"

"Yes, Ma'am," said Sergeant Randall dutifully.

"All right," I said. "It reads: 'The only way to avoid mistakes is to gain experience. The only way to gain experience is to make mistakes.' Sergeant Randall, you ought to think about those words; they might do you some good."

I dismissed him from my office, and sighed as the door shut behind him. I knew I had wanted him to be perfect. I had expected it and was terribly disappointed when I discovered a flaw. But I'd been wrong. Sergeant Randall needed to meet his own expectations, not mine. But I realized, finally, what it meant to become so deeply involved with some soldiers that my own sense of value became predicated on their accomplishments, my identity justified by their existence. The wall of detachment I'd so carefully constructed was beginning to crumble. No matter what might happen in the future, I vowed I would never let myself get that close to one of my soldiers again.

Being exposed to and having to sort out wrenching situations, including those in the private lives of enlisted soldiers, is the moral obligation of an officer. In fact, as a commander, I was not only permitted but also required to involve myself in even their most intimate, and sometimes violent, personal affairs. During my command, I dealt with four separate cases of spouse abuse, child abuse, or both (realizing, of course, that there may have been more cases; those were only the ones reported).

The first two cases were incidences of spouse abuse by two of my male soldiers—an E-4 and an NCO. Though totally unrelated, both stories were practically identical—the guys had come home drunk, turned nasty, and hit their wives. The wives had called the MPs, but when the MPs arrived, neither wife wanted to press charges. So, there was nothing the MPs could do but write up a report. After letting the guys sweat it out for a couple of days, I called them in separately for counseling. I explained to each of them what I felt were the consequences of abusing the women they were supposed to love and care for, and I cautioned them on the role that drinking plays in domestic violence. Both of the men seemed remorseful. They'd already apologized to their wives, and then they apologized to me and promised that a similar outburst would never happen again. And as far as I knew, for as long as I was commander, it didn't.

The third was an ongoing case of spouse and child abuse that I'd inherited, which required periodic review. Both the Army's social services and the Kenner Army Hospital were involved. Although there'd been no proof of physical abuse, these services felt there'd been sufficient grounds to keep the case open. Again, the civilian spouse did not wish to press charges against her soldier husband, but she and her four-year-old child would occasionally come into the hospital to speak with the doctors and have a physical exam. I went to the hospital for at least one of these reviews and also spent some time talking to the husband. While my other two soldiers had readily admitted their wrongdoing, this man would neither confirm nor deny the allegations that had been brought against him. With chilling composure, he just sat out the process.

In the final and perhaps worst instance, the civilian husband of one of my female soldiers was the perpetrator. According to his wife, this man had a drinking problem and considerable difficulty holding a job. He and his wife had an eighteen-month-old baby girl, and while the soldier-mother performed her duty at the 57th Trans, it was supposedly the father's responsibility to stay home and babysit the child.

One day, three of my female soldiers (the child's mother was not among them) came to tell me—for the sake of the baby—that they suspected something terrible was going on at Spec-4 Sullivan's house. They claimed to have seen bruises on the baby during their last visit—hand-marks from being grabbed around the legs and bruises in the middle of her back.

When they first told me the story, I was speechless. In fact, the stunned look on my face prompted one of the women to ask me if I was all right. I knew I had to make sure that the baby was safe, so I summoned Spec-4 Sullivan to my office.

When she arrived, I sat her down and questioned her about her husband's treatment of their daughter. She burst into tears and said that the previous night she and her husband had been in a terrible fight, during the course of which he had threatened the life of the child. She had escaped with the baby to a friend's house, and now she was afraid to go back to the apartment. She said she wished she could spend some time with her parents, but her relationship with them had not been on the best of terms lately.

Immediately I telephoned Sullivan's mother and explained the situation. I said that I was giving her daughter a week's leave, and that she wanted to come home.

Her mother's stern heart melted instantly when she learned of her daughter and granddaughter's predicament, and then she broke down and sobbed over the telephone. She agreed that her daughter should come home with the baby at once.

I sent one of the soldiers in the unit to escort Spec-4 Sullivan to her apartment so she could pack a suitcase for the baby and herself. Sullivan told me that she didn't want her husband to know she was leaving town, and that she intended to divorce him. I wasn't sure I believed her, but at least she left that night.

She returned in a week, as planned. By that time, hostilities had cooled, and she decided not to press charges. Grateful for her return, the woman's husband acted penitent for a while, and she took him back. I could only monitor the couple from afar; apparently none of her friends in the company wanted any further involvement. For a while, all remained quiet.

Then, one night, while Sullivan was on CQ (Charge of Quarters) duty, her husband called her from home—the baby was crying and wouldn't stop. She knew something must be terribly wrong for him to call her, so she ran home and took the baby over to the emergency room at the post hospital. After a complete examination, the doctor told her that the baby would have to be moved to a civilian hospital in Richmond; there appeared to be a problem with the child's intestines. The hospital arranged for both mother and child to be taken there by ambulance at once. As soon as the civilian doctor had examined the baby, he called the police. Her tiny body was showing bruises in several places, and an X ray of her skull had revealed a hairline fracture.

The child was then handed over to civilian social services and placed in a foster home in Petersburg. Because the baby was a military family member (formerly called a "dependent"), an Army social service representative acted as an intermediary between the parents and the civilian social workers. Both Spec-4 Sullivan and her husband were charged with child abuse and neglect, but Mr. Sullivan never appeared in court. When the time came for the hearing, he had simply vanished.

Meanwhile, Spec-4 Sullivan insisted that she had done nothing to hurt her baby and demanded her back. Now that her husband had left her, she sought on-post family housing for herself and her daughter. I arranged for her to move from her apartment into military quarters, reminding her that she wouldn't regain custody of her daughter until an investigation was completed, and only then if the court determined she was a fit mother. Later, Sullivan admitted to me that her husband was a heavy drinker who would occasionally fly into rages and beat her. At times, she told me tearfully, she had tried to fight back.

My role from then on became one of support. Sullivan went through

236

a long process to regain custody of her child. She was required to attend special child-rearing classes given by Army social services at the post hospital, and she had to make numerous appearances in court. I accompanied her to a number of these hearings and met with the social worker who'd been assigned to her case.

Unbelievably, after about two months, Sullivan's husband turned up again, and the couple started living together once more. This was her choice, of course, and there was nothing I could do. Even more incredibly, however, Spec-4 Sullivan became pregnant. I think she must have desperately wanted another child because it was beginning to seem quite possible that she might not get her daughter back.

It didn't take long, unfortunately, for Sullivan's husband to become abusive again. But this time, Sullivan was living in military housing, so I had the power to ban him from post property. Top took care of it for me; he sent the MPs over to Sullivan's apartment to "escort" the man outside the gates. Sullivan's husband must have gotten wind of my intention, though, because by the time the MPs arrived, they found the contents of the apartment had been destroyed, and he was nowhere to be found.

Amid all this turmoil, Spec-4 Sullivan received orders to go to Korea for a year. Korea was considered a "hardship tour," and because the living conditions were poor (the base lacked adequate space to house families, so the soldiers lived together in small barracks rooms), she was informed that she would not be allowed to bring any dependents with her—a military policy impervious to questioning. The Army will accommodate soldiers to a point, but never to the point where the Army's needs don't come first. If you put on the uniform, you accept the "mission" that goes along with it. If parents and children, or husbands and wives, can be located together, fine. If not, then the families will accommodate the Army. In any case, the Army—not the individual—will make that decision. And the soldier will cope.

Now Spec-4 Sullivan had to secure a home for *two* babies. As an E-4, she was allotted—in addition to her regular salary—a small monthly sum designated for the care of her dependents, a category that included both her spouse *and* her children. This sum is fixed according to a soldier's rank and remains exactly the same whether the soldier has two dependents or twenty. (According to the 1990 pay scale, an E-4's dependent benefits total $314.40 per month, certainly not enough to pay for the care and support of two infant children during a year-long enforced absence.)

Sullivan's overseas deployment was temporarily deferred until the end of her maternity leave, and her mother generously agreed to assume guardianship of both children upon her daughter's departure. Fortunately, the court decided to permit the babies to live with their grandmother.

But what if there had been no grandmother? The only alternative for Spec-4 Sullivan—had she been unable to find another guardian for her children—would have been to leave the military with an honorable discharge, on the condition that she sign a "declination of service" statement that simultaneously released her from her overseas commitment and, upon finishing her present tour of duty in CONUS (the Continental United States), barred her from any future reenlistment.

Army regulations clearly state that "the Department of the Army Form 5305-R (Family Care Plan) is the means by which soldiers provide for the care of their family members when military duties prevent the soldier from doing so."

On the Family Care Plan form, soldiers must designate both temporary and permanent caretakers for their dependents during times of temporary deployment, reassignment to posts where family members may not be authorized to follow, and, of course, during times of war. Further, they must include proof that not only do these designated guardians agree to provide care, they have the means and legal authority to do so. This requirement is taken so seriously that if a soldier's care plan appears "inadequate," or if the soldier fails "to manage personal, marital, or family affairs" responsibly, a commander is instructed to initiate proceedings for the "involuntary separation" of that soldier from service, or to prevent him or her from reenlisting.

It is possible, (usually because of some outside influence or intervention) but highly unlikely, that the Army would consider altering its plans in deference to a soldier's family situation. Commanders are instructed to make it clear to their enlisted soldiers that they will not receive any special consideration for duty assignments based on their domestic responsibilities. Only officers and NCOs are "managed" individually, affording them a somewhat greater flexibility in assignments. The number of enlisted soldiers is deemed too large for the Army to consider each assignment individually. Therefore, although the Army possesses information on every soldier's personal circumstances, it is not used as a criterion for determining assignments, with one exception—if the soldier is enrolled in the Army's Exceptional Family Member Program. This program allows soldiers to decline posts that cannot provide the proper facilities for "exceptional" dependents, such as autistic, learning disabled, or physically handicapped children. Otherwise, officers as well as enlisted soldiers are expected to be available for worldwide assignment at all times and to prepare for that eventuality by keeping their "care plan" up-to-date.

And yet, despite these obligations, the Army has come a long way in learning to adapt to the needs of female soldiers. Until 1975, for example, military women on active duty were involuntarily discharged from service if they became pregnant. This policy was abandoned following challenges to its constitutionality. Today, not only may pregnant female officers continue their military careers, but they are required to do so. They must complete their tour of duty regardless of personal circumstances. Pregnant female enlisted soldiers may also continue in their careers if they wish. They, however, are granted an additional option to leave military service at any time. All women are still involuntarily dismissed if they become pregnant during basic training.

From the time a female officer or enlisted soldier first learns she is pregnant, she usually has about eight and a half months to hold off deployment. But she becomes immediately deployable again thirty days after delivery, even though she is technically allowed six weeks to convalesce. (In February 1989, the Army officially extended soldiers' maternity leave from four weeks to six, finally closing the troublesome two-week gap that had long existed between the end of a new mother's maternity leave and the age at which her baby became eligible for daycare.)

Because of their nondeployability, and because of regulations that demand their workload be altered as their "temporary medical condition" progresses, pregnant soldiers are widely regarded as an efficiency problem throughout the services. Concerns over absenteeism, morale, and productivity have been cited by at least one Navy study, although a fourth concern (curiously omitted) should no doubt be included—namely, cost. Improving the frequently poor Ob/Gyn facilities in military hospitals, for instance, has been an important objective of the Defense Advisory Committee on Women in the Services.

Fears about pregnant soldiers persist despite evidence to the contrary obtained from two separate studies—one entitled "Pregnancy in the Navy: Impact on absenteeism, attriting, and work group morale," conducted by the Navy Personnel Research and Development Center in 1977, and a follow-up study of the standard Navy workweek undertaken in 1987.

A third study, currently being conducted by the Navy, entitled "Incidence of Pregnancy and Single Parenthood Among Enlisted Personnel in the Navy," notes these earlier reports, stating that "Women were responsible for fewer days of absenteeism than men, even when pregnancy was included," and "Over two-thirds of the personnel who had worked with a pregnant woman felt that the productivity of the work group had not been impaired." (To date, even though there is widespread concern over the issue, no other service has formally published a pregnancy study. In June 1986, however, the Army completed a "Women in Combat" report, which included a review of Army policies dealing with pregnancy.)

Given such evidence, how do women account for the prejudices that continue against pregnant soldiers? First Sergeant Susan Brown (who, together with her NCO husband, has successfully combined a military career with raising a daughter, now sixteen) sums it up succinctly. "I think people who point to pregnant women as being a big problem for the Army are looking for an escape," she explains. "It's just another way of saying, 'We have too many women in the military.' We take a lot of jobs away from men."

Meanwhile, such pervasive negative attitudes are causing many military women a great deal of unnecessary anguish and embarrassment. One of my soldiers, Spec-4 Maria Gomez, recalls the behavior of a very unsympathetic sergeant who treated the news of her pregnancy as though it were a personal affront. "When I got pregnant and had to be counseled for it," she said, "I had this sergeant—he was 'old Army'—who didn't really agree with having pregnant female soldiers around. When he counseled me, he kept his office door wide open and started screaming, *'What the hell do you think you're going to do now?'* and all this other stuff that everybody in the office could hear, just to humiliate me.

"While the sergeant was carrying on like this," she continued, "I just looked at him and completely maintained my military bearing. As soon as he stopped yelling, I asked him if he was finished. When he said 'Yes,' I said, 'I'm leaving, then.' I acted as though it didn't bother me, but it did, of course. When the day was over, I went up to my room and cried. There was no way I was going to cry in front of that sergeant—even if the sergeant had been a female. Some women do that, but I would never do it. Never."

Later, when asked if she intended to make the military her career, Spec-4 Gomez who paused for a moment and, perhaps remembering this incident, said sadly, "No, I don't. I want to get as much as I can out of it, and then I want to get out before it makes me old."

A West Point classmate of mine, Captain Robin Bach, echoes the sentiments of many officers, both male and female, when she declares, "There *is* a problem with being a commander of a unit that has women in it.

240

Congress currently limits the Army to 780,000 people, but it doesn't say 780,000 *deployable* people. If soldiers are nondeployable for whatever reason—if they break their leg or they're in a drug and alcohol clinic—they're still held against my books. They are assigned to my company and are technically filling a slot, but they are nondeployable and I can't get more soldiers to replace them. The system doesn't compensate for that. So when women soldiers get pregnant and become nondeployable, my unit still has to go out and do all of the things they're supposed to do.

"When I was a company commander," Captain Bach recalls, "I had an excellent Spec-4 who got pregnant. She wanted to work on-line for as long as she could, but the First Armor Division command sergeant major said, for reasons of safety and hygiene, that we couldn't take a pregnant female in her first trimester to the field for more than seventy-two hours, and we couldn't take her to the field after the second trimester at all. I was so pissed I couldn't see straight. This signal operator *wanted* to do her job. But it got to the point where she wasn't allowed to, so they assigned a guy to her rig, and she worked as hard as she could at whatever we found for her to do."

"In *my* company," declares MP First Sergeant Ricki Ellis, "a pregnant woman in her first trimester can work eight hours a day, but she has to get five minutes of rest every hour. The second trimester, she works maybe six hours a day—no more than thirty hours a week—with ten minutes of rest every hour. By the third trimester, she may as well forget it. She can't do this, she can't do that. Practically all the woman can do is sit, breathe, and eat. And that's really degrading for me to see. Besides, the guys aren't stupid; they know how much a woman can get away with when she's pregnant. She comes and goes as she pleases. She doesn't perform any manual labor. She can't use weapons. Nothing. It causes problems."

In contrast to the frustrated and impatient attitude of these two women (neither of whom, it should be noted, have been pregnant themselves), the men occasionally adopt a tone that is more tolerant—even reverent.

"If females are going to be in the military," says Sergeant Michael Sweeney matter-of-factly, "and if the system has already accepted them, then we have to accept what Mother Nature's going to do for them, too. When they get pregnant, it really doesn't bother me because I'm a family man. When I see a family in the making, I understand exactly what that female is going through. I know Mother Nature takes a hellified course to bring in that birth. I recognize the mental and physical pain that a woman endures; I respect it. So I can understand why the system doesn't want to hurt a pregnant female. Some guys think, So, she's pregnant, so what? She can move that goddamn desk. But I think, Hey, now, wait a minute. You know, come on.

"What's more," Sergeant Sweeney continues, "a woman can flunk a PT test six months after she has a baby and be put on remedial PT, and if she flunks the next one six months later, the commander can bar her. He can put her out of the Army. So that's the problem I see—what happens after the delivery, not what happens before.

"The fact is, any active duty soldier who needs to have any type of surgery is going to take some convalescent leave, be it two or six weeks. If I broke my leg today, I'd be hospitalized, and then I'd go on leave. When I finally came back to work, I'd be on crutches and would have to go through physical therapy for an hour a day. And, as far as 'light duty' goes, if I had a bad back and couldn't stand on my feet, I'd get a doctor's slip that said 'Sergeant Sweeney needs to sit behind a desk,' which is really the same as being pregnant. But I'm not going to be barred. I'm not going to have any administrative action taken against me. Man, it's a trip. They should let *me* be in charge of all this; I'd set it straight."

In recent years, perhaps largely due to the emotions elicited by the subject combined with a woeful lack of factual information, pregnancy has been targeted (along with male-female bonding and the impact on mission performance of single parents and dual-career military couples with dependent children) as *the* critical issue concerning women in the military, eclipsing the even more colorful debates over women in combat.

The military women I've spoken with, who are either already mothers or contemplating becoming mothers, remain confident in their professional dedication and abilities. They are less fearful of a hypothetical decrease in their "mission performance" and more troubled by the lack of support in the form of convenient and reliable childcare facilities. Though single-parent families and married service couples have become increasingly common in recent years, the military's not-so-subtle message to female soldiers is that the duties of childrearing still properly rest with them. This attitude is reflected in a number of policies. For example, although all single enlisted parents—whether men or women—have the option of voluntarily leaving military service at any time, only the female member of a married service couple with dependent children is afforded this option. Also, the Army provides women with a six-week postnatal maternity leave but offers no paternity leave to new military fathers.

(Norway, Denmark, and Turkey are, incidentally, the only NATO countries that do.) Finally, even the decision whether or not to have a child can be affected by Army policy. For instance, Army hospitals will not perform abortions, since these facilities operate on U.S. federal funds. (Since 1977, the Hyde Amendment has prohibited all federal funding of abortions, including cases of rape or incest, with only one exception— when a women's life is endangered. The funding restrictions affect all women whose health care is administered by the federal government, and includes not only military personnel and their family members, but low-income women eligible for Medicaid, federal employees and their dependent family members, women in federal prisons, Native American women, Peace Corps volunteers, and residents of the District of Columbia.) Until October 1988, female soldiers had been able to use Army medical facilities to obtain abortions on some military bases in Europe—but only if they paid for them privately. Now, however, even that option has been removed, and the practice is no longer permitted.

My battalion commander, Lieutenant Colonel Edward Schuller, one of the most empathetic men I've heard speak on the subject, recognizes the difficulties faced by female career soldiers with families whose choices are narrowed by a combination of cultural prejudices and policies that often end up being harder on military women than on their male counterparts.

"I would say that the concern over pregnancy in the military has been blown out of proportion," admits Colonel Schuller, "but I don't see pregnancy as a major problem. However, it becomes one when males perceive pregnant females to be even more fragile than those who aren't pregnant. More often than not, this forces the woman in a dual-career military couple to give up her post, if the couple can afford it. So she stays at home and raises the children while her husband continues his military career."

Forcing such choices for military couples is not without precedent, however. As my West Point classmate Captain Diane Yeager explains, "If you're a civilian currently married to someone who is already in the military, and you want to enlist, you can't, if either of you have a dependent child. Meanwhile, we have plenty of Army couples—even single soldiers—who are having kids and doing a great job. Keeping out these married couples isn't helping the situation. It's all a big sham, anyway, because the parents often get around the system by giving custody of the kid to somebody else. Then, a couple of months later, they violate the contract and take the child back. It's a contract that's fairly easy to break.

I see the policy as an anomaly: It's not very reliable from a management standpoint, and it certainly defeats the Army's image of the 'family ideal.' "

Meanwhile, misconceptions abound. My West Point classmate Captain Julie Hawkins says, "I've talked to male officers who claim they've had women in their units who've gotten pregnant just so they didn't have to go to the field, but I don't know of any woman who would do that. I mean, that's a hell of a reason to get pregnant. Do these men really think that women, who have chosen to enlist in the first place, are going to take on a lifetime commitment just to get out of spending a week in the field? The truth is, many men in the military are so afraid of 'women's issues' that they don't know how to deal with them." (Indeed, the Navy has discovered, during the course of its current study, that "male supervisors are largely unfamiliar with policies on pregnancy, and their requirement to counsel pregnant women on their obligations, options, and medical benefits is complied with only about 50 percent of the time.")

An interesting symbol of male ambivalence toward the pregnant female soldier is the military maternity uniform. In 1986 a bulletin in the *Army Times* announced that under no circumstances would soldiers be permitted to call pregnancy uniforms "Maternity BDUs" because BDU means "Battle Dress Uniform" and, at least theoretically, pregnant women aren't going into battle. Instead, people are required to call them "Maternity Work Uniforms." Everyone knows, of course, that they're really BDUs with a big waist.

But the ambivalence goes beyond just the euphemistic nomenclature. To some male officers, the mere concept of pregnant women in combat dress makes them uneasy. "In my unit," recalls my West Point classmate Paula Stafford, "the corps commander made the unilateral decision to prohibit any 'Maternity Work Uniforms' on post. Now, where the hell does a general get off making a policy like that? Naturally, I took him on, because I had three or four women mechanics who were pregnant and who certainly were not going to turn wrenches in their Class B's. I finally got that policy turned around a year later, but only because I was determined to do it. That's the kind of thing women officers always have to do, whether as captains or as generals. I believe we have a moral obligation to take care of the women coming up behind us, so they don't have to go through the same crap that we did. We *are* the pioneers—every day, at every echelon. And we do have power. Remember, I was only a captain at the time, so it couldn't be my policy decision. But, by God, I got *him* to make it for me."

This same classmate also devised a solution to her female soldiers' enforced indolence during pregnancy. "I started a pregnancy PT program," she said, "because the pregnant women used to skip PT and come in late, which caused a big morale problem in the company. I'm not talking about making them do five-mile runs and hundreds of jumping jacks and sit-ups and push-ups, of course, just some basic stretching exercises and some walking. Previously, the pregnant women in the company had been afraid to come to PT because they didn't want to be ridiculed. And the male commanders didn't know what kinds of exercises the women could do, so they just avoided the whole issue. Naturally, it worked out much better when we finally got them out there."

As it happens, Fort Lee has a good pregnancy PT program, initiated and regulated by the post hospital. Every Tuesday and Thursday afternoon the pregnant soldiers on post gather together and do an hour's worth of modified PT.

"I do have some females who are dedicated to the cause," insists Sergeant Sweeney, whose empathy for pregnant soldiers unfortunately does not extend to single mothers. "I had one who was married and had a child, and her husband didn't work. But when she worked for me, she gave 110 percent of her best effort, and I respected the hell out of her.

"On the other hand," he continues, "I had another female who came in two weeks before her, and she was a ruined piece of apple. She'd bitch, complain, and gripe because she was a single parent and her main concern was her son. If her duty extended past normal working hours, she'd always have the excuse that she had to leave because of her son. She might have gotten a sitter, but her first proper thought and responsibility was not to the Army—it was to her child. Even though the same circumstances apply to single fathers, I think they handle it better. They get themselves a nice sitter, and when they have to pull extra duty or work late, the sitter understands. The men understand their mission. They put their duty first and their family second. I know *I* do, and my wife understands."

Though he isn't a single parent, Sergeant Randall is a case in point. "I have a wife and two kids," says Sergeant Randall, "and many, many moons ago, my first priority was my family. But that's when I was an E-3 or E-4, and I didn't have any real responsibility. When I became an NCO in charge of a section, it was my section, and I took pride in being the best. I've explained to my wife that in order to be good you have to make sacrifices—either the duty goes slack or the family goes slack. And if the duty goes slack, it reflects upon me as an NCO. So I didn't always spend enough time at home. But then, knowing that I was doing well at my job kind of made up for that."

It is always the understanding wives, it seems, who make the dreams and ambitions of men like Sergeant Randall and Sergeant Sweeney possible; who enable them to have families *and* careers; who unquestioningly assume the bulk of domestic responsibilities (and sometimes take on the added burden of doing odd jobs for a little extra income) so their men can train to fight "the enemy" by day and come home to a set table, a warm supper, and, perhaps, a brood of angelic children tucked sweetly into bed each night. They are extraordinary women, these wives. If only there were as many understanding husbands.

Of course, the pull of career versus family is not unique to military mothers, nor even to women, although the extra psychological, emotional, and financial pressures on women who attempt to do both often tip the scales of society unfairly against them. In the Army, because of the transience, risk, and inflexibility that are intrinsic to military life, career pressures can be greatly magnified, and the problematic choice every soldier, male or female, must make in deciding whether the Army's priorities are one's own—even at the expense of one's personal life—can sometimes precipitate the downfall of a marriage, a relationship, or a family.

Most soldiers accept this condition of military life with equanimity. "It's an adjustment you have to make," explains my West Point classmate Captain Jane Potter, who once served on active duty as a single parent. "I had my son with me in Germany, and if I had an alert at three or four in the morning, I'd have to go into his room and wake him up. It was hard to look at the little guy and get him all bundled up and take him over to the babysitter's in the middle of a winter night. But I just kept telling myself, He doesn't realize what's going on, and he'll fall back to sleep quickly. He'll be okay because he's a healthy boy. But making that separation between duty and family can be very hard."

"I think there is a point," says another West Point classmate, Captain Kevin Lang, "when you make a more permanent commitment to a career in the military and start to buy into the system. And when you buy into the system, your mind closes to some of the things you may have been open to when you were younger.

"For example, I have seen the state of mind some guys have been in after they've DX'ed their wives [Direct Exchanged—that is, turned them in for a new model] or their wives have DX'ed them, and it seems as if a lot of them must have said, 'The military is more important to me than you are.' I know my mom's talked about it, saying there were times when my father was so caught up in his job as an officer that she didn't want to have anything to do with him.

"My wife and I see the same problem in our marriage. We hope, when we eventually have kids, that our domestic responsibilities will be shared, but my tendency, of course, is to be chauvinistic. It's how I was raised. My mom stayed home. She cooked, cleaned, did the laundry, and took care of the kids while my Dad went to work at five every morning and came home at eight every night. And I have a tendency to expect that type of arrangement, too. It scares the hell out of my wife—who's also an Army captain, and whose work schedule is just as demanding as mine. Although simply sharing the housework from time to time isn't the problem. I do that. Rather, it's assuming *equal responsibility* for the housework. And of course, childrearing becomes even more complicated when both parents are working. So I jokingly tell my wife, when the time comes we'll just have to hire a lactating French maid."

Not all my female West Point classmates are struggling with family issues, however. For some, the struggle was over when they felt compelled to choose between family life and the life of a professional officer. Captain Toby Strong explains, "When I was in England, in September 1980, I attended a conference at Sandhurst where the utilization of women in the British military was being discussed. A British major, who'd prepared a study on integration, invited me to speak, but before I did, he gave me a copy of his study to read.

"One paragraph from the major's covering letter to the commissions board had struck me in particular. Until then, I had held the belief that eventually I could be the perfect wife and mommy and supreme allied commander. But the major's letter, dated 4 September 1980, challenged my hopes when I read: 'If the armed forces are contemplating using women, then they really ought only to consider single women. Working wives, and, to a lesser extent, working mothers, may in society at present be acceptable, even a necessity, but both are really part-time workers with limited employability due to family, marital, and other domestic constraints.'

"Many British officers I spoke with seemed to support the major's opinion that if a woman wanted to apply for a commission, she must be single. For men, of course, the military encouraged a wholesome family atmosphere. Naturally, when I first read those words I was appalled. Now, however, the irony is that my life has ended up just as the major would have predicted.

247

"Years later," she elaborates, "I broke up an engagement over diverging career paths. My fiancé, who was a civilian, could not comprehend my commitment to the military, and at one point he said to me, 'You certainly must have it out of your system by now.'

"But I hadn't. I had recently completed my tour as a company commander, which had been one of the most rewarding experiences of my life. I couldn't remember a morning when I didn't want to get up and go to work, even if I had been up all hours drinking schnapps with my German neighbors the previous night. My soldiers were bright, witty, and engaging people, and though there was always a tremendous amount of stress at work, and policies I disagreed with, the job had so much variety that I never got bored. I simply could not conceive of leaving. I also knew that in order for me to achieve my career goals, my spouse would be doomed to following me around, and I couldn't bring myself to ask him to do that.

"I have now resigned myself to remaining single while I pursue my military career. I think it would take a rare man to put up with the life I have chosen—unless I marry another officer—and yet, even then, someone's career ultimately has to give, and I won't be the one to make that sacrifice. I have come to realize that a network of friends is something to treasure, and that being married is not necessarily the ideal. I've had to become very self-sufficient and a little hardbitten, but I really get a charge out of my work. I bring my nurturing impulses to my unit."

In fact, as a company commander, the opportunities for nurturing are frequent. For example, I decided I wanted my company involved in some community work, and I solicited the voluntary help of some of my soldiers. I asked Sergeant Randall to find out what was around in our area. He came up with the Lafayette House—an apartment complex for the elderly. He and I went to meet Mrs. Simmons, the manager of the building, and arranged a weekly schedule; my only regret was that I didn't start the program sooner. Every Thursday afternoon at 3:00, a handful of soldiers and I would go to Lafayette House and spend about two hours doing odd jobs for the tenants. The front desk would give us the room numbers and a list of errands. Eventually, some of the elderly women began to wait in the lobby for their favorite soldier. We'd do things like vacuum, dust, wash windows, clean kitchens, move furniture—jobs that older people had a lot of trouble doing for themselves and would have had to pay someone else to do. I befriended one seventy-year-old woman named Sara Myers, who had lost part of her leg to cancer and was confined to a wheelchair. I thought she was amazing. She played the piano and had memorized all the tenants' names and apartment numbers—there were over a hundred apart-

248

ments in the building. Each time I went, I either cleaned something for Sara, or I would just drop by for a visit. I think a number of the tenants were simply glad to have visitors. I found out that Sergeant Randall, for instance, kept returning to the same apartment because he liked to eat and watch TV with the woman who lived there.

In a more dramatic illustration, my soldier Spec-4 Bobby Grant and his civilian wife, Mary, were having a great deal of trouble adjusting to the vicissitudes of wedded life. Spec-4 Grant was only twenty years old, and he had married right out of high school. When the marriage went sour, Spec-4 Grant wanted out, but evidently his wife refused to accept it. The couple had one child—an infant son—and my soldier wanted to divorce his wife and obtain custody of the child. His wife, however, couldn't bear to let go.

One night Top received a frantic phone call from the barracks CQ. Mary Grant had been visiting friends in a neighboring company, and some soldiers had walked in and caught her in the act of slitting her wrists. The soldiers immediately called the MPs, who rushed the frightened, bleeding woman to the post hospital. Top called me when he first arrived at the hospital, and then later notified me of the woman's condition once the situation was under control.

Fortunately, Mary Grant survived her self-inflicted wounds. It then became my job to try and smooth relations between her and her husband. I couldn't repair their broken marriage, of course, but I could ensure that my soldier was fulfilling his responsibilities toward his wife and child throughout the divorce proceedings.

Ultimately, Mary Grant was not awarded custody of her son, but she did receive visitation rights. However, her ex-husband refused to let her see the baby. Mary eventually directed her complaints to me, and I subsequently warned Grant that he'd better follow the court order or be prepared to suffer the consequences. As his commander, I could give him an Article 15 for failure to take care of his family members. I could even run him out of the Army or prevent his reenlistment. I also had the power to recommend to the court that Grant's child be taken away from him and handed over to Army social services for placement in a foster home. Spec-4 Grant straightened up very quickly after that.

But Mary Grant's act of suicidal desperation is not an uncommon occurrence on military posts. Reports of psychological disturbances, depression, and suicide attempts—whether among enlisted soldiers, officers, or members of their civilian families—are not unusual. Psychological counseling is available to enlisted soldiers, but in the case of officers, upon whom the pressures of performance and responsibility weigh even more heavily, the unspoken attitude is that they would be very ill advised to seek counseling for themselves. As Major Roberta Crawford, a former West Point tactical officer, explains, "Officers can't see psychiatrists while they're on active duty—the Army will think they're nuts. The smart thing for them to do is to see a civilian therapist and pay privately. If they talk to a psychiatrist at the local Army hospital, those papers certainly will end up in their Army file. What's more, they'll be thought of as soldiers who can't handle stress, which will definitely catch up with them."

Typically, people with no recourse to professional therapy can find some emotional outlet through personal relationships, although the turbulence of Army life can be very hard on developing and maintaining them, particularly for women. Civilian companionship can be limited, and friendships with male officers are not always easily established.

"I would say the hardest thing about being a single woman in the Army is the loneliness," says Lieutenant Susan Webber, a former platoon leader of mine. "When you're an officer, you're surrounded by two hundred people a day, but you're dealing with *their* problems, *their* lives. They're not your friends. You get very wrapped up in other people's lives, and when you go home, they're what you think about. Civilians don't understand this. I have some civilian friends, but none of them understand what it's like, even though some of them are doctors and nurses, and that's all *they* think about. It's funny, you all go out together, and you talk yours, and they talk theirs, and that's all. Until you start talking politics, of course, and then it turns ugly."

Former West Point Tac Major Emily Ferris recalls, "One single female officer I know was completely isolated at Fort Riley, Kansas. After working there as a platoon leader for nearly a year and a half, her company commander and one of his young officer friends finally approached her one day and said, 'We're going over to the Officers' Club for lunch. Would you like to join us?' She said, 'Yes,' but first she had to go into the bathroom and cry because she couldn't handle it. Nobody had invited her to do *anything* during the whole time she'd been there. She told me no one had shown her any kindness for so long that when suddenly someone did, it just ripped her to pieces."

Women who've spent much of their professional life moving around the world occasionally experience a different kind of personal revelation. "I've been sent to Europe three times," says Sergeant Ricki Ellis. "A total of almost seven years. The first two times I never traveled anywhere, except to play softball. I never owned anything German—not a beer stein, a cuckoo clock, a painted candle, a nutcracker, nothing. I gave my family those things, but I never bought them for myself. The third time I went, something clicked inside of me. Maybe it was because I had turned thirty, or maybe I realized there was something missing in my life. Whatever it was, I just went crazy. I started traveling everywhere—to England, Belgium, and Luxembourg. I even went to Paris a couple of times, and to Austria and Italy—every weekend I was gone. And money? I must have spent fifteen thousand dollars. I *bought* things. I bought a color TV, a video camera, a stereo—I've got enough stereo to cover an entire wall. I bought china, crystal, Hummels—all these collectibles. I got a seventy-five-dollar teddy bear that you'd pay a hundred and fifty for in the States. A Steiff. I bought a load of Steiffs, and people would say to me, 'You're thirty years old, why are you buying all these teddy bears?' And I'd say, 'Because I want them. I've worked very, very hard, and I want these teddy bears.' So that's what I did. And I'm still working hard—at being happy."

Sometimes, as I learned at West Point, for women soldiers, loneliness takes the form of wanting to share insights with other women and being frustrated when the opportunity is either unavailable or discouraged. Sergeant Ellis describes an experience that I believe is fairly common. "When I came into the Army in 1974," she says, "law enforcement was a relatively new field for women. And I had no senior women MPs to look to as role models. No one guided me, saying, 'Hey, look, girl, come over here. You're screwing up.' So, I learned most things the hard way.

"For a long time, my mentors were male, and those were the people who trained me. I wasn't treated like a woman, per se. I was treated like a soldier. And I really didn't miss female companionship until I was sent to Europe in 1983 and found myself without any female association whatsoever. In fact, over the last seven or eight years, I've been the only senior enlisted woman in my unit. And I still haven't found any role models. I've been in the Army for sixteen years now, and I do need someone to talk to, to share my problems with, and to understand what I'm experiencing. Only another career Army woman could appreciate that, simply because of what we all endure. It's still a male-oriented military, and no matter how hard you work, or how good your reputation is, you're a woman, and you get slighted for being one. People always question your abilities."

"Neither men nor women like to be under a woman's orders," wrote Simone de Beauvoir in *The Second Sex,* in 1949. "Her superiors, even if they esteem her highly, will always be somewhat condescending; to be a woman, if not a defect, is at least a peculiarity. Woman must constantly win the confidence that is not at first accorded her: at the start she is suspect, she has to prove herself. If she has worth, she will pass the tests, so they say. But worth is not a given essence; it is the outcome of a successful development. To feel the weight of an unfavorable prejudice against one is only on very rare occasions a help in overcoming it."

The ARTEP (Army Readiness Training and Evaluation Program) is one of any company's most important military exercises. It monitors and grades a unit's wartime performance from its first moment of mobilization, through four days of simulated combat, to the unit's final return to garrison.

The ARTEP is generally known among soldiers as one of those "we-have-to-pass" evaluations. All segments are graded as either "go" or "no-go." If units receive a "no-go" in a particular area, they'll usually be given a chance to try again for a "go" before the evaluation is completed. War affords no second chances, of course, but peacetime offers some margin of leniency.

As far as I could determine, throughout the company's history at Fort Lee, the 57th Trans had traditionally conducted its ARTEP at Fort A.P. Hill, Virginia, located directly to the north of Fort Lee, about an hour and a half away. Most of my soldiers knew the roads at Fort A.P. Hill blindfolded. I didn't want to take them over the same boring route, so I decided to take the 57th Trans to Fort Bragg, North Carolina, home of the 82d Airborne Division. Fort Bragg was six hours away by truck, so I knew my guys would get a chance to do what they did best—drive!

It wouldn't be easy, though; 90 percent of my soldiers had never been to Fort Bragg. When I introduced the idea to my junior officer staff, it was met with some resistance by one of my male lieutenants who reminded me that we *had* to pass this ARTEP and insisted we shouldn't take any chances. I knew it was risky going someplace new for this evaluation, but I wanted my soldiers to understand how to deploy to an area they'd never seen. Besides, I was convinced that they would rise to the occasion. I wasn't entirely rash in the way I went about it, either. The ARTEP had been scheduled for the spring of 1987, so in early March I took some of my key personnel down to Fort Bragg for a couple of days to conduct a preliminary reconnaissance of the area.

Through a fellow commander of a truck unit stationed there, I was able to arrange an opportunity for my soldiers to assume some of the company's transportation taskings, in support of a mission for the 82d Airborne. As it turned out, some of the soldiers from the 82d would be jumping into Bragg while we were on post, so it would become my soldiers' job to pick them up at the drop zone and transport them and their equipment back to their units. This, I felt, would at least give my people the feel of performing an actual mission and of being involved in real operations—not just participating in yet another exercise.

Tuesday, 28 April 1987, 0800 hours. One of the biggest thrills I experienced as commander was heading out on convoy. I'd sent an advance party ahead a few hours earlier to prepare the site at Bragg while the rest of us made ready for our departure from Fort Lee. The whir of the deuce-and-a-half's, the smell of the diesel fuel, and the bustling of the soldiers really had me fired up. A deuce-and-a-half makes a low growl when it starts, followed by a high-pitched squeal . . . I was almost overwhelmed. Giving my soldiers the signal to take off was a tremendous rush: The engines broke from a rumble to a roar and we pulled out of the gate, moving the entire lumbering convoy down Route 95 in a giant camouflage parade.

As commander, I was also the last member of the company to leave Fort Lee. En route to our destination, I would dart up and down through the convoy in my little CUCV, like a beetle skimming water in a pond, first racing to the front to make sure everything was okay, then slowing down to wait for the stragglers. Sometimes, though, I'd simply stop by the side of the road and proudly watch the entire procession go by. The teams of soldiers manning each of the huge trucks would wave or honk their horns as they drove past me, and I'd salute them, giving them a high-five in return. Sometimes I'd catch a few of them without their headgear (soldiers are always supposed to wear their camouflage-colored helmets in a military vehicle—partly for safety reasons and partly because it's "uniform"—unless they impair the soldiers' vision while driving), so I'd motion to them to put their helmets back on. I really only cared about enforcing that rule so none of them would get into trouble with someone higher up than me. I knew that in hot weather the webbed inner lining and the chinstraps on those heavy steel pots would start to itch and chafe like mad, and the longer the ride, the heavier and more uncomfortable they became.

Summer comes early in the south, and this day the sun was blazing. None of the trucks had air conditioning, and when we arrived at Bragg in midafternoon, there was no time even to cool off. We immediately had to prepare our camp area and set up a defensive perimeter. One of the first things we did was set up the mess tent, from which we'd be served two hot, cafeteria-style meals a day—breakfast and dinner—known in Army slang as "Hot-A's." We'd "eat tactical," which meant outdoors in the field, dispersed, and hunched over our individual rations like a tribe of monkeys feeding in the jungle, with at least a five-meter distance between each small group. Actually, we had to keep that distance while lining up in the mess tent, too, because if we were attacked during mealtime, the theory went, the enemy (who, in all our training scenarios, was the Soviets) couldn't take us all out at once.

Lunches consisted of something called "MREs"—Meals, Ready to Eat. MREs were "boil-in-a-bag" concoctions that came in dark-brown-and-OD-green plastic bags, about a foot long and six inches wide, which we'd heat up using our electricity generators and portable burners. Packed inside the opaque plastic we might find eight ounces of Chicken à la King, an airtight package of crackers, an ounce and a half of cheese spread, and a hermetically sealed piece of fruit cake, as well as an accessory packet containing the ubiquitous powdered coffee, cocoa, cream substitute, salt, sugar, chewing gum, matches, and toilet paper. I wished they had given us C-Rations instead; the MRE's were bland and tasted like the plastic bags they came in. Being in the field always made me ravenously hungry, though, so I forced myself to swallow every flavorless bite.

Our training area became a giant campground—mostly flat, surrounded by acres of woods and sloping hills cut by trails. Now and then, when the air was still, we could hear the faint popping of simulated gunfire in the distance, a signal that other units were training nearby.

Our soldiers worked well into the night setting up the site and the equipment—pitching and camouflaging enough tents for three platoons (about 140 people) to sleep in, a maintenance tent for the vehicles, a mess tent, and a CP (Command Post) tent, from which the first sergeant and I would control all operations. Eventually, though, the fifteen female soldiers I'd brought with me drifted off to sleep inside a pair of well-insulated arctic tents, which slept six to ten each, while the male crews bedded down in GP medium tents that could comfortably accommodate up to eighteen people. I, however, spent the night curled up inside my own arctic tent—commander's privilege. But I did not sleep alone. Traditionally, during field maneuvers, the first sergeant would sleep inside the same tent as the company commander. I didn't want to behave any differently, so when my first sergeant retired, I climbed in after him. I suppose I was trying to prove a point—that a female commander and a male first sergeant could share a tent without incident. After all, we each had our own separate folding cot, and we each slept in T-shirts and fatigue pants.

Weeks before in Top's office, I had introduced the idea while discussing the administrative details of the trip. "You know, Top," I said casually, "as CO and first sergeant we'll be sharing a tent at Bragg." Slightly embarrassed but not nonplussed, he'd shrugged his lanky shoulders and said, laughing, "Ma'am, I had a feeling you were going to say that."

Of course, this would not be the first time male and female soldiers would sleep together in a field tent or function as a finely tuned team to accomplish a mission without the interference of standard social conventions. I am reminded, in particular, of a story that Colonel Houston once told me.

"When I was a battalion commander down at North Fort Hood, Texas," he said, "that was the National Guard training site and the Reserve training site for the Texas National Guard, 3d Division. My people used to go up there and put up a good-sized tent for that Division— 1,092 of 'em, in fact—and the Texas wind would blow 'em down, and we'd have to go put 'em up again. And that was bestial work. It was awful. And I used to just levee all my companies to provide x number of soldiers to go do this. Of course, after a while, a lot of those soldiers were women.

"Now, it's hotter than the hinges of hell in North Fort Hood in July. I mean, it is some kind of *hot.* And you don't feel like wearing your whole goddamn uniform to do all this work. So, what the hell are we gonna do? Well, I know what we're gonna do, goddamnit. My policy is, if the outside fatigue jacket comes off one of 'em, then they *all* take it off. That's as far as I went. But I said, whatever they do, they're all going to be uniform.

"The next thing I know, my boss—who happened to be the original Neanderthal Man—shows up in a fury. Oh, my goodness, he was beside himself. He had just come from North Fort Hood, and he had seen men and women working together, and they didn't have any shirts on—at all. They didn't even have *T-shirts* on. And I looked him in the eye and said, 'So, what the hell is the problem? The women had bras on, didn't they?' He said, 'Well, yeah.' And I said, 'Well, that's my battalion policy.' And he said, 'What?!' And I said, 'Goddamnit, sir, trust me, sex is the last thing on their goddamn minds. If they've got enough left over for sex, they can use my goddamn office.' He had to agree that I had a point. But he was so shocked and taken aback. Still, I think it may have proved to him that things work if you let them. Once you cut out all the bull and simply leave the men and women alone to do their jobs, they pull together quite well; there doesn't have to be all that 'stuff' in the middle."

The first night of the ARTEP neither Top nor I got too much sleep— maybe four hours, at most—since we had to keep checking the perimeter in the middle of the night to make sure that at least one member of our two-person guard team was awake at all times. Fifty percent security—that was the rule. One night, I even slept on the floor of the Command Post, which was where all our maps and radio equipment were located, because I wanted to stay close to the action.

My job during this entire exercise was to coordinate and supervise the soldiers' training. So, on the second night at Bragg, my plan called for picking up and moving the entire unit to a new location. The area I'd selected was only three miles away, but for training purposes I decided we should follow a roundabout route of fifteen miles.

This driving maneuver was, in fact, a requirement of the ARTEP, but my soldiers told me that other units within the battalion had typically "simulated" the move. I told them I wanted nothing to do with simulations; we moved the unit that night. I knew it would be complicated because we hadn't been able to clear our site before dark, and after nightfall the heavily wooded roads would be much harder to negotiate. We had to take extra care not to run our trucks over any unsuspecting soldiers who might have pitched their camouflaged tents beside the vehicles. We did have one or two sprained ankles at sick call the next morning, but nothing more serious than that.

Although my soldiers were trained in defensive fighting, as a Transportation unit our primary mission was to drive—to haul ammo, equipment, soldiers, and supplies in support of combat units. But on Wednesday night we suddenly heard peals of sniper fire—they were blanks, of course. One of the truck companies at Bragg had decided to act as an aggressor and were trying to infiltrate the camp. They launched one attack and then another and another—in waves—trying to breach the 360-degree perimeter that was our twenty-four-hour line of defense. Their goal was to capture our Command Post. If they had reached that inner sanctum, we would have immediately lost the battle. We were much too clever for them, however. We'd set traps—metal trip wires strung with tin cans from the mess tent, which proved to be a primitive, but effective, alarm system. My soldiers heard the enemy stumbling noisily over the wires in the dark and alerted the rest of us, then sent for reinforcements so we were able to return their fire and head them off in time.

When no outside enemies were conveniently available to attack us, we'd perform that job ourselves. For example, one of our evaluators might walk up to any one of the soldiers and hand him or her a "situation card," and the rest of us would be plunged into a wartime scenario of varying levels of danger and intensity. The situation card might say:

"You are under a chemical attack. What is your action?"

It would then become that soldier's mission to decide the appropriate response to such a message and lead the way for the rest of us. Incidentally, in the case of chemical attack, a soldier's proper immediate reaction would be to pop on a protective gas mask and then start yelling "GAS! GAS!" at the top of his or her lungs. If the sudden proliferation of thick white smoke billowing from the bursting chemical cloud simulators didn't get the message across, then there were other ways to do it. Soldiers might take a visual cue from the leader and whip on their protective masks. Still others might be made aware of the danger by our universal signal for alerting soldiers to chemical attacks—the clamor of metal banging against metal. If, for some reason, soldiers cannot smell or see, they can at least react to the sound.

Generally, the attack would last about two hours. The evaluator would then hand another soldier a card indicating that the area had been cleared. Had the attack been a real emergency, instead of an exercise, a special chemical test kit would have been brought out by the NBC (Nuclear, Biological, and Chemical) NCO, to prove that this was so. We wouldn't expend these kits during a mere practice, but the "decon" (decontamination) teams—who were specialists on the subject—*would* teach the soldiers how to use different chemical showerbaths to act as antidotes to the poison, and the evaluators would quiz them on their knowledge before permitting them to unmask. Then, the NBC NCO would give an all-clear message to the commander, which would be passed along to the rest of the unit through the chain of command.

Thursday was our last night in North Carolina. It rained, so I decided to give the troops a treat. I permitted them to leave the muddy field and go into Fort Bragg proper, where they could take showers in the post gymnasium—their first in three days. Meanwhile, both Colonel Houston and Lieutenant Colonel Schuller (the brigade and battalion commanders) had decided to pay us a visit. Fortunately, our brigade and battalion staff evaluators had been satisfied with our performance and told us we'd be receiving a "go" on each part of the exercise. I was so relieved. My soldiers had busted their butts, and it had paid off. Thankfully, we wouldn't have to do any of our tasks over again, but I knew I wouldn't really relax until Friday night, when the last truck had been driven safely through the gates of Fort Lee's motor pool.

Having led my soldiers through a simulated war, I couldn't help wondering about the real thing. I remembered what Captain Mark O'Neill, a friend of mine from West Point who's now an Infantry officer, once told me. "At the company command level," he explained, "war is no longer about ideologies; it's a matter of self-preservation. The ultimate, of course, is close-in combat, which is what we train for in the Infantry. Frankly, though, I can't quite envision myself actually taking a knife and cutting somebody's throat or sneaking up from behind and stabbing them to death. What drives me, however, is knowing that I'm tactically good: I can lead soldiers and do my job. I don't want war, but if there is one, I want to be there because I'm the better guy for it. I trust myself to take care of it more than I do other people."

But what about women? Do they respond differently to situations of danger? Major Geraldine Frank responds, "I don't think so. I've been in extremely dangerous situations, and I don't think I was responding differently than anyone else.

"We were doing a parachute jump near a disputed border, and we ended up getting shot at. There I was, dangling from a parachute, and when I hit the ground, I had to do the same things as the men. I certainly felt confident because I had the equipment I needed and knew pretty much where I was supposed to go. But if you take anybody and throw them out the door of a helicopter, hang them from a parachute, give them a weapon they don't know which end to point, and start shooting at them, then regardless of their gender, he or she will panic if that individual doesn't know what to do. I understood that we were not welcome where we were going, so my training was crucial to my survival. And survival transcends a lot of so-called gender issues.

"Women can kill just as easily as men," she continues, "but culturally they have been encouraged to be weak, and generally will not choose a violent solution if there's an alternative. Most women haven't been raised with ideas of female conquest, or that their physical prowess may lead to mastery. They don't carry around those lessons or memories. So, teaching women not merely to kill, but to plot it, and to make it happen from near or far, is something that requires knocking down more barriers. It might take a little longer, and some may need help in overcoming a few more instincts, but it is really quite possible for them to learn. Even so, the concept of a powerful woman who could actually kill somebody frightens women, as well as men. In fact, it is still too frightening for most people to grasp, much less accept."

Of course, men's reasons for not wanting women in the military are legion and varied. Many cite "attitudes they've grown up with" as a primary justification, particularly those gleaned from Hollywood. John Wayne's name comes up a lot. Some men say they fear women will have a negative impact on mission performance because of physical differences

("Women can't lift heavy things"). Some cite psychological or relationship differences between the sexes ("Women can't bond with men the way men can bond with men"). Others observe that women represent an economic threat ("Men lose jobs"). And then there is always the sexual threat ("Women 'use' sex to get over and take advantage of the system"). Some men mention feeling that their egos are being threatened, therefore their self-esteem is compromised ("If a *woman* can do this, then what good am *I*?"). Assuming global sexism, they also fear the backlash from other countries and the damage women's inclusion could potentially pose to the image of the American military throughout the world ("How does it look if we allow women to fight our battles for us?").

Other justifications include the reluctance to "wipe out a generation of baby-bearers," the persistent belief that women are inherently unable to "handle" killing and aggression or to endure "physical pain and hardship," and the theory that women will suffer from a "lack of hygiene." "Can women 'go' in the woods?" is a constant argument.

But even if we put aside individual fears and prejudices, there is also a completely different type of challenge facing American military women. Colonel Houston offers one perspective. "In utilizing women," he explains, "I am not convinced that our political masters are doing anything other than solving a very pragmatic numbers problem. Demographically, we have a 'he' deficit right now. There aren't enough draftees, if you will, or military-age men to serve the country's needs. Until nineteen ninety-two through ninety-three, the U.S. will remain in that deficit posture. But from then through the balance of the century, we'll begin to have enough young men again. The Soviets are facing the same problem, as a matter of fact. So, in some sense, it becomes a question of when the two windows merge and balance.

"And yet, what happens if we suddenly have a sufficient number of men and don't need women anymore? I mean, are they here to stay or not? Are they a realistic part of our national policy? Personally, I sense a lot of ambiguity on that issue; I don't believe these questions have been answered."

Sergeant Michael Sweeney offers his opinion. "Really," he says, "the only thing that bothers me about having females in the military is that if a woman and I train together, if we work together and go to the field together, and war suddenly breaks out, I don't want her separated from me. I want her to go where I go. You mean I go up on the line and she stays back two thousand miles? I think that's bullshit."

On the other hand, according to Sergeant Ricki Ellis, Sergeant

Sweeney's fears are unfounded because in the event of a conflict women are going to stay put. "We had a battalion commander when I was in Europe," recounts Sergeant Ellis, "and some of the women used to say to him, 'We know females will be moved to the rear and sent back to America as soon as the balloon goes up.' And this guy would march up and down in front of all the NCOs and say, 'If any of you females think that you'll be leaving, you're crazy. We're not even sure if we can get the soldiers' family members out in time, so how can you think we'll be taking *you* out?' "

Colonel Mitchell Douglas takes the battalion commander's point a step further. "Where does the combat zone end?" he asks. "For example, what are we going to do with the Signal Corps gals in the mountains of Korea when the North Koreans attack—put them all in trucks back to Seoul? Of course not. So, even though Signal Corps is not called Combat Arms, if the balloon goes up in Korea, you're going to have a whole lot of women coming home in body bags. There's no doubt about it; I don't care *what* branch they're in."

Colonel Houston is equally straightforward in voicing his opinions on the subject of women in combat. "My concern," says Colonel Houston, "is not that women will get killed. Tough shit. *I* might get killed. That's the way it goes. I hate to see any soldier hurt. It's my charge to conserve human life—American life and the life of my allies—particularly if it's entrusted to my care. And I'm very, very serious about that. But death isn't my greatest fear about women in combat. My greatest fear is the same thing that happened to us in Vietnam, and let me digress for a minute. I was an administration and logistics advisor out in the bush with the South Vietnamese. And we had word that prisoners were being carried around in bamboo cages, having sharp bunji and bamboo sticks poked at them and being subjected to all sorts of tortures. So we would lunge and lunge and lunge and mount more attacks to try to get through. Every time we could confirm a rumor, we'd mount a combat operation. We *spent* ourselves trying to recapture those men.

"My concern in a similar situation would be if females were captured, because that would enrage American men. You're not only screwing with one of our people, you're screwing with one of our *women.* And, by God, you're not going to get away with that. I think the emotional commitment to the women's recapture, and the degree of intensity to which those rescue operations would be carried out, would be so extreme that it might cause the fighting to escalate even further. And that is what worries me."

Captain Bill Thomas, an Infantry captain, and a graduate of West

Point's class of '79, does not seem to share the colonel's fear of overprotective zeal but has his own reservations, nonetheless. "I know I could take a squad of five women and four men," declares Captain Thomas, "and with the proper training, probably do anything a squad of nine men could do. I might have to handpick the men and women who would be in that squad, but I can accept that. I've seen what the women at West Point have been able to accomplish, and I've seen women performing outstanding jobs in the Army. But not everyone thinks that way. I imagine the large majority of Infantry and Armor soldiers would not accept women in their ranks. So there'd be a huge barrier to overcome. I suppose we could get over it in time, but I don't think we're ready yet."

Sergeant Ellis, however, voices her impatience with this attitude. "Frankly," she says, "I think that proving I can do a job should entitle me to do it. I realize that not every woman can pick up a rucksack and hump it twenty or fifty miles. Not every guy can do that. But why shouldn't I be given the chance to try?

"A lot of male soldiers I know say they don't believe a woman could handle combat. Well, I don't really know *how* I'd feel about shooting people. I go to traffic accidents and get sick when I see dead bodies. But is that abnormal? I don't think anybody really relishes seeing other people's bodies being torn apart and their guts hanging out. Most people go into the bushes and puke—male or female. But the guys will still say, 'Oh, there's Sergeant Ellis. Ha, ha—we saw you throwing up in the bushes.' But is that a reason to keep me from doing a job that I'm qualified for?

"When I was at Fort McClellan in the mid-seventies," she continues, "I remember some of the little bitty guys they were bringing in to be MPs. And I didn't want to work with someone puny. I didn't want to work with a wimp. I didn't want to work with a little kid who was afraid of his own shadow. But the Army didn't see it that way because he was a guy, so that was okay. But a female? Some of the male officers would say, 'I can't work with a female.' And I'd say, 'You wouldn't work with *me*, Sir? I'm five foot eight, one hundred fifty-five pounds, and I can hold my own. The fact is, I don't want to work with *you*. You're short, and a flyweight, and you couldn't back me up in a fight.' But the Army still took men who were small and paid very little attention to their abilities—I mean, I had guys in my unit who couldn't read, I had guys who cried, I had guys who tried to jump out a second-story window when we got locked up to go to the Middle East. But I've always thrived on that stuff. If the Army's going somewhere, I say, 'Hey, take *me* along. Because I'm ready.' "

· · ·

261

I belong to a profession in which killing is solemnly accepted as standard procedure. This being the case, I have never found it useful to dwell on the sadness, or the permanence, of death. For most of my life, I had determinedly avoided all funerals but one—for the mother of a high school friend. In August 1987, however, I found myself suddenly faced with the distressing prospect of attending the funeral of a stillborn baby of Private First Class Virgil Walker, one of my truck mechanics.

The Walkers were a young couple, not quite twenty-one, and this infant would have been their first child. They'd been offered the choice of either allowing the doctor to discreetly dispose of the fetus or giving the baby a regular funeral. When Private Walker stopped by my office to inform me of his plans, I'm not sure why, but I assumed he'd choose the former option. Still, I understood how he and his wife must be feeling. "I lost a brother a long time ago," I said. "If you ever need to talk to someone, I'm here to listen." He told me, then, that he and his wife had decided to give their baby a proper burial, and that they very much wanted me to come.

Suddenly I became uneasy; the palms of my hands grew cold. My first impulse was to politely decline the invitation and then perhaps send the couple a wreath of flowers, or a sympathy card. I knew I wasn't obligated to attend the funeral. As commander, I could have found any number of excuses for being "unavailable." But when Walker told me that his parents and in-laws were on their way to Petersburg in joyful anticipation of a birth, I had a vision of their faces as they received the terrible news when they got off the plane. I thought of my own father and mother, and my heart lurched. I told Private Walker I'd be there.

As soon as my soldier had gone, I left my office, walked down the hall to the Supply Room, and sat at Sergeant Randall's desk. When he came in and saw me, he knew at once that something was wrong. He pulled up a chair and sat beside me; the other clerks took his cue and left. I told Sergeant Randall I had heard about the baby's death and was planning to attend the funeral, but I really didn't know if I could handle it. He seemed surprised at this admission, but then I told him about Dick, my older brother who'd been killed in a car crash at nineteen.

I explained to Sergeant Randall how I'd been awakened early one August morning in 1973 by the sound of footsteps outside my parents' bedroom and by my father's voice calling out the haunting words, "Get up! Dick's been in a bad accident." I told him how my brother Mitchell had been driving home from a camping trip, and, while listening to the radio, had received his first report of Dick's injuries over the local news. I told him how my younger sister, Janice, and I had stayed home that morning watching silly cartoons on television, anxiously waiting for our eldest brother, Jeff, to call with news from Dick's bedside at the hospital. And I told him about my parents when they came home at noon from the hospital with the unspoken final word—how my mother was inconsolable; how my father collapsed into a chair beside the kitchen table, cradled me in his arms and wept, unable to let go, as though fearing that if he did, perhaps he'd lose me, too. Finally, I told him how I'd refused to attend my brother's funeral, how I'd seen no point to it—or so I'd told myself at the time. I had wanted to remember my brother alive and would not permit death's intrusion on that memory. I didn't share my secret with anyone, but deep down I felt almost as if I'd been thrust into some strange and terrifying competition, and I had absolutely no intention of allowing death to win. I was only fourteen.

I admitted to Sergeant Randall that I was afraid of going to the baby's funeral; I feared it would return me to that painful time. Sergeant Randall received this, as he did everything I confided to him, quietly. He offered no words of advice or consolation, but he and I both knew he didn't have to say anything. It was his presence—and his silence—that I needed.

Once I'd gotten these worries off my chest, I was able to steel myself for the ordeal ahead. I would once again rely on the technique I had developed so many years ago at West Point. Whenever too much emotion threatened, I would simply blot out my feelings and make myself as numb as stone. It was the only way I could endure.

The morning of the funeral was swelteringly hot. It was a weekday, and I was wearing my heavy green polyester Class A uniform. Already, by midmorning, beads of perspiration were beginning to drip down my forehead. Fortunately, the cemetery was only a fifteen-minute drive from Fort Lee, and a procession of seven or eight cars, their headlights competing with the brilliant morning sun, wound their way over the Virginia back roads, finally coming to rest in a dirt parking lot just outside the cemetery gate.

The entrance to the cemetery was flanked by a pair of three-foot stone pillars; inside, a gray nineteenth-century chapel stood about a hundred yards to the right. Across the main dirt road that cleaved the churchyard in two, a small white canopy had been set up, bordered on one side by rows of folding chairs. Drawing closer to the canopy, I could see that a small plot had been dug beneath it. A miniature black casket, about the size of a large mailbox, rested gently on the ground beside that dark hole in the earth.

I quietly greeted Private Walker and his wife as they approached the gravesite. I asked them how they were holding up, and Walker choked out, "It's very hard, Ma'am, but we're doing okay." Friends, relatives, and some of Walker's fellow mechanics from the motor pool began to drift toward the chairs that faced the tiny plot. I remained with the gathering of mourners long enough to briefly offer my condolences to Walker's family, but I couldn't sit down. Instead, I deliberately found a place to stand well in back of the assembly, in case I felt the need to leave. Sergeant Randall stood beside me.

When everyone was present, the funeral began. I tried to focus on what the pastor was saying, but all I could think about during the thirty-minute ceremony was my brother. I kept trying to imagine his funeral; I kept seeing my own family beside his grave. I was fighting hard not to cry, but I could hear the young mother sobbing softly, and I had to walk away from the gravesite to hide my tears. I would have given anything to leave at that point, but felt I had to hang in and be strong for my soldier and his wife. And for me.

At last, the service was over. I had driven to the cemetery alone, and I departed alone. I told Sergeant Randall to go ahead, I'd catch up with him. On my way back to Fort Lee, however, I decided to stop at a small coffee shop in Hopewell to have a cup of tea and collect myself before returning to the company. By the time I entered, the tears had dried.

Command was the point in my life when I finally began to feel comfortable with myself, with how I fit into the military world. It had taken me years to be able to relax, both in and out of uniform. Of course, I wasn't the only one of my female West Point classmates who'd been struggling to find her place. I had run into Michelle Mathews—my old plebe year room-mate—who is no longer in the Army. She told me she'd been having some trouble readjusting to civilian life. She said, "I'd hate to think that my greatest accomplishment in life came when I was twenty-one years old." I understood exactly what she meant.

Still, I'd learned a tremendous amount during my nineteen-month command—mainly, that my soldiers expected a lot from me. I'd also been required to set an example for my soldiers as a platoon leader in Germany, but I felt much more targeted to be a role model as a CO. I had the final word of authority, in most cases, on matters that could shape their entire futures. I had control, and that was scary sometimes. Yet, I was in my element. I have to admit, I like to be in control.

Major Constance Andrews explains the impulses that sometimes draw a person to the military. "I didn't necessarily want to *do* things in my life," she says. "I wanted to *be* things. I never figured I was going to be so smart that I'd invent something worthwhile or become the greatest athlete or the greatest dancer or the greatest anything. What I wanted, was to be someone who improved my immediate area. In other words, to be a good leader. It was important to me to learn how to manage people, to assist them in making decisions and developing their qualities. I also wanted to learn how to be a strong person. Being a woman in the Army has made me very strong. But if you don't have the commitment to service, after five or ten years you will leave. By that time, the money has leveled off and your civilian friends are probably living more comfortably than you are. If this other thing, this commitment to leadership, isn't in you, you've got no reason to stay. You may as well move on."

Had I not been an Army officer, I probably would have been an athletic coach. But then, that is what I do in the military. As Major Joan Parker once said, "The Army is, really, a place to be coached. I mean, there are a lot of times when you look at the soldiers around you and say, 'Gosh, why did *this* person come into the military?' The Army takes people who are sometimes confused and molds them and then watches the transformation that occurs as they develop into soldiers. What makes it rewarding is that you get so close to these people; you learn so much about them. You see some of them go through so much hell that when they come out looking great and loving every minute of it, you grow a lot with them. It sounds corny, I know, but it is intense."

24 February 1988. An outgoing commander always has some type of social gathering given in his or her honor. Mine was a dinner sponsored by my soldiers. I think it was a bit different, though, because in addition to the usual rubbery chicken and sentimental speeches at the NCO club, my guys brought in a DJ to spin records and we danced the night away. I danced with my soldiers, and I don't know too many other military commanders who can say they've done that.

As they made their speeches, each platoon of soldiers presented me with gifts, which I had not expected. None of them were too serious—a giant pillow (so I'd have something soft to sit on when I returned to a cushy staff officer's job), a toilet seat with my picture framed inside it (who knows why), some hats, an Army watch with a webbed, OD green band (instead of a gold one because I was retiring), and a beautiful maroon-and-gold company guidon. Perhaps best of all, however, was the aerobics certificate, presented to me by Top, which read:

"In recognition of Carol A. Barkalow, CPT, TC Commander, a fine aerobic exerciser . . .

On Wednesday morning don't be tardy,
Because Captain B wants your body.
She'll twist it, bend it, and damn near break it,
You might even feel that you can't take it.
But just bear with it until the last song,
Because when it's over, we'll all be stronger.
Now she's leaving, and we'll all be blue
But we all know what we won't have to do . . . AEROBICS.

I relinquished command of the 57th Trans on 26 February 1988. The Change of Command ceremony, which took place in the post gymnasium at 0900 hours, was a mirror image of the one I'd participated in nineteen months earlier, except this time, of course, I was the one leaving. After the ceremony, in a somewhat unprecedented move, I invited my soldiers over to my house for a final farewell party. It was a very sad day for me. Now that I was leaving, I was leaving everything that was familiar to me. I felt like I was losing a piece of myself.

At home on leave a week later, I tried to make some sense of my emotions. *"It's now been a week since I gave up command,"* I wrote, suddenly picking up the thread of a diary that had ended nearly eight years earlier. *"I was at the battalion yesterday, but I couldn't go down to the company. I'm not sure why. I don't think I wanted to invade. Or else, maybe I was afraid to see the company as his. I'll always think of it as mine. It sounds childish, I know—crying because something was taken away. But I knew when I took over nineteen months ago that someday I'd have to let go of that guidon."*

Looking back as a commander, I realized I had accomplished what I'd set out to do at seventeen. I'd held positions of leadership and been responsible for people's welfare. I realized, too, that the years I'd spent at West Point had been essential to that achievement. Despite its limitations, the Academy had helped to define me, and it's still the compass by which I steer.

Appendix

★

According to a Fact Sheet issued by West Point's office of Public Affairs, "The admission of 119 women on July 7 to the United States Military Academy (USMA) at West Point has been termed a 'military and sociological phenomenon.' This phenomenon carried with it the advance preparation normally given to an important, well-planned military maneuver." Indeed, planning for the arrival of women began before the law directing that they be admitted was even signed.

With the passage of the Stratton Amendment by the House of Representatives on 20 May 1975 (the amendment called for women to be admitted to the service academies on the same basis as men, and the vote was 303 in favor, and 96 opposed), the USMA Planning Committee was formulated the following day. On 6 June 1975 the Hathaway Amendment (a slightly modified version of the Stratton amendment, which made women eligible for appointment and admission to the academies) was passed by an overwhelmingly favorable voice-vote in the Senate, and between the months of June and September 1975 data collection ensued. On 15 September 1975 "Operations Plan 75-1," a report assessing the location and scope of the construction necessary to accommodate women at the Academy, was published. The plan had projected that in October 1975 briefing for the congressional committees would start and, obviously anticipating their positive response, had planned that by 15 November 1975 an information pamphlet would be published for distribution to women applicants. On 17 November 1975 a prototype of uniforms was to be presented to the superintendent who, together with the superintendent of the United States Naval Academy, would make an appearance on nationwide television during the Army-Navy game that year "to show and explain the uniforms that women cadets and midshipmen would be wearing" (the *Washington Post*, 22 December 1975). Further, Operations Plan 75-1 projected that on 1 January 1976 the construction contractor would begin work, and later that month, women physical education instructors were scheduled to arrive at the Academy to report for duty. In February 1976 the Physical Aptitude Test would be administered to women applicants, and in the period from March to April 1976 the women would be selected for admission. By 26 June 1976 the construction contractor was to have completed work, and on 7 July 1976, just three days after the nation's bicentennial, women cadets would be admitted to USMA. (One hundred nineteen women were admitted to the Military Academy, 81 women to the Naval Academy, and 157 to the United States Air Force Academy. Air Force, meanwhile, was conducting its own integration study, called "The Women's Integration Research Project—Project 'Blue Eyes.' ")

As the Academy had expected, on 7 October 1975 President Gerald R. Ford did sign Public Law 94-106. It read as follows:

". . . The Secretaries of the military departments concerned shall take such action as may be necessary and appropriate to insure that female individuals shall be eligible for appointment and admission to the service academy concerned, beginning with appointment to such academy beginning in calendar year 1976, and the academic and other relevant standards required for appointment, training, graduation, and commissioning of female individuals, shall be the same as those required for male individuals, except for those minimum essential adjustments in such performance standards required because of physiological differences between male and female individuals."

At once, planning at the United States Military Academy intensified. In order to determine the projected physical capabilities and limitations of the incoming women, an extensive study had been undertaken in the summer of 1975. It was called Project 60, named for the sixty high school women who had volunteered to participate, and was designed "to determine the effect of various physical exercise programs, the physical capabilities of women in comparison with men, and whether the requirements of the Physical Aptitude Exam [throwing a basketball for distance, performing a standing long jump, doing a shuttle run between two lines for a total distance of three hundred yards, and performing a minimum of six pull-ups] was a valid predictor of female performance in the simulated summer training environment."

Close on the heels of Project 60 came Project 60A, a study conducted by the Department of Tactics to determine "the ability of women cadets to withstand the rigors of military training during the first summer's Cadet Basic Training."

Another study, the "Research on Psychological Differences," was undertaken by a group that was tasked by the Office of Military Leadership to examine the "psychological, sociological, and cultural differences between men and women."

Project 211 was yet another in the long line of studies on women. This one was instituted by the Office of Institutional Research "to assess attitudes of cadets and faculty toward female equality." The study was later incorporated into Project Athena.

And, finally, there was Project Athena—a study conducted by the triumvirate of the Office of Military Leadership, the Office of Institutional Research, and the Army Research Institute, which examined the effect that attending USMA had on female cadets in comparison with male cadets, and, conversely, the effect that admitting women had on USMA. Among the civilian researchers were Dr. Nora Scott Kinzer (who later included a chapter on the women of the class of 1980 in her book *Stress and the American Woman*), Dr. Charles Moskos of Northwestern University, Dr. Janet Spence of the University of Texas at Austin, and Dr. Morris Janowitz of the University of Chicago. Their study, which West Point's then Superintendent, Lieutenant General Sidney B. Berry, called "the only research authorized into the psychology and sociology of women's assimilation into the Corps of Cadets," was pursued throughout the four-year tenure of the class of 1980.

With the first stirrings of recruitment, fledgling efforts were made on the public relations front. A *Washington Post* article, dated 22 December 1975, and titled "Military Colleges Wooing Women for Class of '80," noted that "In an effort to drum up interest in West Point, three hundred cadets were sent home two days early on their Christmas leave this year with orders to spend the time in their hometowns rounding up qualified women applicants." And in his letter to parents, General Berry noted, "Preparations for media coverage are well under way with civilian media representatives actively assisting and advising in the development of ground rules. One individual from each news agency is being briefed in depth to insure that reports are informed and in context. Media access to the men and women cadets will be in the form of staged interviews on Reception Day only. The next planned exposure of men and women cadets to the news media is at the end of Cadet Basic Training."

During one of these "planned exposures," in response to a reporter's question about whether women would be allowed to cry, and what would happen to them if they did, General Berry replied, "Yes, if a woman cadet feels she has to cry she will be allowed to go off somewhere and shed tears. Then, of course, she'll be expected to come back and do what she was required to do in the first place." (7 July 1976—"Dressing Up the Staid Old Plains: A Long, Gray Curvy Line at West Point," by Peter Coutros)

Applications were received from 867 women. From this number, 631 had received nominations, and 148 were offered admission. Twenty-eight women declined their appointment; one woman was medically disqualified.

In considering who was qualified, the wording of Public Law 94-106 had raised two critical questions for the Academy:

1. "What are the 'physiological differences' between men and women?"
2. "What '. . . minimum essential adjustments in . . . performance standards . . .' are needed between men and women?"

The Academy claimed that "a review of the literature" satisfactorily answered the first question. "Literature" referred to Dr. James Peterson's unpublished report, "Physiological Differences Between Men and Women, 1975." The Academy noted, however, that the "literature" did not provide solutions to the second question. So Project Summertime was devised to determine the impact of physiological gender differences on physical training by taking measures of such quantifiable characteristics as arm and shoulder girdle, leg strength, hand grip strength, power endurance, cardiorespiratory efficiency, and body composition. Thirty men and 30 women new cadet trainees were "randomly" selected to participate in this study at the beginning of Beast Barracks. The 30 men represented 2.2 percent of the total number of male basic trainees (1,366), while the women who were chosen represented 25.2 percent of the total number of women (119). The mean age, height, and weight for the men was 20.18 years, 69.64 inches, and 71.06 kilograms, respectively. For women, it was 19.41 years, 65.70 inches, and 59.63 kilograms. From the original study groups of 30 each, 26 men successfully completed the training (86.7 percent), as did 23 women (76.7 percent).

Despite these mutually high success rates, the tests nevertheless determined that there were indeed "significant physiological performance differences between women and men, evident in upper body and leg strength, power, power endurance, and grip strength." No difference in cardiorespiratory efficiency was indicated.

270

During Beast Barracks, Project Athena, an "in-depth socio-psychological study on the impact the admission of women would have on the Corps of Cadets," was begun. After the first summer, Academy statistics indicated that 17 women (14 percent) and 137 men (10 percent) had resigned. According to the Academy, a 10 percent attrition rate by the end of the first summer is normal. The commandant's new policy, however, was revolutionary—that those cadets who were "doing their best" would not be expelled from the Academy at the end of Cadet Basic Training, regardless of their achievement level in physical training.

As of 5 October 1976 (three months after being admitted) 21 women (out of 119) and 197 men (out of 1,366) had resigned.

Regarding male attitudes toward women, Academy surveys claimed that they had improved markedly from August 1975 to March 1976 (after the administration had been forced to reverse its negative position on the issue, and before the women had actually arrived), but that, from March 1976 to November 1976 (prior to the women's arrival and four months following it), fewer males felt positive about the overall effect of women on the Corps. Companies without women held the most negative attitudes toward women. Among those attitudes were:

1. The belief that women don't belong in military academies.

2. An awareness that top leadership had originally opposed the admission of women.

3. The perception that USMA officials "overreacted"—scheduled too many lectures, surveys, briefings on the subject.

4. The perception that women received more favorable treatment than men.

5. The belief that accepting women was "inconsistent with the combat mission of USMA." [Technically, the official mission of the Academy contains no specific references to preparation for combat, although many cadets continue to refer to the Academy as a "Combat Arms School."]

6. The belief that "women should have their own academy."

7. General hostility and prejudice toward women.

As of December 1976 a PAO report documented that women had a slight edge over men academically. As of 13 December 1976, of the 119 women who had entered the Academy on 7 July, 25 had resigned. At this time, the attrition rate for women was 21 percent, as compared with 16 percent for men. The main reason cited for leaving was the same for men and women—"a high anxiety due to change of environment, strong parental pressure to come to West Point, and a lack of desire for a military career," elsewhere phrased as a "lack of commitment to the military way

271

of life." (There were some variations—women balked at the excessive regimentation, according to Project Athena, citing "too much discipline" as their primary reason for leaving, whereas men cited "the lack of privacy" as their main reason for quitting. Women cited "lack of privacy" last.)

By the beginning of the second semester of the first year, 91 women remained. Thirty percent of these women stood in the top one-quarter of the class academically. More women cadets qualified for advanced classes in English and foreign languages compared with men, and the percentages were equal in mathematics. In leadership evaluations, the top woman in the class was eighth in class standings and ranked first in her company. Two women were ranked first in their respective companies.

In physical education, 69 percent of the women rated the self-defense courses from "above average" to "of great value." Women took the same swimming courses as men, but their gymnastics course was modified to eliminate many of the upper-body-strength activities, substituting balance and agility exercises. According to the Academy's "First Semester Report," because "the Military Academy is interested in equal effort rather than equal performance," men and women are graded on separate scales in testing such as on the two-mile run and the Physical Aptitude Test.

As of 16 February 1977 admissions applications for the class of 1981 were down, with 9,321 applicants received as compared to 10,553 at the same time in 1976.

By March 1977 29 of the plebe women (24 percent) and 283 plebe men (20 percent) had resigned. According to the Academy's report, from the end of Beast Barracks until March 1977, the attrition rate for both sexes had leveled off to about 7 percent.

A Chronology of American Army Women in the Twentieth Century

1901: The Army Nurse Corps is established.

1908: The Navy Nurse Corps is established.

1918: By the end of World War I, 34,000 American women have served in the Army and Navy Nurse Corps, the Navy, Marine Corps, and Coast Guard.

May 14, 1942: Congress approves the creation of the WAAC (Women's Army Auxiliary Corps). Two days later, Oveta Culp Hobby is sworn in as the organization's first director. In her opening speech to the first class of officer candidates, Director Hobby says, "You have taken off silk and put on khaki. You have a debt to democracy, and a date with destiny." As an auxiliary of the Army, however, women who enter the WAAC have no military status.

January 1943: Massachusetts Congresswoman Edith Nourse Rogers (who had introduced the first bill to establish the WAAC) initiates bills in both houses of Congress to permit the enlistment and commissioning of women in the Army.

July 1, 1943: President Franklin D. Roosevelt signs a law changing the name of the WAAC to the WAC (Women's Army Corps), thereby establishing the Corps as a part of the Army. Four days later, Hobby is administered the oath as the first WAC director, with the rank of colonel. Six months before women achieve military status, the first WAAC contingent arrives at Allied Forces Headquarters in Algiers, North Africa. Women serve overseas during 1943 in England, India, Italy, and Egypt.

January 1944: The first WACs arrive in the Pacific.

July 1944: WACs land on Normandy beach, and at the same time, other WACs begin assuming duties in the China–Burma–India Theater, and also go to Oro Bay, Hollandia, Casablanca, Chungking, and Manila.

August 1945: Enlistment of women into the WAC ends, and WAC school/training center closes. With the end of World War II and the rapid demobilization of men after the war, the Army finds itself with a critical shortage of skilled personnel. The War Department is compelled to reconsider its position on the use of women.

1946: The Army announces that the chief of staff has directed the preparation of legislation to make the WAC a permanent part of the Army.

June 12, 1948: President Truman signs the Women's Armed Services Integration Act (Public Law 80-625), establishing the WAC as a permanent part of the Regular Army and Reserve.

July 1948: The first enlisted women enter the Regular Army.

December 1948: The first WAC officers receive Regular Army appointments.

August 1950: With the beginning of the Korean War, women again are needed in greater numbers in the Army than in peacetime. The Army begins a voluntary recall of WAC enlisted Reservists and company grade officers. When adequate numbers do not return to active duty, the Army involuntarily calls WAC Reservists.

1951: General George C. Marshall, Secretary of Defense, invites fifty civilian women to Washington, D.C., to form an advisory committee on matters pertaining to women in the Armed Forces and on obtaining women for the Services. The Defense Advisory Committee on Women in the Services (DACOWITS) is formed at this meeting. The group's first objective is to assist the Defense Department in a unified recruiting campaign to get 72,000 more women to join the Armed Forces by June 1952. This ambitious objective is not met; however, there is a net increase of about 14 percent in the number of women in the Armed Forces. (By 1952, nearly 50,000 are serving.) New WAC detachments are established, and the strength of those already in existence, particularly in the Far East (Japan, Okinawa, and the Philippines), is doubled. Although no WAC unit is established in Korea, a number of individual WACs fill administrative positions in Pusan and later in Seoul.

1953: Following the Korean Armistice, a new charter is proposed (and adopted) to change the DACOWITS mission from an intensified recruiting program to one of helping the Military Services to promote further acceptance of military service as a career for women. The Committee also begins to advise the Department of Defense on legislative matters affecting the welfare of military personnel, and specifically, on matters of concern to women (i.e., retention rate, housing, pay and allowances, job opportunities, and the identification of institutional barriers that limit the full utilization of military women).

September 1954: Fort McClellan, Alabama, is dedicated as the permanent center and home for the Women's Army Corps.

March 1962: The first WAC officer is assigned to Vietnam. During the course of the war, between 7,500 and 11,000 women serve in Vietnam, mostly as Army, Air Force, and Navy nurses. (In a Fall 1988 *Minerva* article, entitled "Women Veterans from the Vietnam War to the Eighties," June A. Willenz writes that "more than three quarters [of these women] had exposure to combat. This is in contrast to the proportion of one-tenth of the women who served in World War II who had similar combat exposure.")

November 8, 1967: With the passing of Public Law 90-130, Congress removes promotion restrictions, thus making possible the appointment of women officers in the various services to the flag/general officer rank. The 2 percent restriction on the number of Regular Army WACs is also removed.

June 11, 1970: While serving as the seventh WAC director, Elizabeth P. Hoisington becomes the first WAC to be promoted to brigadier general.

1971: General Hoisington retires. Her successor, Mildred C. Bailey, is appointed as a brigadier general.

October 12, 1971: The House of Representatives approves the Equal Rights Amendment by a vote of 354 to 23.

1972: The Army begins accepting women into ROTC on a test basis. In March, the Senate completes congressional approval of the Equal Rights Amendment.

June 1973: The draft ends, and with the advent of the All-Volunteer Army, the Army begins a major expansion in the numbers of women needed to help maintain its required strength.

July 1974: All WAC officers are permanently detailed to other Army branches, except Infantry, Armor, and Field Artillery. By moving into the male-occupied branches, women may now compete for the same assignments and schooling, and be promoted equally with their male counterparts. There are 430 out of 467 enlisted Military Occupational Specialties (MOS) available to women; 37 combat MOS remain closed.

1975: The ninth and last WAC director, Mary E. Clarke, is promoted to brigadier general.

June 1975: Involuntary discharge for pregnancy/parenthood is discontinued for women not in an initial training status. The Army authorizes a maternity uniform.

July 1975: Defensive weapons training becomes mandatory in WAC basic training.

October 7, 1975: President Gerald R. Ford signs Public Law 94-106, admitting women into the nation's service academies.

July 7, 1976: One hundred and nineteen women become the first to enter the U.S. Military Academy at West Point as cadets; 62 graduate in 1980. (Eighty-one women enter the U.S. Naval Academy at Annapolis, Maryland, and 157 enter the U.S. Air Force Academy at Colorado Springs, Colorado.)

October 1976–June 1977: The MAXWAC [Maximum Women Army Content] Study is conducted, in which a variety of support-type companies are pumped up to between 15 percent and 35 percent women during a three-day, standard peacetime field exercise. Participating officers are asked to give their opinion on the importance of "percentage of women" as an influence on a company's ability to perform its mission (it receives fewer points than any of the other factors listed). According to a report by Joel M. Savell and Cecil D. Johnson of the U.S. Army Research Institute for the Behavioral and Social Sciences, presented at the 88th Annual Meeting of the American Psychological Association in Montreal, Canada, in September 1980, the results of three sets of analyses provide "no evidence that the companies' performance during the exercise suffered as a result of having had women assigned."

December 31, 1976: WAC center and WAC school close as a result of integration of basic and officer training for men and women. The number of positions potentially open to females has increased dramatically from 19,000 in 1972 to 160,800 in 1976.

1977: While there are no statutory restrictions on the utilization of Army women in combat (as there are within the Navy, Air Force, and Marine Corps), in keeping with the practice of the other services, the

Army's Combat Exclusion Policy is developed. Under this policy, selected assignments are further opened to women in brigade positions, medium and high altitude air defense artillery positions, rocket field artillery positions, and all aviation positions except aerial scout and attack helicopter pilot.

Fall 1977: Women begin to train with men in the same basic training battalions at Fort McClellan, Alabama; Fort Jackson, South Carolina; Fort Dix, New Jersey; and Fort Leonard Wood, Missouri.

REFWAC—a follow-up study to MAXWAC—is conducted, in which male and female enlisted cohorts are compared with respect to their performance during the REFORGER '77 field exercise. This exercise keeps units deployed in the field for several weeks, and there is no evidence in this study that performance by the women is poorer than performance by the men.

May 1978: General Mary E. Clarke, assigned to commanding activities at Fort McClellan, Alabama, is promoted to major general. She remains in command at Fort McClellan until August 1980.

Fall 1978: The extent to which women have been assimilated into men's training, assignments, logistics, and administrative management appears to remove the need for a separate corps for women. A congressional act, signed by President Carter in September, disestablishes the Women's Army Corps, effective October 20, 1978. Meanwhile, WAC strength has grown from some 16,000 officers and enlisted women in 1972 to 56,841 by September 30, 1978.

1979–1980: The Military Personnel Subcommittee of the House Armed Services Committee holds hearings on a proposal to repeal the Air Force and Navy laws prohibiting the use of women in combat missions. The hearing turns into a heated debate over women in combat, with emphasis on ground combat, and ends with no decision on the repeal. The 1980 law requiring reinstitution of the draft specifically excludes women from the draft. Congress's decision not to pass registration of women for the draft is legally challenged on the grounds of sexual equality.

September 1980: Hazel Winifred Johnson becomes the first black woman to achieve the rank of brigadier (one-star) general.

1981: The U.S. Supreme Court rules the government may exclude women from the military draft and registration for the draft.

A woman successfully completes the Green Beret course, but is unable to use her training because of the Army's combat exclusion policies.

During the Carter years, women's participation in the military had been projected to rise from 8.5 percent to over 12 percent by 1986; plans had been made to access another 91,000 women servicewide over the next five years, potentially bringing the number of Army women up from 69,700 (in 1980) to 99,000 (in 1986).

January 19, 1981: According to Maj. Gen. Jeanne Holm (USAF, Ret.), on this date, the service *Times* reported that "the Army and Air Force had secretly submitted to the Reagan transition team in December a proposal that the female enlisted strength goals set by the Carter administration be scrapped until women's impact on force readiness could be determined."

The Army decides to institute an overall study, allegedly spurred by the concern of some Army field commanders regarding women soldiers' effect on readiness, and by a 1976 General Accounting Office Report, which had criticized some aspects of women's performance and noted their high attrition rates.

May 1981: The Army sets up a task force called the "Women in the Army Policy Review Group" to review the performance and place of women in the Army.

July 1981: Mildred P. Hedberg becomes the fourth woman officer (less Medical Department officers) to be promoted to brigadier general.

Summer 1982: Army Basic Training returns to separate training for men and women.

October 1982: After several delays, the WITAPRG's study report is finally issued. An important change in the Army's approach to women is the study's recommended institution of the Direct Combat Probability Coding system as a replacement for, and essentially a broader interpretation of, the 1977 Combat Exclusion Policy. The DCPC system rates every position according to its probability of direct exposure to combat.

DCPC consists of seven codes—P1 through P7—with P1 representing the highest probability of being engaged in combat and P7 the lowest. These probabilities are based, in part, on battlefield location as a criterion for potential exposure. Although DCPC only codes positions—not units or MOS or AOC [Areas of Concentration]—according to the new coding system, twenty-three military occupational specialties (meaning thousands of jobs) that previously had been open to women are closed off, raising the total number of specialties closed to women from thirty-eight to sixty-one.

The WITAPRG study also introduces the Military Entrance Physical Strength Capacity Test (MEPSCAT) for both men and women, which rates MOS according to the estimated number of pounds a soldier will be required to lift in order to perform a given specialty. It is recommended that, regardless of gender, an individual soldier's performance on the MEPSCAT test determine which MOS he or she is permitted to enter. The study acknowledges, however, that no way has yet been devised to satisfactorily ensure the accuracy of the weight estimate categories, which range from "Light" (occasionally lift up to a maximum of 20 lbs. and frequently lift up to a maximum of 10 lbs.) to "Very Heavy" (occasionally lift greater than 100 lbs. and frequently lift greater than 50 lbs.). The study notes that, in many cases, the physical demands data may be overestimated and therefore prove unnecessarily restrictive.

December 31, 1982: The Equal Rights Amendment fails to be ratified by the required number of states.

1983: The DACOWITS advises the Secretary of Defense regarding the dangers of implementing the recommendations of the 1982 Women in the Army Study. The Committee suggests that the implementation of both the reinterpreted combat exclusion rules and newly devised physical demands provisions of all services must be monitored to insure that artificial or institutional barriers to women's career progression are systematically eliminated.

Consequently, the Army announces a revalidation of the findings of the Women in the Army Study, and thirteen of the original twenty-three military occupational specialities (MOS) are reopened and one additional closed; numerous units that were closed under the Direct Combat Probability Coding System are reopened (5,100 of the Army's then 10,000 units), and the recommended physical strength capacity test (MEPSCAT) is established as an "enlistment counseling tool," rather than a bar to certain job skills.

October 1983: Women MPs from Fort Bragg participate in the U.S. invasion of Granada. Upon reaching Granada they are recalled to the States, and then, three days later, returned to duty in Granada. The commander of the 82d's XVIII Airborne Corps asserts the initial decision to evacuate the women was incorrect. "If there's a battle," he says, "the women will stay to complete their mission."

January 16, 1984: The MEPSCAT is implemented for all active Army and Army Reserve applicants and those Army National Guard personnel who process through Military Entrance Processing Stations. These MEPS are in sixty-eight locations throughout the U.S., including Hawaii, Alaska,

Guam, and Puerto Rico. The Army will eventually drop the MEPSCAT as a job placement tool, however, since its criteria cannot be consistently validated.

August 1985: A report is published by Louis Harris and Associates, entitled "Survey of Female Veterans: A Study of the Needs, Attitudes, and Experiences of Women Veterans." It is the first comprehensive survey of women veterans to be commissioned by the VA.

1986: Army female helicopter pilots and military police participate in the airlift of Honduran troops during the Nicaraguan incursion. Air Force women serve in flight crews in aerial refueling operations during the U.S. mission over Libya.

Statistics indicate that women comprise 10.4 percent of all uniformed Army personnel; 43.4 percent of all enlisted women are black; 2.5 percent of all enlisted women are Hispanic (from a paper by Cynthia Enloe, "United States Country Report: Women and Militarization in the Late '80s," published in *Minerva,* Spring 1988). The DACOWITS celebrates its 35th anniversary.

October 3, 1986: Senator William Proxmire (D–Wis.) and Senator William S. Cohen (R–Maine) introduce legislation that would provide for the permanent assignment of women to all units that have as their mission the direct support of combat units. Noting that, according to current DOD statistics, women are capable of holding at least 88 percent of all MOS, but only 63 percent are open to them, Senator Proxmire asserts that current assignment policies do not really protect women from the dangers of combat, and are a waste of talent. Senator Cohen remarks, "What we need to see is more women promoted and given the opportunity to serve in decision-making roles. . . . Every position should be available to every individual who possesses the necessary experience, skills, qualifications, and motivation, regardless of gender."

November 6, 1986: Construction of the "Women in Military Service Memorial" (as distinct from the "Vietnam Women's Memorial") in Washington, D.C., to recognize the contributions of women who serve or have served in the Armed Forces, is authorized by Public Law 99-610. Congresswoman Mary Rose Oakar of Ohio and Senator Frank Murkowski of Alaska sponsor the legislation.

November 26, 1986: The Secretary of the Army reaffirms DCPC as the Army policy concerning the assignment of women. He also approves a recommendation to open Forward Support Battalions (FSB) as a fine-tuning adjustment to current DCPC policy. As a result, all positions in the FSB Headquarters, Medical, Maintenance, and Supply companies are now able to be filled by either males or females. However, Infantry and Tank system support team positions, because of their habitual locations with maneuver battalions, will continue to be designated "male only."

September 28, 1988: A report on sexual harassment, whose findings are based on a 1988 summer tour of Army bases in Southern Europe, is prepared by the DACOWITS and submitted to the Department of Defense for review. The results of this study include reports of explicit sexual harassment, racial problems, poor medical care for servicewomen, and inadequate daycare for children. An edited version of the report is released on February 17, 1989.

October 1, 1988: Brigadier General Evelyn P. Foote becomes the only woman currently in command of a major Army installation, and the first woman commander at Fort Belvoir, Virginia, which employs approximately 15,000 people. She is one of nine women serving as general or flag officers (or, 1.2 percent of the total "one-star" brigadier rank, according to a Summer 1989 article in *Minerva: Quarterly Report*, by Perry D. Luckett, on "Military Women in Contemporary Film, Television, and Media." There are no women two-, three-, or four-star generals. Further, Luckett documents, women hold but 2 percent of colonel, 3.5 percent of lieutenant colonel, and 7.1 percent of major ranks. Percentages of senior enlisted grades are reported to be similar, ranging from 0.4 percent of chief master sergeants to 5.6 percent of technical sergeants).

November 1988: A yearlong Defense Department review of hundreds of thousands of Army jobs results in the opening of 3,128 active duty, 6,274 National Guard, and 1,736 Reserve positions to women (and about 16,000 jobs servicewide). A new standard, known as the "Risk Rule," is approved by Secretary of Defense Frank C. Carlucci for determining which military jobs women may or may not hold.

Definition of DOD Risk Rule: "Risks of direct combat, exposure to hostile fire, or capture are proper criteria for closing non-combat positions or units to women, providing that the type, degree, and duration of such risks are *equal to or greater than* the combat units with which they are normally associated within a given theater of operations. If the risk of non-combat units or positions is less than comparable to land, air, or sea combat units with which they are associated, then they should be open to women." The services are now in the process of reviewing their combat support positions in light of this revised rule of risk.

1989: Canada abolishes its laws barring women from combat and opens all military jobs, except on submarines, to females. Canadian women may now serve as Infantry troops, fighter pilots, and sailors on Navy destroyers.

August 1989: Twenty-one-year-old Kristin Baker is announced as the first female selected to hold the U.S. Military Academy's highest cadet rank—brigade commander, or "first captain."

September 1, 1989: Brigadier General Evelyn P. Foote retires from service.

December 1989: During the U.S. invasion of Panama, twenty-nine-year-old Captain Linda Bray, company commander of a Military Police unit, becomes allegedly the first woman to command American troops in battle. It is reported that she leads a force of thirty soldiers—male and female—to capture a kennel holding guard dogs that turns out to be defended by the Panamanian Defense Forces. She and her troops are engaged in an unexpected firefight. (The incident, however, draws conflicting reports.) Prior to the attack, about 620 Army women are stationed in Panama. Once the attack is launched, 170 more women are sent there.

January 23, 1990: Representative Pat Schroeder of Colorado introduces a bill to Congress, HR-3868, "to direct the Secretary of the Army to carry out a 4-year test program to examine the implications of the removal of limitations on the assignment of female members of the Army to combat and combat support positions." The legislation, which would have experimentally tested American women in direct combat roles, is voted down.

May 28, 1990: An article by correspondent Margaret Roth, entitled "Will Deployability Determine Who Is Forced Out?" appears in the *Army Times.* According to the article, "The Army's deputy chief of staff for personnel has ordered a review of how soldiers with special needs, from pregnant soldiers to dual career couples, will fit into a [smaller, highly trained] force. The director of military personnel management for the deputy chief of staff for personnel has asked the major commands to comment on existing deployability criteria and policies for six groups with special needs. The six groups are: single parents, dual-service member couples, soldiers with Exceptional Family Members [i.e., dependents with handicaps], pregnant women, soldiers infected with the AIDS virus, and soldiers with unspecified health or medical problems that affect readiness and deployability." Army spokespeople say the call for the information paper seems to be driven by budgetary concerns.

June 1990: The Department of Defense is planning to transform the status of the DCPC system from a policy to a regulation. DACOWITS has requested a briefing on a draft of the new regulation in June. Finalization is planned for the fall of 1990.